The Fabulous Budapest Gambit

Viktor Moskalenko

The Fabulous

Budapest Gambit

New In Chess 2007

Introduction

Surprise your opponent with the Budapest Gambit!

1.d4 ♘f6 2.c4 e5

Lasker, Rubinstein, organizer Kagan, Schlechter and Tarrasch during the Berlin tournament in 1918, where the Budapest Gambit was born at grandmaster level.

Prologue: History and Origins (1896-2007)

At the beginning of the 20th century, openings with the queen's pawn offered solid possibilities of playing a strategic game without many complications. In those times most openings did not have much interesting depth. The most common opening was the Queen's Gambit. Black players were in need of something more attractive.

The first game with the Budapest Gambit appears to have been Adler-Maroczy (see Chapter Three, Game 80), Budapest 1896. In 1916 Stephan Abonyi developed the ideas behind 2...e5, together with his compatriots Zsigmond Barasz and Gyula Breyer, who played it against the Dutch surgeon Johannes Esser in a small tournament in Budapest.

Protagonists and Heroes

Akiba Rubinstein became the first grandmaster in history to face the Budapest Gambit. In a strong double round robin tournament in the city of Berlin in April 1918, Milan Vidmar sprung it on him in Round 3. Rubinstein's reply was 4.♗f4!? and the position became very complicated. On move 13 Rubinstein committed an error and he lost the game in 24 moves, an outright sensation. The four-player tournament continued, and the two other rivals of Akiba Rubinstein, Carl Schlechter and Jacques Mieses, scored one and a half point more after spectacular games. With this success, the fabulous Budapest Gambit was born.

Easy Development

The Budapest Gambit has maintained its good reputation until the present day. Its prestige is defended by great masters like Peter Svidler, Nigel Short, Vladimir Epishin, Ian Rogers, Jeroen Piket, Normunds Miezis, Boris Savchenko, Shakhriyar Mamedyarov, Georg Mohr and many other high-level players.

The gambit is also very popular at club level, yet it has never become a main defence against 1.d4. However, it continues to be a weapon of great practical value, since it allows easy development of the black pieces.

Basic Ideas of the Gambit and General Advice

The main idea of the Budapest Gambit is to win back the pawn with simple developing moves. Black's knight immediately attacks White's extra pawn in the main line with 3...♘g4. White has enough moves to defend the pawn on e5: ♘f3, ♗f4, ♕d4/♕d5, but move order is of paramount importance here.

The Budapest Gambit forces players to demonstrate a good level of calculation and a good feeling for piece play (in many Budapest games Black makes only 2-4 moves with his pawns in the opening phase).

Black's main weapon is tactics. Opportunities for this are offered by the typical Budapest Gambit pawn structure, with lots of free space and smooth development, which allows the black pieces to make unexpected manoeuvres. If Black continues actively and does not allow his rival to dictate the game, then his possibilities will be equal to White's.

If White spends tempi defending the e5 pawn, then Black must take advantage of this and seek the initiative, following the strategic ideas in each given variation.

When we analyse the Budapest Gambit games from the period 1918-1930, arguably by some of the classical players of the time, it becomes obvious that all of them tried to control the proceedings in their own way: Alekhine and Bogoljubow attacked; Euwe studied the details; Capablanca overcame his opponents technically; Rubinstein played 4.♗f4, pressing strategically.

Especially against the 4.e4 variation (the Alekhine System) some masters playing with the black pieces, like Richard Réti and Savielly Tartakower, tended to make too many significant mistakes at key moments, possibly due to their style or maybe because of lack of knowledge.

The problem with the Budapest is that few high-level games have been played with it in the past years. Most professionals do not dare to take so much risk and decide on a solid Queen's Gambit instead. The same happened at the beginning of the 20th century – see my discussion with Mr. Bohigas presented at the end of Chapter One, Part I. We hope that this will soon change and new gentlemen will appear who adopt the Budapest Gambit!

Statistics Report

In his active career, Ian Rogers had the best performance with the Budapest Gambit

General Statistics

Whereas in other closed openings the game tends to develop slowly, in the Budapest Gambit, especially in the lines with 4.♗f4 or 4.e4, the critical phase already starts from moves 6-8 onwards. Between moves 9-12 both sides must make important decisions, and by move 15 an assessment of the position can be made. Between moves 18-22 we already know how the game will finish, although it can continue for 20 or 30 more moves. The majority of games with this opening are decided between moves 6-15, which means that it must be thoroughly studied from both sides. Without knowledge of the tactical possibilities and the typical plans for both sides, the game may become too difficult in no time, even for very strong players.

Typical Endgames

Most of the games with the Budapest Gambit finish quickly. It is a gambit to all intents and purposes! However, we have to say something about the endgames that can arise. In the majority of endgames, White obtains the better perspectives thanks to his advantage of the bishop pair and his more dynamic pawn structure. But when Black emerges out of the opening and the middlegame in good shape, there are possibilities of good counterplay, mainly in the centre and on the queenside, where White has some weaknesses in his pawn structure. See the games Bareev-Rogers (Chapter One, Part I), Gurevich-Miezis and Garcia-Rogers (Chapter One, Part II).

Statistics report and some notes

With the Megabase, which contains approximately 3.5 million games, I have been studying the results of the BG in practical chess.

I have found 12.029 games with the moves 1.d4 ♘f6 2.c4 e5. That is approximately one BG game in every 300 games in the Megabase.

In total the results were:

White wins:	43%	(5195 games)	= 56%
Draw:	27%	(3179 games)	
Black wins:	30%	(3647 games)	= 44%

Average Elo white players: 2146 - Rating Performance = 2130
Average Elo black players: 2095 - Rating Performance = 2054
In other words: playing the BG hardly affects your Elo!

What does White play against the Budapest Gambit?

The key move in the modern BG is White's 4th, when he determines his opening strategy. The most popular moves are the various defences of the extra pawn on e5: with the knight (4.♘f3) or the bishop (4.♗f4), and then there are moves like 4.e2-e4 and 4.e2-e3.

A key problem in the BG is that White gains most of his points with simple, well-known moves. Therefore Black looks for risky lines and may look for gambit moves like ...d7-d6 or ...f7-f6 in many lines.

What are the tendencies in the Budapest Gambit?

In the 21st century, the BG is played much less than, for example, in the 1920s-1930s or the 1980s-1990s.

I would be interested to know if with the passage of time, certain players have gained or lost more points with the BG. White has won the same percentage of games at all times, the amount of draws has increased slightly through the years, whereas the amount of black victories has decreased slightly.

In all periods, the white player was on average stronger than the black player, so they would probably have won anyway, with or without the BG. The Budapest Gambit is played more and more by weak players, which does not help to advance or develop the theory.

Here the key question is: why do strong players hardly ever play the BG? Because it is a weak defence, or because they do not approve of it theoretically? A possible answer is that its theory is insufficiently developed and it is somewhat easier to play with the white pieces. There is much more risk for the black player, and several historic defeats have given the BG a bad reputation.

So maybe for these reasons, strong players prefer to devote their attention to more universal opening systems.

12

Who plays the Budapest Gambit today?

An opening is developed according by those who play it, therefore this is an important question.

Among the players of today Slovenian GM Georg Mohr and Australian GM Ian Rogers stand out above the others. They have not only played a greater number of games with the BG, they have also obtained extraordinary results with it, against very strong opposition.

The BG was very popular for some time during the 1980s and 1990s, but later this popularity decreased. What has happened?

Probably, when an elite player tries his hand at this gambit, many will imitate him. In the year 1992 in the World Championship Candidate Semi-Final in Linares, Nigel Short launched the Budapest Gambit against Karpov and although he lost the game, this gave a world-wide boost to the gambit.

Shortly before, a young Miguel Illescas had played the Gambit against Boris Spassky in Linares. He also lost the game, but it had a great impact on all BG fans all the same.

By the way, Veselin Topalov played a BG against Alexey Dreev in 1989!
Still, there there are not many elite players who employ the BG, and the number of the games with this opening has decreased.

Classification of Budapest Gambit players

Perhaps the motifs of BG players can be classified into the following four types:
  A) youthful love of romantic chess;
  B) the surprise factor;
  C) the avoidance of theory;
  D) love of risks (romantic style).

Many strong players have ventured the BG when they were young. It seems that it is good for a growing player to adopt a gambit because it helps him to learn more about the value of the pieces. When these players arrive at elite level, they adopt a less risky repertoire.

The second type is, for example, represented by Short in the above-mentioned example. Nowadays, a BG is still a surprise, but less so than before. Although it is not played often, many 1.d4 players know its main strategic landmarks and it is difficult to surprise them.

Perhaps this background information may explain moves like ...d7-d6 or ...f7-f6 in many lines, which are like surprises within a surprise!

Another type is the player who wants to avoid theory. When he does not have much time to study, he will prefer quick deviation from the main lines to more popular openings that are in continuous revision.

Finally, players who are enchanted by risk will favour this opening. In one line we have commented: 'It's quite as if you've landed in a roller coaster fairground attraction'. Steep ascents, slippery slopes and litres of adrenalin!

Today, the BG has reached such a theoretical level that it has turned insipid, that is to say, the main lines lead to positions where Black must struggle to make a draw, and this is not what risk-lovers want.

Still, we have seen a pair of BG games played by Shakhriyar Mamedyarov lately. Will it remain a youth love, did he speculate on the surprise factor, or is Mamedyarov an ardent risk-lover? We will have to wait and see, but hopefully his devotion to this gambit will prove true, and it will not be just a device to steer clear of the trodden paths.

Times are hard for the Budapest Gambit player. But I think that the problem is not this opening – rather a change in chess philosophy. He who plays the Budapest Gambit should learn to play universally – more 'modern', that is – and not fear to enter lines where the game acquires a strategic character.

I have discovered that BG players with the black pieces are trying to follow aggressive and devious lines, whereas white players often prefer to follow positional schemes. We can conclude that both parts need to improve their level and their knowledge of main ideas. I am sure that in that case the Budapest Gambit will become a modern and universal opening, as it contains a plethora of resources.

Chapter One

Bishops against Knights

Rubinstein Variation – 1.d4 ♘f6 2.c4 e5 3.dxe5 ♘g4 4.♗f4

A Bit of History

Actually, Rubinstein's move 4.♗f4 has remained one of most popular answers to the Budapest Gambit. Karpov, Kortchnoi, Shirov, Ivanchuk, Bareev, Ivan Sokolov, Van Wely and Mikhail Gurevich are some of the elite players who pre-

Akiba Rubinstein (1888-1961), one of the greatest chess personalities of the 20th century, was the first grandmaster that faced the BG. His favourite reply was 4.♗f4!?.

fer this line. The character of the game after this move is solid and positional, trying to prevent Black from becoming active.

Strategies

One of the main ideas of 4.♗f4 is to try and defend the e5 pawn. 4.♘f3 allows 4...♗c5!?, attacking f2!. Now 5.e3 is the only answer, but this temporarily closes in the bishop on c1.

The attempt to break open the position with c4-c5 is a classic resource. This advance allows the white bishop on f4 to become active on the h2-b8 diagonal.

Black must defend well against the c4-c5 break and prepare his counter-attack mainly in the centre

Directions

There are three main directions after 4.♗f4:
1) ambitious play with 6.♘c3 (Part I – The Schlechter Knight);
2) solid play with 5/6.♘bd2 (Part II – The Solid ♘bd2);
3) the sharp 4...g5 (Part III – Black Jet).

We start Part I with the famous Games 1-3, which can be considered the origin of 4.♗f4.

After 6.♘c3 ♛e7 7.♛d5 ♗xc3+ 8.bxc3, 8...f6! is the modern reply. The alternative is Vidmar's adventurous move 8...♛a3!?, immediately attacking the weak squares on the queenside. It is still playable but also risky – see Games 1 and 3 and Game 4, O'Kelly-Heidenfeld, of a much later date.

The key game with 6.♘c3 is Game 2, Rubinstein-Schlechter, which introduces the important idea of the Schlechter Knight. Schlechter's strategy was different than Vidmar's and Mieses's in Games 1 and 3; instead of moving the queen to a3 to attack White's weak queenside pawns, Black is aiming for a blockade, taking advantage of his better piece coordination and space advantage. Schlechter exchanged all the pieces, ending up with a strong knight on c5 against White's poor bishop. The knight blocks the two doubled pawns, protects b7 and e5, controls e4 and harasses d3. It is a great knight, and it is untouchable. Schlechter completed his strategy by controlling the semi-open e-file with his major pieces. He didn't bother capturing any of the doubled pawns, White's main weaknesses, as they facilitated his blockading strategy.

Game 2 Rubinstein-Schlechter
after 12...♘e4!

The magnificent king's knight goes to c5 via e4, threatening the c3 pawn and the f2-square on the way. This knight manoeuvre has been repeated on many occasions and is named the 'Schlechter manoeuvre'.

During the years 1919-1930, white players like Alekhine, Bogoljubow and Euwe, and even Capablanca, started aiming for a sharp fight with 4.e4!? (see Chapter Two). Akiba Rubinstein, however, followed his own concepts and dedicated himself to the development of the line 4.♗f4.

16

Against 4.♗f4, 6.♘c3 (Part I), Rubinstein's opponents – especially Schlechter – developed a strategy that has survived the years. But in Part II it is Rubinstein who outlines the strategy of the variation.

I enjoyed analysing the two Rubinstein games with which Part II opens a lot, seeing how many ideas that determined the future development of the line, were born in them. Perhaps the most significant is the advance of the white pawn to c5:

Game 19 Rubinstein-Daniuszewski   Game 20 Rubinstein-Tartakower

Many games in Part II revolve around this advance, and Rubinstein had already seen it in 1927.

It is surprising that such a strong player as Miezis in 1996, that is to say, 70 years later, forgot about Rubinstein's games and failed to prevent the move c4-c5 (Game 24).

Game 24 Gurevich-Miezis
after 11.c5!

Rubinstein's strategy consists in domination of the queenside and the centre and thereby to force weaknesses on Black's kingside, where the final clash will take place. This is a strategy of total board domination. Unlike Part I, the game is very dynamic here.

The sharpest way to challenge the Rubinstein Bishop is the 'Black Jet' move 4...g5, which at the same time aims to fianchetto the bishop on f8 (Part III).

Part I – The Schlechter Knight

1.d4 ♘f6 2.c4 e5 3.dxe5 ♘g4 4.♗f4, 6.♘c3

Introduction
After 1.d4 ♘f6 2.c4 e5 3.dxe5 ♘g4 4.♗f4, the main line continues 4...♘c6 5.♘f3 ♗b4+. Now, 6.♘c3!? is a move that complicates matters, and the fight for the initiative and for the e5 pawn continues.

The first attempts with 6.♘c3 in history failed for white players because of lack of knowledge, and lack of practice (see Games 1-3). But, in fact, it is one of White's best options, as time has revealed.

Directions
The most common sequence is 6...♕e7 7.♕d5 ♗xc3+ 8.bxc3.

Now we reach a position that has been critical for this opening since the game Rubinstein-Vidmar, Berlin 1918 (Game 1).

White maintains the extra pawn. But let's have a look at the costs:
- two pairs of doubled pawns;
- a weak queenside where the black pieces can invade;

- his king in the centre and at least two tempi required for castling (Black is ready for castling);
- the queen in the centre is subject to attack, which will cause White to lose more time.

Vidmar's move 8...♛a3!? has been replaced by the modern 8...f6! and after 9.exf6 ♘f6 10.♛d3 d6 White is well advised to play:

A) 11.g3!

Here Black has several options: 11...0-0, 11...b6 or Schlechter's 11/12...♘e4.

A1) 11...0-0

We begin our treatment of this line with the classical game Kashdan-Pilnick (Game 5). In the strategy devised by Schlechter (see Game 2), the movement of the black knight from f6 to e4 and c5 was an essential part of the plan. This knight movement is harder to realize when White puts his bishop on g2.

In the game Kashdan-Pilnick, after the big mistake 13...♗f5? (better is 13...♘c5! with complicated play), the black knight on e4 is temporarily under attack by the bishop on g2, allowing the tactical shot 14.♘h4, which forces the destruction of Black's kingside pawn structure after 14...g6 15.♘xf5.

We continue with Rogers-Miezis (Game 6), a game between two great present-day experts of the Budapest Gambit. Black develops his bishop to d7, allowing White to play c4-c5, but also permitting Black to gain space with ...c4!?. In this game we see a theme that is not very frequent after 6.♘c3: an attack on the white king.

Game 6 Rogers-Miezis
after 22.♖d5

The first step is the exchange of bishops on h3, then in my annotations to Black's 22nd move there follows the exchange sacrifice on f4, removing the g-pawn from the protection of its king. This sacrifice was already played by Vidmar (Game 1), although in that game the pawn that supported the bishop was the king's pawn and the file opened was the e-file.

After 12.♗g2, an aggressive options is 12...♗g4!?, as in the recent game D. Gurevich-Pacheco (Game 7), in which the blockade could have been achieved by the c-pawn (see my annotation to Black's 15th move). Another important example is Dlugy-Epishin (Game 8). Here Black's strategy is different than Schlechter's. It consists of an attack on the centre and on the doubled pawns.

Game 8 Dlugy-Epishin
after 14.♖ae1

After 14...♔h8! Black moves his bishop with much agility. From g4 it X-rays the e2 pawn, then it goes to g6 via h5, and from there it attacks the queen from the e4-square, and then finally it goes to f7 to attack the doubled pawn. By the way, here White plays the thematic pawn push to c5 and captures the pawn on d6, when Black recaptures with the rook and controls the d-file. See also Hoffman-Amura (Game 9).

A2) 11...b6
This move was played in Game 10, Kortchnoi-Mohr.

Game 10 Kortchnoi-Mohr
after 11...b6

In this game, Black puts his bishop on b7 to exchange it for the g2 bishop, reducing White's control of the light squares. This doesn't prevent White from pushing his king's pawn to e5.

On the other hand, this is one of the few games in which Black attacks the white kingside with his pawns, but this attack is countered by the strong advance of White's king's pawn.

Included in the notes to Kortchnoi-Mohr is the recent game Krasenkow-Wippermann. After the exchange of bishops on the long diagonal, Black occupies the e-file with both of his rooks and uses his knight and queen to attack the pawns on the queenside. Here, the white knight goes to d2, defending from there the e4 and c4 pawns, while the f-pawn infiltrates Black's position, destroying the kingside.

Another interesting game with 11...b6 is Shabalov-Wippermann (Game 11).

A3) 11...♘e4
Schlechter's move 11...♘e4 can be found in Barsov-Roofthoofd (Game 12). To avoid the problems that occurred in Game 5 (Kashdan-Pilnick), the knight leaves the e4-square as soon as the white bishop goes to g2, and heads to c5. On this square the knight threatens the white queen, which has to move to e3. This queen move is only possible because the pawn has not yet moved to e3, obviously.

Game 12 Barsov-Roofthoofd
after 22.♛e3

The queen on e3 threatens to exchange itself for the powerful black queen. Both the game and the 13th move alternatives are very disheartening for Black.

By the way, both this game and the games mentioned in its notes introduce a new strategy for White: the attack on the queenside, taking advantage of the bishop on g2, the knight and the open b-file. Another illustration of this theme is Bareev-Rogers (Game 13). Here again, we see Schlechter's knight manoeuvre, the exchange of queens and the aggressive break c4-c5!?. Black escaped with half a point but White's advantage was very clear.

To conclude: after White's fianchetto (11.g3!), it looks as if the blockading idea with ...♘e4-♘c5 isn't as effective as in the case of 11.e3.

B) 11.e3
White's alternative 11.e3 is not as troublesome for Black as 11.g3!. Black has sufficient resources to obtain a good game.

The 'Schlechter manoeuvre' is aptly illustrated in the key game Rubinstein-Schlechter (Game 2). We can observe the same strategy in Game 14, Vukic-Rogers. The blockade is accomplished by the advance of the d6 pawn which ends up on e4 after the exchange of the bishop for the e5 knight. This pawn controls the centre and the white pawns, with the help of the bishop on c6 and the knight on c5. This game features a new strategy, which is confirmed in my annotations, based on the attack on the white king with the help of the black rook on the sixth rank.

Good examples of victims on the white side of the board are Kishnev-Mollekens (Game 15) – where Black makes a very useful bishop movement, from f5 to g6 and then to e8, winning the queen! – and Pogorelov-Andres Gonzalez (Game 16), where the comment on move 17 suggests another interesting plan for Black.

A more recent example is Pinter-Cebalo (Game 17). In this original game we see that against 11.e3 Black uses a strategy that has already been used against 11.g3: putting the bishop on b7 to dominate the long diagonal. On c5 he places not the king's knight, like Schlechter, but the queen's knight, after the manoeuvre ...♘c6-e5-d7-c5-e6. Black's position looks good.

Game 17 Pinter-Cebalo
after 18.♗g5

It is a pity that he didn't play 18...♘xd3! and 19...♛e4!, as I mention in my notes on move 18.

I also include a bad example (for Black). In the game Reshevsky-Olafsson we see the antithesis of the previous games. White is able to push his doubled pawns forward and exchange them, obtaining an extraordinary space advantage in the centre and great piece mobility. For example, the dark-squared bishop, which is normally quite static, dominates the board in this game.

Our investigation of 6.♘c3 concludes with an amazing game: Inkiov Djukic (Game 18).

⚠ **Keep in Mind!**

- **In general, in the 6.♘c3 line you must remember that if White is able to carry out the typical manoeuvre ♘f3-d4!?, then Black can answer with ...♘e5! and the game is balanced.**
- **The prophylactic ...♚h8!? may be a useful resource for Black.**

The Schlechter Knight – Games

GAME 1
□ **Akiba Rubinstein**
■ **Milan Vidmar Sr**
Berlin 1918 (3)

1.d4 ♘f6 2.c4 e5 3.dxe5 ♘g4 4.♗f4 ♘c6

If now 4...♗c5?, 5.e3 and White is much better, because the bishop on f4 protects the pawn on e5, the queen threatens the knight on g4 and Black does not have time to attack the e5 pawn with more pieces.

5.♘f3 ♗b4+!

This continuation has the objective of gaining a tempo to prepare ...♕e7, attacking the pawn on e5. White has two answers which are quite different in character. The choice depends on the style or taste of the player.

6.♘c3!?

Complicating matters. The fight for the initiative and for the pawn on e5 contin-

Milan Vidmar Sr. (1885-1962) played the first grandmaster game in the history of the Budapest Gambit. Despite its many mistakes, the great potential of the gambit was already demonstrated in this game.

ues. A more calm and solid alternative is 6.♘bd2, but then Black will soon recover the e5-pawn with 6...♕e7 – see Part II.

6...♕e7 7.♕d5

Fighting to defend the pawn.

7...♗xc3+ 8.bxc3 ♕a3!?

Vidmar immediately attacks the weak squares on the queenside. The most common move today is 8...f6!.

9.♖c1!?

This move is preferred even nowadays. Very interesting is 9.♖d1!?, for example: 9...♕xc3+ (9...f6 10.exf6 ♘xf6 11.♕d2 d6 12.♕e3+±) 10.♕d2!? ♕xc4 11.h3 ♘h6 12.e3 ♕b4 13.♕xb4 ♘xb4 14.a3 ♘c6 15.♗c4 with very good compensation for the pawn.

9...f6!

9...♕xa2?! 10.h3 ♘h6 11.e4 ♕a3 12.♗e2±.

10.exf6 ♘xf6 11.♕d2

The idea is to defend the pawn on a2, but here the queen is passive.

A) 11.♕d3 0-0!? 12.g3 (12.c5!?) 12...d6 13.♗g2 ♕xa2 (13...♘e7!? 14.♘d4 ♘g6⇄) 14.c5?! (14.♘g5!?) 14...dxc5 15.♗xc7 ♖e8 16.0-0 ♕xe2 17.♕b1 ♕e7?! (17...♕c4!∓; 17...♕e4!?) 18.♗f4∞ Yakovich-Coret Frasquet, Sevilla 1992;

B) 11.♕d1!? d6 (11...♕xa2? 12.♗xc7 ♕xc4 13.e3±) 12.♕b3±.

11...d6 12.♞d4 0-0 13.e3?

A serious error. The only move was 13.f3 in order to avoid ...♞e4.

13...♞xd4! 14.cxd4?

White does not see the danger. If 14.exd4 ♞e4 15.♕e3 ♜e8 16.♗e2 ♕xa2, with initiative for Black.

14...♞e4

The attack begins! For just one pawn Black has great compensation on account of his lead in development. Perhaps, before taking the knight to e4, the following pawn thrust deserved attention: 14...g5! 15.♗g3 ♞e4 16.♕c2 ♕a5+ 17.♔e2 (17.♔d1 ♜xf2!−+) 17...♜xf2+! 18.♗xf2 ♗g4+ 19.♔d3 ♕a3+ 20.♕b3 (20.♔xe4 ♜e8+ 21.♔d5 c6 mate) 20...♕xc1 21.c5+ ♔h8 22.♔xe4 ♜e8+ 23.♔d3 ♗f5+ 24.♔e2 ♗c2! and White can already resign.

15.♕c2 ♕a5+ 16.♔e2

16...♜xf4!

White's king position is opened up by this exchange sacrifice.

17.exf4 ♗f5 18.♕b2 ♜e8! 19.♔f3 ♞d2+ 20.♔g3 ♞e4+ 21.♔h4??

The white king had to return: 21.♔f3 h5! with a strong attack: 22.g3 (22.h3 h4) 22...♞g5+!−+.

21...♜e6!

Now mate is inevitable.

22.♗e2 ♜h6+ 23.♗h5 ♜xh5+! 24.♔xh5 ♗g6+

White resigned in view of 25.♔g4 ♕h5 mate.

GAME 2

□ **Akiba Rubinstein**
■ **Carl Schlechter**
Berlin 1918 (4)

1.d4 ♞f6 2.c4 e5 3.dxe5 ♞g4 4.♗f4 ♞c6 5.♞f3 ♗b4+ 6.♞c3 ♕e7 7.♕d5 f6!

Contrary to Vidmar and Mieses in Games 1 and 3, Schlechter bases his strategy on a blockade.

8.exf6 ♗xc3+ 9.bxc3 ♞xf6 10.♕d3

The best square for the queen.

10...d6 11.e3

Rubinstein plays the natural move and again it is a mistake! The most powerful

Carl Schlechter (1874-1918) was the originator of the important knight manoeuvre to e4 and c5.

alternative is the modern idea of the fianchetto with 11.g3! (see Game 5 onwards).

11...0-0

11...♘e4!? with the idea of 12.♘d4 ♘c5 13.♕d2 ♘e5 14.f3 0-0 15.e4?? ♖xf4!.

12.♗e2

12...♘e4!

Starting what has come to be known as the 'Schlechter manoeuvre'.

13.♕c2

More common is 13.0-0 or 13.♘d4 – see the games with 11.e3.

13...♘c5!

With the idea of 14...♗f5. Another option was 13...♕f6!?, intending 14.♘d4 ♘xc3! 15.♕xc3 ♘xd4.

14.♘d4!

Domination! This leap is White's main resource in this line, as the Great White Knight controls all the important squares and is also untouchable.

14...♘e5!

Black fights back! This is the best defence. The fight between the minor pieces continues. It is the key to the Schlechter Knight method.

15.0-0 ♗d7!

68 years later 15...♕f7!? was played on this move: 16.♗g3 ♗d7 17.♖ad1 ♘xc4 18.♘b3 ♗f5 19.♕c1 ♘e4 20.♘d4 ♗d7 (20...♗g6!?) 21.♕c2 ♘c5?! (21...♖ae8!) 22.♘b3 ♗f5 23.♕c1 ♘e4 24.♘d4 ♗d7 25.♕c2 ♘c5 ½-½ Dolmatov-Malaniuk, Soviet Championship, Kiev 1986.

16.f3?!

16.♕d2 ♖ae8∞.

16...♖ae8

16...♘g6! 17.♕d2 ♖ae8 18.♖fe1 ♘xf4 19.exf4 ♕e3+ 20.♕xe3 ♖xe3.

17.♗g3 ♕f7 18.♗xe5?! ♖xe5 19.e4 a6

19...♕f4!? with the initiative.

20.♖ae1 ♗e6 21.♘xe6 ♕xe6 22.♖f2 ♖e8 23.♗f1 ♕d7 24.♖d2 ♕c6 25.♖b1 ♕d7 26.♖d5 ♕f7 27.♕d2 b6 28.♖d1 h6 29.♕f2 ♔h8 30.♕e3 ♕f6 31.g3
½-½

An extraordinary strategic encounter between two of the best players of their time.

GAME 3
☐ **Akiba Rubinstein**
■ **Jacques Mieses**
Berlin 1918 (5)

1.d4 ♘f6 2.c4 e5
Fighting for the initiative from the second move onwards!
3.dxe5 ♘g4 4.♗f4 ♘c6 5.♘f3 ♗b4+ 6.♘c3 ♕e7 7.♕d5 ♗xc3+ 8.bxc3 ♕a3

9.♕d3
Against Vidmar in Round 3, Rubinstein had played 9.♖c1!? (Game 1).
9...♕a5
9...♕e7!?.
10.♖c1 ♘gxe5 11.♘xe5 ♘xe5 12.♕g3!
The exchange of queens does not promise much: 12.♕d5 ♕xd5 13.cxd5 d6 with an equal ending.
12...d6 13.♕xg7 ♘g6 14.h4!
It seems that White is better, but there are complications. White has weak

pawns on the queenside and is slightly lagging in development.
14...h5 15.e4 ♗e6 16.♗g5 ♔d7!

17.f4?
Very aggressive, but too risky. The correct answer was 17.♕d4!, returning the queen to the centre; 17...♖ae8 18.♗e2±.
17...♖ae8!
Black has dangerous counterplay. This rook is ready to attack along the e-file and the white king remains exposed.
18.♗e2?!
It is already too late for 18.♕d4 ♗f5! with the initiative on Black's side.
18...♕xa2↑ 19.0-0?

Jacques Mieses (1865-1954) was the first master to play the Budapest Gambit on a regular basis.

Rubinstein loses the thread of the game and commits the decisive error. 19.♕d4 ♗g4! 20.♗f3 f6! 21.♗xf6 ♗xf3 22.gxf3 ♘xf4 23.♕d2 ♘g2+ 24.♔d1 ♕xd2+ 25.♔xd2 ♖hf8∓.

19...♖hg8!

A winning intermediate move.

20.♕d4 ♕xe2 21.f5

21...♗xc4!?

Black could have won here with a surprising tactic: 21...♘xh4!! 22.fxe6+ fxe6 23.♖f7+ ♔c8 24.♖f2 ♖xg5! 25.♖xe2 ♘f3+–+.

22.fxg6 ♖xe4

22...♖xg6!? 23.♕xa7 ♕xe4–+.

23.♕xa7 ♖xg6 24.♖f2 ♕d3 25.♕xb7 ♖e2 26.♖xe2 ♕xe2 27.♖a1 ♖g8

27...f6!? 28.♖a7 ♕e1+ 29.♔h2 ♕e5+ 30.♔h1 d5∓.

28.♖a7 ♕e1+ 29.♔h2 ♕e5+ 30.♔g1?

30.♔h1 ♕c5∓.

30...♕c5+ 31.♔h1 ♗d5!　　　　**0-1**

After these three famous games in a grandmaster tournament in wartime Berlin, the Budapest Gambit developed fast. It gained popularity and great respect of many chess players, until the point where same players stopped playing 2.c4 for fear of it!

These first three grandmaster games in the history of the Budapest Gambit, played some ninety years ago, are excellent examples for theoreticians and practitioners of 2...e5 to this day. They contain all the necessary material for the study of the main ideas.

We conclude the treatment of 8...♕a3!? with a game played 38 years later.

GAME 4
□ Alberic O'Kelly de Galway
■ Wolfgang Heidenfeld
Dublin Zonal 1956 (4)

1.d4 ♘f6 2.c4 e5 3.dxe5 ♘g4 4.♗f4 ♗b4+ 5.♘c3 ♘c6 6.♘f3 ♕e7 7.♕d5 ♗xc3+ 8.bxc3 ♕a3 9.♖c1

9.♕d2 ♕e7.

9...f6!

Black has also tried to make use of the position of the white queen in other ways:

A) 9...d6?! 10.exd6 ♗e6 11.♕b5 cxd6 (11...0-0 (Rothenstein-Richter,

Berlin 1928) 12.h3!±) 12.♕xb7 ♖c8 13.♕b3 ♕c5 14.e3± Dlugy-Mills, Chicago 1989;

B) 9...♘e7 10.♕d2 ♘g6 (Gilfer-Vajda, Folkestone Olympiad 1933) 11.♗g3 h5 12.h3 h4 13.♗f4±.

10.exf6

More than 80 years after Berlin, 10.♖c2!? ♘e7?! (≥ 10...♕a4!? 11.♖d2 ♕a3⇄; also interesting is 10...♕e7!? 11.exf6 ♘xf6 and the game begins) 11.♕d2 fxe5 12.♘xe5 ♘f6 13.♘d3 d6 14.g3 (14.c5!?) 14...♗e6 15.♗g2, with unclear play, happened in Inarkiev-B.Savchenko, Krasnodar 2002.

10...♘xf6 11.♕d2 d6!

If 11...0-0 12.e3! (12.♗xc7?! ♘e4⇄) 12...d6 13.♗d3±.

12.♘d4

12.e3?! ♗f5! (12...♘e4!? 13.♕c2 ♘c5⇄) intending 13.♘d4 ♘xd4! 14.exd4 ♘e4↑; 12.♕e3+ ♘e7 is unclear.

12...0-0 13.f3!?

Defending against the threat of 13...♘e4 and preparing the advance e2-e4. 13.e3? was played by Rubinstein in 1918.

13...♘e5!

Black should try to attack the weak pawns on the queenside. 13...♗d7 is too slow: 14.e4 ♖ae8 15.♗e2 ♘e5 16.♖b1±. Also insufficient is 13...♘a5?! 14.e4 ♕c5 15.♘b3.

14.e4 ♕c5 15.♘b3 ♕c6 16.♗xe5!?

Heidenfeld repeated the game up to now against Holford (1946), where White lost quickly after 16.c5? ♘xe4! (making use of the rook's pressure against the ♗f4!) 17.♕e3 (17.fxe4 ♕xe4+−+) 17...♘g6 18.♗d3 ♘xf4−+.

16...dxe5 17.♕g5 ♖e8 18.♗e2

18...h6

Black had to try and attack the queenside, leaving White's queen out of play on the other side of the board. More active was 18...a5!? 19.0-0 a4 20.♘d2 ♕b6+ 21.♔h1 h6! 22.♕g3 ♕b2 and Black will have a dangerous passed a-pawn. More in the spirit of the line (play against the weak c-pawns) is the solid 18...b6!? 19.0-0 ♗a6 20.♖fd1 ♗xc4 21.♗xc4+ ♕xc4=; but not 18...♗e6? 19.♕xe5 ♗xc4 20.♕c5+−.

19.♕e3 b6

19...♘h5!? with the idea of 20...♘f4.

20.g4?

20.c5 ♗e6 21.0-0±.

20...♗e6?!

White will answer the attack on the c4 pawn with a counterattack on the kingside. The move 18...h6 helps White to open the g-file. More promising was 20...♗a6!? 21.g5? ♘h5! 22.gxh6 ♘f4 .

21.g5 hxg5?

21...♘h5.

22.♕xg5 ♘h7

22...♗xc4 loses a piece after 23.♖g1 ♖e7 24.♗xc4+ ♕xc4 25.♕xf6.

23.♕xe5 ♗xc4 24.♗xc4+ ♕xc4 25.♕d4 ♕f7 26.0-0 ♖ad8

Black has no real compensation for the pawn, and this attack is a last attempt to trouble the waters.

27.♕e3 ♖d6 28.♖cd1 ♖g6+ 29.♔h1 ♘g5 30.♖g1 ♖f8 31.♘d4 ♘xf3 32.♖xg6 ♘xd4 33.♖xg7+ ♔xg7 34.♖g1+ **1-0**

Almost 100 years later, 8...♕a3 is still playable, but now it is Black who must study all the resources deeply!

GAME 5
□ **Isaac Kashdan**
■ **Carl Pilnick**
New York ch-USA 1942 (1)

1.d4 ♘f6 2.c4 e5 3.dxe5 ♘g4 4.♗f4 ♘c6 5.♘f3 ♗b4+ 6.♘c3! ♕e7

It is advisable to exchange the bishop immediately: 6...♗xc3+ 7.bxc3 ♕e7.

7.♕d5

White can take advantage of his bishop pair combined with his superior pawn structure by the natural 7.♖c1!? ♘gxe5 8.♘xe5 ♘xe5 9.a3 ♗xc3+ 10.♖xc3, obtaining a slightly better position, Lugovoi-Novitsky, St Petersburg 2000.

7...♗xc3+ 8.bxc3 f6!

The modern reply.

9.exf6

The best choice is to take. 9.e6 doesn't promise much: 9...dxe6 10.♕h5+ g6 11.♕xg4 e5 12.♕g3 exf4 13.♕xf4 ♗d7!? and Black is better prepared for the attack on either side of the board.

However, the typical counterblow 9.c5!? may be interesting: 9...fxe5 10.♗g5 ♘f6 11.♗xf6 gxf6, with a complicated position.

9...♘xf6 10.♕d3! d6

We have arrived at the position that is currently considered to be the most important in the line with 6.♘c3.

11.g3!

The best method of development. White has scored well with this line so far. The alternative 11.e3 is also popular – see Games 14-18.

11...0-0

A natural move. Other interesting possibilities are 11...b6 and also 11...♘e4. We will analyse those below in Games 10/11 and 12/13.

12.♗g2 ♘e4!?

Pilnick uses Schlechter's idea against 11.e3 (Game 2). After 12...♘a5!? there followed 13.0-0 (it may be better take advantage of this turn and try 13.♘g5!? h6 14.♗d5+!? ♔h8 15.h4 and the situation is very irrational) 13...♗e6 14.♘d2 ♘d7!? in Van Wely-Blatny, New York 1996; 14...♕f7?! 15.c5!? dxc5 16.♕b5; or 14...♖ae8!? are also unclear.

13.0-0 ♗f5?

This is too simple. Black usually continues 13...♘c5!? and if 14.♕e3!?, now there are several alternatives: 14...♕f6!, keeping the queens on the board (14...♗e6?! 15.♘d4! (one of the advantages of having more material is that you can return it at the right moment!) 15...♗xc4 16.♘xc6 ♕xe3 17.♗xe3 bxc6 and we will soon reach an endgame that is technically winning for White, Seirawan-Wessman, New York 1990; 14...♗g4 15.♕xe7 ♘xe7 16.♘d4 (16.♗e3!?) 16...♖ae8 17.♖fb1 ♘g6 18.♗e3 c6 19.h3 ♗c8 20.♘b3 ♘a4 21.♖c1 ♘e5 22.c5 ♘c4 23.♗d4 d5⇄ Kortchnoi-Faure, Zürich simul 1988) 15.♘d4 ♘d8? (much better is 15...♘xd4!? 16.cxd4 ♘e6 17.♗d5 ♔h8 18.♗xe6 ♗xe6⇄ or also 15...♗d7!? 16.♕d2 ♘a5⇄) 16.♕d2 ♔h8 17.♘b3 ♘de6 18.♗e3± Barsov-Demetrios, Val Thorens 1994.

Also interesting is 13...♗d7!? intending 14...♖e8.

14.♘h4!

An unexpected reaction.

14...g6 15.♘xf5 gxf5 16.♖ab1!

The old masters have arrived at a position with a clear advantage for White.

16...♖ab8 17.♖b2 ♔h8 18.♖fb1 b6 19.♕d5 ♕e8 20.♗e3!

Kashdan now increases his advantage with great mastery.

20...♘e7 21.♕d4+ ♘f6 22.♗h6 ♖f7 23.♗g5 ♘g8 24.♗d5+− c5 25.♗xf7 cxd4 26.♗xe8 dxc3 27.♖c2 ♖xe8 28.♗f4! ♖c8 29.♖xc3 d5 30.♖bc1 ♖e8 31.♗e3 ♘e7 32.♗d4 ♔g7 33.♖e3 1-0

Summary of 12...♘e4: after 13.0-0 it is necessary to continue 13...♘c5!? or 13...♗d7!? although, in my opinion, Schlechter's blockading idea is more effective against 11.e3.

GAME 6
□ **Ian Rogers**
■ **Normunds Miezis**
Reykjavik Open 2004 (8)

This is a typical example of correct opening play: two great present-day specialists of this opening dispute an important theme. Indeed, this game provides us with some answers about the main motifs of the 6.♘c3!? line.

1.d4 ♘f6 2.c4 e5 3.dxe5 ♘g4 4.♗f4 ♘c6 5.♘f3 ♗b4+ 6.♘c3! ♕e7 7.♕d5 f6 8.exf6 ♗xc3+

Also interesting is 8...♘xf6!? as in another spectacular game between two classic masters: 9.♕d3 d6 (9...♘e4!?) 10.♘d2?! (10.♗g5!?) 10...0-0 11.g3 ♗g4 (11...♘e5!?) 12.♗g2 ♖ae8 13.f3

analysis diagram

13...♗f5? (13...♗xc3! 14.bxc3 ♗e6⩲
△ ...♘d7, ...♛f7) 14.e4 g5? 15.♗xg5
♘xe4 16.♛d5+! ♔h8 17.♗xe7 ♘xc3
18.bxc3 ♖xe7+ 19.♔d1 ♗xc3 20.♖c1
♗b2 21.♘e4 ♗xc1 22.♔xc1 ♗xe4
23.fxe4 ♖f2 24.♖f1! 1-0 Spielmann-
Réti, Vienna 1921.

**9.bxc3 ♘xf6 10.♛d3 d6 11.g3 0-0
12.♗g2 ♗d7!? 13.0-0 ♖ae8**

The black pieces are neatly concentrated
in the centre.

14.c5!?

A typical sacrifice.

14...dxc5!

Grandmaster Miezis starts an innovative
and very interesting plan. In the only
known earlier game the following happened: 14...♘e5 15.cxd6! cxd6
16.♛d4±, Legky-Altisen Palmada,
Cannes 1999; 16.♘xe5!? dxe5
17.♗g5±.

15.♗xc7 c4!

This is a new position in which Black
seems to have a choice between several
moves, but a total lack of practical expe-
rience makes it hard to determine
which is the better plan. In case of
15...♛xe2 16.♛xe2 ♖xe2 17.♗d6±
White wins the pawn on c5.

16.♛d1!

Of course not 16.♛xc4+?? ♗e6−+.

GM Normunds Miezis, one of today's great
experts of the Budapest Gambit.

16...♘e4 17.♖c1

A slightly more adventurous alternative
is to reactivate the queen with
17.♛d5+!? ♛f7.

17...♖f7 18.♗f4

How to interpret this situation? The
best way is to analyse and try to find a
way to move the black queen to strategically important squares.

18...♛c5!?

Obviously Black has good compensation for the pawn – his pieces are ready
to attack. But we must not forget that
we live in times of modern chess and

there is a small problem: White is also in good shape – an extra pawn, two bishops, a good pawn structure. There is a lot of play for both sides. Alternatives are 18...♕f6!? and 18...♕a3!?.

19.♕c2!

With the idea of ♘d4!.

19...♕h5

The black queen approaches the enemy king. If 19...♗f5 20.♕b2±.

20.♖cd1?!

The critical moment of the game. It was better to try and activate the minor pieces with 20.♘d4!?, when in the case of 20...♘f6 21.e4! ♘g4 22.h3 ♘ge5 23.♕e2! White has the advantage.

20...♗h3! 21.♗xh3 ♕xh3 22.♖d5 h6

Losing an important tempo. More forceful was 22...♕e6! (exploiting some tactical motifs) 23.♖fd1 ♖xf4! 24.gxf4 ♕g4+ 25.♔f1 ♕h3+ 26.♔g1 (26.♔e1?? ♕g2–+) 26...♕g4+ with a draw by repetition of moves.

23.♗e5!

The fight continues.

23...♘g5

23...♕g4 24.♗d4.

24.♘xg5 hxg5 25.♗d6!

The bishop is perfectly placed on this square. It constricts the black knight and defends its own kingside!

25...♖e6?

Intending to give mate with 26...♖h6 and 27...♕xh2. But this does not work. Better was 25...♖f6! 26.f3 (26.e4 ♕h7!?) 26...♕e6! 27.♖d2 (27.e4 g4!) 27...♕e3+ and nothing is decided yet.

26.f3!

Preparing g4 or e4.

26...♖d7

26...♖h6 27.e4±.

27.♖fd1

The balance is tipped in White's favour.

27...♖f7 28.g4!

Fixing the g5 and g7 pawns.

28...♖e3 29.♖xg5

29.♗c5+–.

29...♕h7 30.♕d2 ♖e6 31.♗g3 ♕h6 32.h4 ♖e8 33.♖h5?!

In spite of several errors, White maintains his advantage until the end.

33...♕e6?

The last chance was 33...♕e3+ 34.♕xe3 ♖xe3 35.♔f2 ♖xc3 36.♖d2±.

34.♕c2+− ♖f6 35.♕h7+ ♔f7 36.♖g5 ♖g8 37.♔f1 ♕e3 38.♖f5 ♘e7 39.♖xf6+ ♔xf6 40.♕h5 g6 41.♕b5 ♕xc3 42.♕g5+ ♔f7 43.♗e5 ♕b4 44.♗d6 **1-0**

A very combative game in which both players demonstrated superior knowledge of this variation. Probably the knowledge of these lines will soon advance.

GAME 7
□ **Dmitry Gurevich**
■ **Daniel Pacheco**
Buenos Aires 2005 (2)

1.d4 ♘f6 2.c4 e5 3.dxe5 ♘g4 4.♗f4 ♗b4+ 5.♘c3 ♘c6 6.♘f3 ♗xc3+ 7.bxc3 ♕e7 8.♕d5 f6 9.exf6 ♘xf6 10.♕d3 d6 11.g3 0-0 12.♗g2 ♗g4!?

This natural plan is probably the most aggressive. Black mobilizes his pieces quickly!

13.♘d4?!

This is one of the key moves of White's counterplan, but it's too early yet. Better is 13.0-0, see the next games.
Another idea is 13.♖b1!?.

13...♖ae8!

Fighting for the initiative. Also interesting is 13...♘e5!?.

14.♘xc6 bxc6

14...♕xe2+? 15.♕xe2 ♖xe2+ 16.♔f1 bxc6 17.f3 ♖b2 18.fxg4 ♘xg4 19.♔g1 ♘f2 20.h4 ♘xh1 21.♗xh1±.

15.♗e3

An important moment: 15.e3 ♕d7!?.

15...♗d7?!

With 15...c5!, blockading the c3/c4 structure, Black could have obtained better perspectives: 16.0-0 ♕f7 with two attacking threats: ...♗e6 or ...♕h5.

16.♗g5

16.0-0 was preferable.

16...♕e5

16...♗f5!?.

17.♗xf6 ♖xf6

In the end the game loses its course. Many mistakes are made, and one way or another it all ends in White's favour.

18.e3 ♕c5

18...♕h5!?.

19.♕d4 ♕h5 20.♖d1 ♗g4 21.♖d2 ♗f3 22.♗xf3 ♕xf3 23.0-0 a5 24.♖b2 h5 25.♖b7 ♖e4 26.♕d1 ♕f5

26...♕xd1 27.♖xd1 ♖xc4=.

27.♕e2 h4 28.f3

28.♖xc7!?.

28...hxg3! 29.hxg3 ♖e7

29...♕h3!? 30.♕g2 ♕xg2+ 31.♔xg2 ♖xe3⇄.

30.♔g2?

30.e4.

30...♖h6 31.g4? ♕g5?

31...♕h7!–+.

32.♖b8+ ♔f7 33.♕f2 ♖xe3 34.♖e1 ♖he6

34...♕f4!.

35.♖xe3 ♖xe3 36.♖b7 ♖e7 37.♖b2 ♕c5?

37...♕c1∓.

38.♕d4?

38.♕xc5 dxc5 39.♖b7±.

38...♕g5 39.♔g3 ♕c1 40.♕f4+ ♕xf4+ 41.♔xf4 ♖e5 42.g5 ♖c5 43.♔g4 ♖xc4+ 44.f4 ♖xc3 45.♖b7 g6= 46.♖xc7+ ♔f8 47.♖c8+ ♔e7 48.♖c7+ ♔f8 49.♖c8+ ♔e7 50.♖c7+ ♔e8?? 51.♔g7 ♖d3 52.♖xg6 ♔f7 53.♖f6+ ♔e7 54.♖h6 c5 55.f5+– c4 56.♖h7+ ♔d8 57.f6 ♔e8 58.g6 ♖d4+ 59.♔f5 c3 60.♖c7 ♔d8 61.g7   1-0

Summarizing 12...♗g4!?: clearly the plan with ...♗g4 and ...♖e8 is a good possibility to fight the 11.g3 fianchetto. All Black's pieces are active and prepared to attack White's weaknesses, the pawns on c3/c4, e2 and a2, and also the centre and the kingside (see Games 8 and 9).

GAME 8
□ **Maxim Dlugy**
■ **Vladimir Epishin**
New York Open 1989 (1)

1.d4 ♘f6 2.c4 e5 3.dxe5 ♘g4 4.♗f4 ♘c6 5.♘f3 ♗b4+ 6.♘c3 ♗xc3+ 7.bxc3 ♕e7 8.♕d5 f6 9.exf6 ♘xf6 10.♕d3 d6 11.g3 0-0 12.♗g2 ♗g4!? 13.0-0

Castling is more logical than 13.♘d4?!, as played in the previous game.

13...♖ae8 14.♖ae1!?

14.♖ab1!?.

14...♔h8!

This move is very useful, as it prevents a possible check or a pin on the a2-g8 diagonal. 14...♗h5!?.

15.♘d4!?

The typical knight manoeuvre.

15...♘a5!?

Black prefers to keep the game complicated by avoiding exchanges. To achieve the balance, correct was 15...♘e5! 16.♗xe5 dxe5 17.♘b3 c5 and White's position is blocked; after 18.h3 the game J.Piket-Reinderman, Rotterdam ch-NED 1999, was agreed drawn.

16.♗g5 ♕e5 17.♗xf6 ♖xf6≅ 18.e3 ♗h5

18...♕h5!? with the idea ...♖h6 or ...♕f7.

19.♘b3 ♗g6 20.♕d4

20.e4!?.

20...♘c6 21.♕d2?! ♕e7 22.e4 ♗f7 23.♕e2 ♕e6 24.c5 ♕c4 25.♕d2 a5⌓ 26.cxd6 ♖xd6 27.♕b2 ♖d3 28.♖c1 a4 29.♘d4 ♘xd4 30.cxd4 ♕xd4 31.♕xd4 ½-½

We see that the plan with ...♗g4 and ...♖e8 successfully reduces the effect of the powerful knight move to d4. If Black remains alert, he will get enough counterplay to keep the balance: 31...♖xd4 32.♖xc7 ♗xa2 33.♖xb7 a3.

As always in this line, if White plays ♘d4!?, Black replies ...♘e5!, after which he has the same number of pieces in the centre.

GAME 9
□ **Alejandro Hoffman**
■ **Claudia Amura**
Potrero de los Funes 1995 (8)

1.d4 ♘f6 2.c4 e5 3.dxe5 ♘g4 4.♗f4 ♘c6 5.♘f3 ♗b4+ 6.♘c3 ♗xc3+ 7.bxc3 ♕e7 8.♕d5 f6 9.exf6 ♘xf6 10.♕d3 d6 11.g3 0-0 12.♗g2 ♗g4 13.0-0 ♖ae8

14.♖fe1

In this game White moves his kingside rook. One must try everything! 14.♘d4?! ♗xe2?! (better is 14...♘xd4 15.♕xd4 ♗xe2 (15...b6!?) 16.♖fe1

♕f7⇄) 15.♘xe2 ♕xe2 16.♕xe2 ♖xe2 17.♗f3!?± Barsov-Chatalbashev, Val Thorens 1996; 17.♖fb1!? ♘a5 18.c5!.

14...♘d7!?

Creating two possibilities, ...♘c5 and ...♘e5. In another game, Black achieved more than just equality by using Epishin's 'mysterious' move 14...♔h8!? 15.♘d4 ♘e5!

analysis diagram

16.♕b1 c6 17.♕b3 ♘h5 18.♗e3 ♕f7 19.c5 ♘c4↑ 20.♘f3 ♘xe3 21.♕xf7 ♖xf7 22.fxe3 dxc5∓ 23.e4 ♘f6 24.♖ad1 h6 25.♘d2 ♖d7 26.♘b3 ♖xd1 27.♖xd1 ♘xe4 28.♗xe4 ♖xe4 29.♘xc5 ♖xe2 30.♘xb7 ♖xa2 31.♖d4 ♗h3 32.♘d8 ♖g2+ 0-1 Gralka-Murdzia, Polish Championship, Augustow 1996.

15.♘d4!

As we know, this is White's programmed manoeuvre in this position. The knight is untouchable on d4.

15...♘ce5!

But the knight on e5 also!

16.♕b1 ♘b6

Careful! 16...b6? 17.h3 ♗h5 18.♘e6! loses on the spot.

17.a4

17.♗e4!?.

17...c5!?

With complicated play that ends in a draw. Another option is 17...a5.

18.♘c2

18.♘b5!? ♘bxc4 19.♗xe5 ♘xe5 20.♘xa7±.

18...♗f5 19.e4?! ♗e6 20.♗xe5 dxe5 21.♘e3 ♘xc4 22.♘d5 ♕f7 23.♕c2 b6 24.♖ad1 ♗d7 25.♗f1

25...♗xa4!?

25...♘d6!?.

26.♕xa4 ♕xf2+ 27.♔h1 ♘b2 28.♕a1 ♘xd1 29.♕xd1 ♔h8 30.♕e2 g6 31.♕xf2 ♖xf2 32.♗e2 ♖ef8 33.♔g1 ♖2f7 34.♘e3 ♖d8 35.♗c4 ♖b7 36.♗d5 ♖e7 37.♘c4 ♖f8 38.♔g2 ♔g7 39.h4 h5 40.♖a1 ♖f6 41.♘a3 a6 42.♘c4 b5 43.♘a5 ♖c7 44.c4 ♔h6 45.♖b1 g5 46.cxb5 axb5 47.hxg5+ ♔xg5 48.♖xb5 h4 49.♘c4 hxg3 50.♖b3 ♖f4 51.♘xe5 ♖xe4 52.♗xe4

♗f4 53.♗c2 ♔xe5 54.♖xg3 ♖f7 55.♗d1 ♔d4 56.♗e2 ♖f4 57.♖d3+ ♔e4 58.♖d8 ♔e3 59.♗f3 c4 60.♖e8+ ♔d2 61.♔f2 c3 62.♖d8+ ♔c1 63.♔e3 ♖f6 64.♗e4 ♖b6 65.♖h8 c2 66.♖c8 ♖b3+ 67.♔d3 ♖b2 68.♖c7 ♔d1 69.♗e2+ ♔c1 70.♖c6 ♖b6 71.♖c5 ♔b2 72.♔d2 ♖d6+ 73.♗d3   ½-½

GAME 10
□ **Viktor Kortchnoi**
■ **Georg Mohr**
Ptuj Zonal 1995 (8)

This game provides a good illustration of the type of middlegame that often arises in this variation. Viktor Kortchnoi is known as a middlegame specialist. Here we have a demonstration of his talent.

1.d4 ♘f6 2.c4 e5 3.dxe5 ♘g4 4.♗f4 ♗b4+ 5.♘c3!? ♗xc3+!

It is better to exchange the bishop immediately.

6.bxc3 ♘c6 7.♘f3 ♕e7 8.♕d5 f6 9.exf6 ♘xf6 10.♕d3 d6 11.g3 b6!?

The start of an interesting plan.

12.♗g2 ♗b7 13.0-0 ♘a5!?

If 13...0-0 14.♘g5!? or 14.♘d4!?.

14.♘d2!?

White defends his extra pawn on c4 and prepares a frontal attack.

14...♗xg2 15.♔xg2 ♕e6!?

15...0-0 16.♗g5! ♖ae8 17.e4 ♕d7 (17...♔h8!? 18.♖ae1 ♘b7) 18.♗xf6 ♖xf6 19.f4 ♖fe6 (19...c6) 20.♖ae1 ♕a4? (20...♘b7 21.f5 ♖e5 22.♘f3 ♖a5 23.♖f2±) 21.f5 ♖e5 22.f6!→ Krasenkow-Wippermann, Baden-Baden 2005.

16.♗g5!

With the idea to exchange the bishop and to push the pawns to e4 and f4. 16.♕e3!?.

16...♘d7!

16...0-0 17.♗xf6 ♖xf6 (17...♕xf6 18.♘b3±) 18.♕d5 ♖e8 19.e4±, and the ♘a5 is vulnerable.

17.♕d5! ♔f7□

17...♕xd5+ 18.cxd5 h6 19.♗e3 intending 20.♗d4+−.

18.♕f3+ ♔g6!?

18...♘f6 19.♗xf6 ♕xf6 20.♕d3 and now the ♔f7 as well as the ♘a5 are misplaced.

19.h4 ♖ae8

19...♘xc4? 20.♕d3++−.

20.e4

The tensest moment of the game. The position is complicated and Black must find a plan to create effective counterplay.

20...h6

20...♘e5!? 21.♕e2 h6! 22.f4 ♕g4!∞.

Legendary GM Viktor Kortchnoi had to fight against the BG in many games, always choosing 4.♗f4.

21.♗f4 ♘f6

21...♘e5 22.♗xe5 ♕xe5 23.♕d3→; 21...♘xc4? 22.♘xc4 ♕xc4 23.♕g4++−.

22.♕d3 ♔f7 23.♖ae1 g5!?

The beginning of complications which will develop in White's favour. If 23...♘d7 24.♕d5±.

24.e5!□ gxf4

24...dxe5 25.♗xe5 ♖d8 26.♕c2→.

25.exf6 ♕xf6 26.♘e4

26...♕d8?

Necessary was 26...♕g6 27.♕f3 ♘xc4 (27...♖hf8 28.♕xf4+ ♔g7 29.♕e3±

♘xc4 30.♕d4+ ♘e5 31.f4) 28.♕xf4+
♔g7 29.h5 ♕f7 30.♕g4+ ♔f8!±.

**27.♕f3+− ♖hf8 28.♕xf4+ ♔g7
29.♕g4+ ♔h8**

Or 29...♔h7 30.h5 ♖g8 31.♕f5+ ♔h8
32.♘f6+−.

30.♕g6   1-0

This wasn't the first time that Viktor
Kortchnoi obtained victory after a tense
struggle!

GAME 11
□ Alexander Shabalov
■ Till Wippermann
Bad Wiessee 2002 (3)

**1.d4 ♘f6 2.c4 e5 3.dxe5 ♘g4 4.♗f4
♘c6 5.♘f3 ♗b4+ 6.♘c3 ♕e7 7.♕d5
♗xc3+ 8.bxc3 f6 9.exf6 ♘xf6 10.♕d3
d6 11.g3 b6 12.♗g2 ♗b7 13.0-0
♘a5!? 14.♖fe1!?**

With the idea e2-e4. Now, not so good
is 14.♘d4 ♗xg2 15.♔xg2 0-0 16.♗g5
♖ae8 17.♖ae1 ♕f7 (eyeing c4)
18.♗xf6!? gxf6 19.e4= Ljubojevic-
Ivanchuk, Monaco blind 1999, but interesting may be the direct 14.e4!? and
if 14...♗xe4?! 15.♕d1! 0-0 16.♖e1.

14...0-0?!
Necessary was 14...♗e4.
15.e4! ♘h5

After 15...♗xe4? 16.♕d1 Black will
lose on account of the pin along the
e-file: 16...♕d7 17.♖xe4 ♘xe4
18.♕d5+±; 15...♖ad8!? 16.♖ad1 ♗a6
offers mutual chances.

16.♗c1 ♕f7 17.c5! dxc5 18.♕c2 h6?

Probably the decisive mistake, after
which White's kingside majority becomes mobile, a factor which decides
the game. Better was 18...♖ae8 or
18...♕e8!?.

**19.♘e5! ♕e6 20.f4 ♖fe8 21.♕e2 ♘f6
22.♕f1 ♖ad8 23.♗h3 ♕e7 24.♗f5
♕f8 25.♖b1!?**

With the idea of ♖b2 and ♖f2.

**25...♗c8 26.♗g6 ♖e7 27.♖b2 ♗b7
28.♖f2 ♖d6 29.♗f5 ♕a8 30.♕g2 ♖d8
31.g4! ♗c8 32.g5 hxg5 33.fxg5 ♘e8
34.♘g6 ♖f7 35.♕h3   1-0**

GAME 12
□ Alexey Barsov
■ Marcel Roofthoofd
Antwerp Open 1996 (2)

**1.d4 ♘f6 2.c4 e5 3.dxe5 ♘g4 4.♗f4
♘c6 5.♘f3 ♗b4+ 6.♘c3 ♗xc3+
7.bxc3 ♕e7 8.♕d5 f6 9.exf6 ♘xf6
10.♕d3 d6 11.g3 ♘e4**

An attempt to activate the Schlechter
Knight before castling.

12.♗g2 ♘c5

For 12...0-0 see Game 5, Kashdan-Pilnick.

13.♕e3

13...0-0!?

For 13...♘a5 see the next game, Bareev-Rogers. Alternatives are:

A) 13...♕xe3?!, but after the queen exchange White won quickly: 14.♗xe3 0-0 (if 14...♘a4?! 15.♘d4! ♘e5 16.♘b5+− Exposito Cabrera-Glavina Rossi, Cordoba 1990) 15.♘d4 ♘a5 16.♘b5 ♘a6 17.♗f4 ♗e6 18.c5!+− Shirov-Bang, Neuilly sur Seine simul 2001;

B) 13...♘e6!? 14.♘g5!? (14.♘d4? ♘cxd4 15.cxd4 g5!) 14...♘xf4 15.gxf4 ♕xe3 16.fxe3 ♘a5 17.c5! dxc5 18.♘e4± Tukmakov-Del Prado Montoro, Cordoba 1991.

14.♘d4!

Taking advantage of his turn, White, instead of castling, prepares a counterattack in the centre and on the queenside. On the squares d4 and b3 the knight is untouchable! Less strong was 14.♕xe7!? ♘xe7 15.♘d4±.

14...♘e5 15.♘b3! ♘cd7

16.c5! ♘f6 17.0-0 ♔h8 18.♘a5
18.cxd6!? cxd6 19.♖ad1+−.

18...♘fg4 19.cxd6! cxd6 20.♕d4+− ♕c7 21.♕b4 ♗d7 22.♖ad1 ♖ad8 23.h3 b6 24.hxg4 bxa5 25.♕xd6 1-0

We can conclude that after the fianchetto 11.g3!, the blockading idea ...♘e4-♘c5 doesn't seem as effective as in case of 11.e3.

GAME 13
□ **Evgeny Bareev**
■ **Ian Rogers**
Germany Bundesliga 1999/2000 (3)

This is another typical game that may be useful for learning the basic ideas of this variation.

1.d4 ♘f6 2.c4 e5 3.dxe5 ♘g4 4.♗f4 ♘c6 5.♘f3 ♗b4+ 6.♘c3 ♕e7 7.♕d5 ♗xc3+ 8.bxc3 f6 9.exf6 ♘xf6 10.♕d3 d6 11.g3 ♘e4 12.♗g2 ♘c5 13.♕e3 ♘a5

14.♕xe7+

Not 14.♘d2?! ♗e6⇄ 15.♗d5 0-0 16.♘b3 ♘axb3 17.axb3 ♕f7 18.b4? (18.♗xe6 ♘xe6 19.♕d2=) 18...♗xd5 19.cxd5 ♕xd5 20.0-0 ♘e6∓ 21.♖xa7?? ♖xa7 22.♕xa7 ♖xf4! 23.gxf4 ♘xf4 24.f3 ♕g5+ 25.♔f2 ♘h3+ 0-1 Röschlau-Blasek, Schöneck 1988.

14...♔xe7 15.♗g5+!

15.♘d2!?.

15...♔e8 16.♘d2 ♗e6 17.♗e3!

In the ensuing battle of three minor pieces against three, White's bishop pair prevails in the end.

17...♘a4

18.c5

As always an important resource – one of the advantages of the two bishops is that one of them can be exchanged advantageously at the right time! But per-

haps this time this push wasn't necessary for a change. In fact, now was the time to open fire on the other flank: 18.h4!? c6 (18...♘xc3 19.♗d4±) 19.h5 h6 20.♖h4!±. The rook enters the game, increasing White's advantage.

18...♘xc5 19.♗xc5 dxc5 20.♘e4 ♗d5 21.0-0-0

Worthy of attention was 21.♘d6+!? ♔d7 (21...cxd6 22.♗xd5±) 22.♗xd5 ♔xd6 23.0-0-0 and White is very comfortable in this ending.

21...♗c6 22.♖d3 ♔e7 23.♗f3 b6 24.♘g5 ♔f6 25.h4↑ h6 26.♘e4+

26.♗xc6!? ♘xc6 27.♖f3+ ♔g6 28.♘e6↑.

26...♔e7 27.♘d2 ♖hd8 28.♖e3+ ♔f7 29.♖d1 ♖d6 30.♗xc6 ♘xc6 31.♘c4 ♖xd1+ 32.♔xd1 ♖d8+ 33.♔c2 ♔f6 34.g4 ♖d7 35.♖f3+ ♔e6 36.h5 b5 37.♖e3+ ♔d5 38.♘d2 c4 39.f3

39.f4!? ♖f7 40.♖f3±.

39...♘e5 40.♖e4 c5 41.♘f1 ♖f7 42.♘e3+ ♔d6 43.f4 ♘c6 44.♘f5+ ♔d7 45.♔d1 ♘e7

46.♖e5

The pawn ending after 46.♘xe7 ♖xe7 47.♖xe7+ ♔xe7 is a draw.

46...♘xf5 47.gxf5 ♔d6   ½-½

48.♖e6+ ♔d7 49.e4 ♖e7!=.

Although in the end Rogers managed to draw, he was forced throughout to fight with all his might just to survive. I believe that Bareev did not manage to convert his advantage properly at several critical points, for example with 18.h4! or 21.♘d6+!?.

GAME 14
□ **Milan Vukic**
■ **Ian Rogers**
Reggio Emilia 1983/84 (2)

1.d4 ♘f6 2.c4 e5 3.dxe5 ♘g4 4.♗f4 ♘c6 5.♘f3 ♗b4+ 6.♘c3 ♗xc3+ 7.bxc3 ♕e7 8.♕d5 f6 9.exf6 ♘xf6 10.♕d3 d6 11.e3

This is the main alternative to 11.g3!. See also the stem game Rubinstein-Schlechter (Game 2).
11...0-0 12.♗e2 ♘e4 13.♘d4
Another sharp game saw 13.♖c1?! ♗g4 (13...♘c5!?) 14.♕d5+ ♔h8 15.♘d4?? (15.0-0 ♘c5∞) 15...♘xf4! 16.exf4 ♘xd4? (16...♘f6!–+) 17.♕xd4 ♗xe2 18.♔xe2 ♘g3+ 19.♔f3 ♘xh1 20.♖xh1 ♖e8↑ Vanek-Schirmbeck, Litomysl 2005.
13...♘c5!
13...♘xf2?! 14.♔xf2 g5 15.♖hf1±.
14.♕d1 ♘e5!? 15.0-0 ♔h8!?
One of the most useful moves here.

16.♖c1 ♗d7 17.♕c2 ♕f7
17...♗e8!?.
18.♗xe5 dxe5 19.♘f3 ♕e7 20.♘d2 ♗c6 21.♗f3 e4 22.♗e2 ♖f6∞
For the pawn, Black has an initiative on the kingside.

23.♘b3 ♖h6
Rogers prefers to finish off with two major pieces, forgetting that he has a rook on a8. This allows his opponent to escape defeat... Preferable was 23...♖af8!?, involving all the pieces in the attack.
24.♘xc5 ♕xc5 25.♖cd1 ♕e5
25...♕g5!?.
26.h3 ♕g5 27.♗g4 ♖g6
27...♖f8!?.
28.♕e2! ♕a5?!   ½-½
28...h5? 29.f4! exf3 30.♗xf3 ♖e8 31.♗xc6 ♖xc6 32.e4±; ≥ 28...♖e8=.

GAME 15
□ **Sergey Kishnev**
■ **Roeland Mollekens**
Antwerp Open 1993 (3)

1.d4 ♘f6 2.c4 e5 3.dxe5 ♘g4 4.♗f4 ♗b4+ 5.♘c3 ♗xc3+ 6.bxc3 ♘c6 7.♘f3 ♕e7 8.♕d5 f6 9.exf6 ♘xf6 10.♕d3 d6 11.e3 0-0 12.♗e2 ♘e4 13.0-0!?
This is more natural than 13.♘d4.

13...♗f5!?

13...♘c5!?.

14.♕d5+ ♔h8 15.♖ac1 ♗g6!?

Preparing an interesting trick.

16.♘d4 ♘d8! 17.♖fe1 a5!

With the idea to hunt down the white queen! 17...c6!?.

18.♕b5

Looking for the exit!

18...♘c5!

It seems everything is blocked...

19.♘b3??

...aha!!

19...♗e8!–+ 20.♕xa5 ♖xa5 21.♘xa5 ♗g6   **0-1**

GAME 16
□ **Ruslan Pogorelov**
■ **Alberto Andres Gonzalez**
Mondariz Open 2000 (6)

1.d4 ♘f6 2.c4 e5 3.dxe5 ♘g4 4.♘f3 ♘c6 5.♗f4 ♗b4+ 6.♘c3 ♕e7 7.♕d5

f6 8.exf6 ♗xc3+ 9.bxc3 ♘xf6 10.♕d3 d6 11.e3 0-0 12.♗e2 ♘e4 13.0-0 ♗f5 14.♕d5+ ♔h8 15.♖ac1 ♘c5!?

This move also seems good.

16.♘d4 ♗e4 17.♘xc6 bxc6

17...♕e8!? 18.♕d2 ♗xc6⇄.

18.♕d2 ♘d7 19.f3 ♗f5 20.e4 ♗e6 21.♗e3 c5! 22.♖b1 ♘b6⇄ 23.♖fe1 ♖ae8

23...♘xc4=.

24.♗f2 ♕f7 25.e5 ♗f5 26.♗d3 ♖xe5?

26...♗xd3 27.♕xd3 ♘xc4 28.exd6 cxd6 is equal.

27.♖xe5 dxe5 28.♗xf5 ♕xf5 29.♖e1 ♘xc4 30.♕d5 ♘b2 31.♗xc5 ♘d3 32.♗xf8 ♘xe1 33.♗c5 h6

34.♕d2??

A great mix-up. 34.♗xa7! ♕b1 35.♕a8+ ♔h7 36.♕e4++–.

34...♕b1!–+ 35.♕d8+ ♔h7 36.h3 ♘d3+ 37.♔h2 ♘xc5 38.♕xc7 ♘d3

39.♕xa7 ♕c1 40.♕a8 ♕f4+ 41.♔g1 ♘c1 42.a4 ♘e2+ 43.♔f2 ♘xc3 44.a5 e4 45.♕d8 e3+ 46.♔g1 ♘e2+ 47.♔h1 ♘d4 48.♕b6 e2 49.♕b1+ ♕f5 50.♕e1 ♕d3   0-1

GAME 17
□ Jozsef Pinter
■ Miso Cebalo
Rabac tt 2004 (1)

1.d4 ♘f6 2.c4 e5 3.dxe5 ♘g4 4.♗f4 ♘c6 5.♘f3 ♗b4+ 6.♘c3 ♗xc3+ 7.bxc3 ♕e7 8.♕d5 f6 9.exf6 ♘xf6 10.♕d3 d6 11.e3
If 11.♕e3 ♗e6! 12.♖b1 0-0!⇄.
11...0-0 12.♗e2

12...b6!?
A new idea against 11.e3, which was previously used against 11.g3; 12...♘d8?! 13.c5! was played in another famous game: 13...d5 14.c4 (14.♗e5!?) 14...♘e6 15.♗e5 ♘xc5∞ 16.♕d4 dxc4 17.♕xc4+ ♗e6 18.♕h4 ♘ce4 19.0-0 ♗g4 (19...♗d5!?) 20.♗b2 ♖ad8 21.h3 ♗e6 22.♖fd1 ♖xd1+ 23.♗xd1 ♕b4 24.♗e5 c5 (24...♕c5) 25.♗c2 ♘d2?? 26.♗xf6+– Reshevsky-D. Olafsson, Reykjavik 1986.
13.0-0 ♗b7 14.♘d4?!
Not good this time; 14.c5!?.

14...♘e5!⇄ 15.♕c2 ♖ae8 16.♖ae1 ♘ed7!? 17.♗d3 ♘c5 18.♗g5?
The critical moment of the opening. Better was 18.f3 ♘xd3 19.♕xd3 ♘d7.

18...h6?!
An excellent opportunity to achieve a clear advantage was 18...♘xd3! 19.♕xd3 ♕e4! 20.♕xe4 ♘xe4∓.
19.♗xf6 ♕xf6 20.e4 ♕e5 21.♖e3 ♘e6
21...a6.
22.♖fe1 ♕c5 23.♗f1

23...♖f6??
23...♘xd4 24.cxd4 ♕xd4∓.
24.♘b3??
24.e5!+–.
24...♕e5
The game continued with many mistakes and in the end White won...
25.g3 g5 26.♗h3 ♖ef8 27.♗f5 ♘g7 28.♘d4 ♕c5 29.♕a4 a6 30.g4 ♕e5

31.♕d1 a5 32.h3 ♖e8 33.♘f3 ♕f4
34.♕d4 ♖ff8 35.♘d2 ♘e6 36.♗xe6+
♖xe6 37.♖1e2 ♕e5 38.♔g2 ♖e7
39.f3 ♗a6 40.♖e1 ♖fe8 41.♖h1 ♖h7
42.♕d5+ ♔g7 43.♘b3 ♕f4 44.♖he1
♖e5 45.♕c6 ♕f7 46.♘d4 ♕xc4
47.♘f5+ ♔f7 48.♕a8 ♖e8 49.♕a7
♔g6 50.h4 h5 51.gxh5+ ♖xh5
52.♖d1 gxh4 53.♖xd6+

53...♔g5?
53...cxd6?? 54.♕g7 mate;
53...♔h7!-+.
**54.♖d1 ♖hh8 55.♘d4 ♔f4 56.♖ed3
♖h7 57.♘e2+ ♔g5 58.♖d5+ ♔h6
59.♘f4 ♖g7+ 60.♔f2 ♔h7 61.♖d7
♖ee7 62.♖7d4 ♕b5 63.♖d5 ♕c4
64.♕a8**
64.♖h5+ ♔g8 65.♕b8+.
64...♖e5 65.♖xe5 ♕xa2+ 66.♔e3 1-0
After analysing this game (and also after careful study of all the games of this
survey) I have the impression that GM's
also make mistakes – especially in the
Budapest Gambit!
Anyway, the idea 12...b6!? deserves
consideration.

In order to complete this part, I would
like to present one of the most interesting and mysterious games with the Budapest Gambit.

GAME 18
□ **Ventzislav Inkiov**
■ **Zeljko Djukic**
Bor 1983 (9)

1.d4 ♘f6 2.c4 e5 3.dxe5 ♘g4 4.♘f3
♘c6 5.♗f4 ♗b4+ 6.♘c3 ♗xc3+ 7.bxc3
♕e7 8.♕d5 f6 9.exf6 ♘xf6 10.♕d1?!
The best move is 10.♕d3.

10...d6 11.e3 0-0 12.♗e2 ♘e4! 13.♖c1
Usually Black's target is the weak pawn on
c4. Possible now is 13...♘c5, planning
...♗e6 and ...♕f7 or ...♘a5. But master
Djukic has an immediate attack in mind.
13...♔h8!?
Preparing to attack with his king's pawns.
14.0-0
Better was 14.♗g3 ♗g4!? 15.♘d4
♗xe2 16.♕xe2 ♘e5 17.♘b3?! b6
18.0-0 ♘xg3 19.hxg3 ♕e6 20.♘d2
♖ae8 Campos Moreno-Rogers, Valjevo
1984.

14...g5!? 15.♗g3 h5!

Already obligatory.

16.♗d3

Or 16.h4 ♘xg3 17.fxg3 gxh4 18.♘xh4 ♕xe3+ 19.♔h1 (19.♔h2 ♖g8) 19...♖xf1+ 20.♕xf1 ♔g7!.

16...♘c5 17.h4

Trying to set up a block. If 17.h3 h4 18.♗h2 g4!→.

17...♖xf3!

This exchange sacrifice obviously came as an unpleasant surprise for White, and promptly there follows a mistake.

18.gxf3

18.♕xf3 ♗g4 19.♕d5 ♗e6 20.♕f3 ♘xd3 21.♕xh5+ ♕h7−+.

18...gxh4 19.♗h2??

The decisive mistake. It would not have been easy for Black to continue his attack after 19.♗f4 ♗h3 20.♔h2! with an unclear position.

19...♗h3 20.♔h1

White is ready to return the exchange, but Black plays for a win:

20...♖g8! 21.♖g1 ♖xg1+!

The most mystifying aspect of this game is its history. I have found three (!) more games that were identical up to here. Here, in the game Lanzani-Rogers, Nuoro 1984, White was tired of defending his bad position and resigned. The third game, Knechtel-Besner, Pfarrkirchen Open 1989 (0-1), followed the text game until move 27. How is this possible??

22.♕xg1

Or 22.♗xg1 ♘xd3 23.♕xd3 ♕g7 with mate to follow.

22...♘xd3 23.♖d1 ♕f7 24.♗f4

24.f4 ♗g4!.

24...♘xf4 25.exf4 ♕xf4 26.♕g6 ♕xf3+ 27.♔h2 ♕xd1 28.♕f6+ ♔g8

0-1

White has no perpetual check: 28...♔g8 29.♕g6+ ♔f8 30.♕f6+ ♔e8 31.♕g6+ ♔d7 32.♕f7+ ♘e7 33.♔xh3 ♕h1 mate.

Summary of Strategies 11.e3/11.g3

White

The main plan is to push forward the e- and f-pawns up to the 4th or 5th rank, gaining space which allows for better piece manoeuvring and a possible attack on the kingside. Alternatively, in some cases White can exchange queens and attack on the queenside. White will also try to exchange his weak queenside pawns .

* 1. The alternatives 11.e3 and 11.g3 allow different developments of the kingside bishop. In the former case it will go to e2, in the latter to g2. Statistics indicate that after the former move Black has equal results, but White's performance after the latter move is overwhelming.

   Why is the position of the light-squared bishop so important? All the squares on the h1-a8 diagonal are important in this variation, whereas the defence of the c4 pawn, which is the main function of the bishop on e2, has not proved to be very useful. Therefore, it seems that the development of the bishop to g2 is more in accordance with the needs of White's position than on e2.

* 2. The g1 knight must go to d4. This knight cannot be captured because this improves White's pawn structure. The knight threatens its counterpart on c6, it can leap to b5 and it can also become annoying on e6 or f5. It allows White to mobilize his kingside pawns, gaining space and controlling central squares. In the variation with 11.g3, this pawn supports the advance of the f-pawn to f4 and the bishop supports the e-pawn.

* 3. The pawn push c4-c5 attacks, along with the bishop on f4, the pawn on d6. If the latter captures on c5 or advances to d5, the e5-square is weakened and White will control it with his f4 bishop and his knight. This plan harmonizes with the previous idea.

* 4. White can also pursue the plan of exchanging queens and attacking on the queenside with the two bishops and the rook on the b-file.

Black

Black has two plans at his disposal: blockading the position with the help of the Schlechter Knight, or attacking White's doubled pawns on the queenside. I think that if White develops his bishop to e2, then the best plan is to play for the blockade, while if the bishop goes to g2, then Black must play more actively and attack the doubled pawns and the e2 pawn. Alternatively, an attack on the white king is possible in some positions, when Black has a space advantage.

* 1. Blockade of the doubled pawns, generally with the g8 knight via ...♘f6-e4-c5. Sometimes the blockader is the b8 knight or even the c-pawn.

* 2. Major pieces on the e-file – in general the queen and the a8 rook.

* 3. The most versatile piece is the black bishop, which can be situated on the long diagonal by a queenside fianchetto or via d7-c6; it can also saunter along the c8-h3 diagonal: we have seen it appear on d7, e6, f5 and on g4. It has been

seen on g6 and f7 as well. The objective varies on each square: for example, it can be exchanged for the white bishop, it can attack the doubled pawns on c4, or it can attack the queen on d3 or the pawn on e2.

* 4. The attack on the doubled pawns is carried out by the b8 knight from a5 or e5, the queen on f7 and the bishop on e6 or f7.
* 5. In some games, the attack on the white kingside is carried out by a rook on the sixth rank, the knight threatening the bishop from e6, and the queen on g5. The kingside pawns were only advanced in one game so far.

⚠ Keep in Mind!
The player who knows how to use his light-squared bishop better will dominate the game.

Conclusion 4.♗f4, 6.♘c3

It is possible that Rubinstein's line 4.♗f4 is less aggressive than, for example, 4.e4 (see Chapter Two) or 4.♘f3 (see Chapter Three), but its intention is to preserve the advantage that White has already obtained: the extra pawn on e5. Besides, the bishop is very well posted on the h2-b8 diagonal, where it attacks the weaknesses in Black's fortress.

A particularity of the variation 4.♗f4 ♘c6 5.♘f3 ♗b4+ 6.♘c3 is the tendency that it can cause Black some difficult moments (for a little while) and force him to act quickly and alertly. Black has many plans and moves to choose from, but White's position remains very solid and it is hard to surprise him.

Back to 8...♛a3!?

When my Survey on this chapter was published in Yearbook 80, Mr. Luis Bohigas, former president of the Catalan Chess Federation and an avid Budapest Gambit fan, wrote a letter to the Forum Section of Yearbook 81 entitled 'The Quick, the Alert... and the Tenacious'. Mr. Bohigas wrote that the article had 'caused him great sadness':

> 'In 1918 the Budapest Gambit was played by the world elite: Vidmar, Mieses, Schlechter, and with it one of the best players of all time was beaten: Akiba Rubinstein. But in the 21st century, 'normal' players have lost all six most recent games.'

He went on to mention that Black had made a 50% score against 11.e3, but only 25% in 11 games with 11.g3.

> 'In 1998, Bogdan Lalic in his book on the Budapest considered 11.e3 equivalent to 11.g3, eight years later the latter appears to be clearly superior.
> True, nowadays in the Budapest the black player tends to have an inferior Elo, and would therefore probably lose in any case, but isn't it also because White's game is more fluid than Black's?*

I believe that the fundamental reason for the difference is the situation of White's light-squared bishop. In the 11.e3 line, this bishop becomes bored on e2, only defending the pawn on c4 and not having any good squares to go to, especially if White builds up a centre with f3 and e4. On g2, on the other hand, the bishop dominates the long diagonal, controls e4, exerts influence on d5, attacks the c6 knight and presses on the b7 pawn. It can even move to h3 in some cases. A great bishop! The only disadvantage is that the c4 pawn is without protection, but this is a doubled pawn, and in addition, it can be sacrificed magnificently on c5! (...)

Many recent games with 11.e3 still follow [Schlechter's] scheme. But the 'Schlechter' knight manoeuvre to e4 and c5 is disastrous after 11.g3 (in Kashdan-Pilnick, the knight remained on e4), because White can move his queen to e3 (which is not possible when White has put his pawn there on the 11th move), exchange queens and then the bishop pair will attack the queenside. (...)

That leaves only 12...♗g4, which harvests a defeat and four draws. This is by far the best result, but it is still not very encouraging. The only game that I like is Dlugy-Epishin, the manoeuvre by the light-squared bishop over g4, h5, g6 and f7 is brilliant. It at least balances the power of its white counterpart.

After reading your article I am contemplating playing 8...♕a3. This move may not be fashionable today, but at least the great Akiba was beaten with it!'

These comments prompted me to take another look at this subject.

In general Mr. Bohigas was right. Today in most Budapest games the white player is the stronger, improving the statistics in White's favour. But in Part II the situation will already be different. Moreover, Mr. Bohigas's conclusions were based on the outcome of the games and not the positions!

This is my reply to Mr. Bohigas's questions:

* 1. The statistics do not tell the whole story. Analysing a great amount of games I have found numerous strategic and tactical errors.
* 2. I think that in each line there are enough complications, and no game was won easily by White. I have included some wins where masters faced amateur rivals, but does that mean the variation is bad for Black or just that the opponent was?
* 3. The line with 11.e3 seems bad for White. In Game 19 of Part I, Black was better until he played 18...h6?. In spite of the bad statistics with 11.e3, I have mentioned in the games' comments that Black was always doing well.
* 4. 11.g3! is the best option, but even in this line things are not very clear. The bishop on g2 is more active, but the c4 pawn is weaker. Almost all games in this line were hotly disputed. Black had good resources at his disposal.

Not only 12...♗g4 is interesting; all lines are and there is a lot of play in each and every one of them, if you study the analyses carefully.

In another sense, Mr. Bohigas was right. On a professional level, players tend to try too solid lines and produce quite boring games.

We will see if this changes!

Part II – A New Glance at the Solid ♘bd2

1.d4 ♘f6 2.c4 e5 3.dxe5 ♘g4 4.♗f4 and 5/6.♘bd2

Introduction

In this part, we shall investigate the line 4...♘c6 5.♘f3 ♗b4+ 6.♘bd2, as well as the sharp sideline 4...♗b4+ 5.♘d2 d6.

In the first variation, the option of 6.♘bd2 is more solid than 6.♘c3, which was discussed in Part I. 6.♘bd2 is my recommendation, which is seen frequently in practice. It contains specific plans and gives the game a quite different character. A good understanding of the middlegame by both sides plays a fundamental role here.

Directions

There are several hidden strategic ideas, such as:

- The bishop on b4 does not have any comfortable squares, which is why Black is practically forced to exchange it for the knight on d2.
- White gives back the e5 pawn, but in return he gains the advantage of the two bishops and obtains a good pawn structure for an attack.
- The c4-c5 break is always a convenient option in this variation; see Games 19, 20, 22, 23, 24, 25, 26, 28 and 31.
- As a result of the abovementioned motifs, most of the endgames are favourable for White – Games 23, 24, 26 and 30.
- Game 26 is very appropriate for the study of the endgame characteristics of this opening, in which Rogers shows masterful play.
- Black must defend well against the c4-c5 break and prepare counterattacks in the centre and on the kingside – Games 21, 22, 23, 24, 25, 27, 33 and 34.
- In certain games in which the white pawn is placed on e4 (Rubinstein-Schlechter in Part I, Browne-Speelman in Part II, Gligoric-Bakonyi and Dreev-Topalov in Part III), Black gets good counterplay on account of the fact that, among other things, the white light-squared bishop remains passive.

The white bishop on f1

While in the line with 6.♘c3 White's light-squared bishop is a passive piece, after 6.♘bd2 it becomes very strong.

The first game by Rubinstein amazed me: the way his light-squared bishop dances all over the board, eventually to become a decisive factor in the attack on the black king. The bishop doesn't leave its original square until move 13, and only really enters the game at move 20, attacking Black's pawn. At move 21 it goes on attacking the kingside, next it retires to b1, to form a battery with the queen on c2 on the next move, causing another weakening of the black kingside. At move 25 it makes its last move, dominating the a2-g8 diagonal. Black resigns on the following move:

Game 19 Rubinstein-Daniuszewski
after 25...♔g7

With 26.♕c3+ the white queen dominates the great diagonal. Two white pieces situated on the queenside are threatening to mate the black king from a distance. Another beautiful detail of this game is the placement of the white pieces; on move 18 all of them (except the 'dancer') occupy dark squares, precisely the squares of the bishop that Black does not have any more.

The movement of White's light-squared bishop appears, years later, in more modest form, in Karpov-Short (Game 27). Karpov plays it to g4 on the 15th move, attacking the knight on d7. A similar move also appears in Garcia Palermo-Rogers (Game 26), where, on move 19, White locates his bishop on square c4, dominating the diagonal a2-g8. But Rubinstein made all these bishop moves in a single game.

The black bishop on f8

A crucial question for Black is what to do with his dark-squared bishop. The check on b4 is fundamental in this line (and in the entire Budapest Gambit), and White's reply ♘d2 is its first success. Indeed, the knight is worse placed on d2 than on c3; for example, on this latter square it has direct access to d5, from where it would dominate the board and pose Black a lot of problems. The knight on d2 also limits the mobility of the queen on the d-file, but these disadvantages will disappear the moment White castles and moves the knight. Then the bishop on b4 is left 'hanging in the air'.

51

Following Rubinstein's idea, White can force the exchange of the bishop for the knight with a2-a3, gaining the bishop pair and domination on the dark squares, which allows him to carry out the strong break c4-c5.

But more recently, White has discovered that he can gain a tempo with e2-e3, moving the bishop to e2 and castling, thereby neutralizing the power of the bishop on b4. By moving the d2 knight to b3, White leaves the black bishop on b4 'hanging in the air', just as Rubinstein did in his game with Tartakower (Game 20):

and then repeated in Karpov-Short (Game 27):   and Mikhalevski-Chabanon (Game 29):

Black has experimented with four methods of supporting his suspended bishop:

1. (Game 27 Karpov-Short) The idea of ...b6 was not applied very effectively in the Karpov-Short game, but it has its advantages. I maintain that the best move of the black light-squared bishop is ...♗b7 – I will return to this later – and for this, ...b6 is required. Therefore, this move is not necessarily bad.

2. (Game 28 Ivanchuk-Epishin) 9...d6 and 10...♗d7 or 10...a5!?. The plan with ...♗d7 has the advantage of developing a piece, and also the bishop can trouble the white knight on a4. Ivanchuk played 11.a3, forcing the exchange of the bishop for the knight.

3. (Game 29 Mikhalevski-Chabanon) After 9...0-0, 10...a5!? White has won (Game 27), lost (Game 29) and drawn games (Game 28 and 30). Although one case does not make the norm, I also prefer ....a5!?, as in the following examples:

instead of 10...♗d7!? in Game 28, as in the notes to Ivanchuk-Epishin:

played on move 10 in Game 29 Mikhalevski-Chabanon:

In many lines, the black a-pawn advances in order to control the queenside and also to support its bishop. It can advance further to a4, harassing the knight (in some of my Internet games with the CapNemo handle – see the notes in Game 28 – we can see it advancing as far as a3, after which the black bishop ended up dominating all the dark squares on the queenside).

4. (Game 30 Stohl-Blatny) 10...♘g6 and 11...♗d6. This plan seems to be a loss of time, although Stohl-Blatny ended in a draw.

5. (Game 25 Solozhenkin-Miezis, and Game 26 Garcia Palermo-Rogers) Some strong players, like Rogers and Miezis, systematically exchange the bishop for the knight on d2 as soon as White castles.

Personally, I do not like this option, because the bishop might still have a game ahead, but mainly because it prevents c4-c5! Although, in case this advance does take place, the c7 pawn still defends d6.

The white pawn on e5

The second strategic idea (see 'Directions') is the white pawn on e5, which, in this line, White cannot defend with his queen because the knight on d2 impedes its movements on the d-file. This pawn is lost for White, but to recover it, Black must spend several tempi and exchange pieces. I think that the elimination of the e-pawn by exchanging it for another with ...f6 or ...d6, maintaining an advance in development, is more in accordance with the spirit of the Gambit. At the end of this part we will return to this subject.

The white break c4-c5

The move c4-c5 is the key to White's strategy. It is another idea of Rubinstein, who used to play it as soon as it was possible, even before castling.

This push attacks the d6 pawn, which gives new life to the bishop on f4, it opens the c-file for White and clears the light squares for the white bishop. This can be annoying for the black king, if it has not castled. As a consequence, Black's strategy must be to prevent c4-c5. The basic moves are ...d6 and later ...b6, but even then White often prefers to sacrifice the pawn because of the advantages that the advance brings him. Another way for Black to fight against c4-c5 consists in maintaining his dark-squared bishop. In some other games we see Black placing a rook on d8, to capture on c5 with the d-pawn, with an attack on the enemy queen. In order to avoid this, White puts his queen on c3, but then the c4-c5 advance is not so strong. In other games we see Black going ahead and playing ...c7-c5, which weakens the pawn on d6 but, on the other hand, controls the dark squares.

In general, if Black cannot prevent c4-c5, he takes it:

with the b-pawn, to avoid the attack on c7 by the white bishop on f4 (Game 23 Lesiège-Svidler after 12.c5).

or with the d-pawn: to maintain a structure without weaknesses (Game 26 Garcia Palermo-Rogers after 14.c5).

Endings

The endgame Garcia Palermo-Rogers (Game 26) is very nice. Years ago, Ian Rogers wrote a Survey about the BG in Yearbook 24, where he presented this same game.

In this Survey he also presented his game against Dreyer in Auckland 1992, where he plays the same variation with white, but on the 19th move he improves:

Game 26 Garcia Palermo-Rogers
after 18...♖ac8

19.cxb6!, and White won in the end. Not only is Rogers good at endings, he also knows how to correct his ideas with time and to win with both colours!

The black counterattack in the centre and on the kingside
As illustrations of the black counterattack, the games 21, 22, 23, 24, 27, 33 and 34 are all very interesting. The first three have in common Black's development of his light-squared bishop to b7, where it dominates the long diagonal and attacks White's castled king.

- Browne-Speelman (Game 21) shows a very attractive idea: if Black develops the bishop to b7 and the queen to e7, he can castle both sides. In 95% of the BG games, Black castles kingside, removing his king from the centre as soon as possible. Nevertheless, an attack on the black king in the centre occurs on very few occasions, since the white pieces are not well enough arranged to produce such an attack:

Game 21 Browne-Speelman
after 13...0-0-0

'Then why not castle queenside?', Jonathan Speelman asked himself. This way, an attack on the white kingside can be prepared without being hindered by having his own king on the same side. This thought scared Browne, who also preferred castling queenside and this resulted in one of the rare occasions where both sides castled queenside in the BG. Still, the attack was started on the kingside, where there were no kings (!), and it ended in Black's favour.

● (Game 22 Bareev-Mohr). Here Black lashed out with an attack on the kingside, leaving his own king in the centre, demonstrating that White did not have the means to attack it:

Game 22 Bareev-Mohr after 12.b4
(12...♗b7, 13...♘g6, 14...h5)

Another very interesting idea of Mohr's is to attack the white dark-squared bishop with the kingside pawns.

● (Game 23 Lesiège-Svidler). Here we see how the activity of Black's light-squared bishop situated on b7 and the rooks on the central squares compensate for the white attack with c4-c5.

Game 23 Lesiège-Svidler
after 14...♗b7

Wresting the Initiative and Tactics

At the end of Part II we will analyse two moves that have in common a search for the initiative by Black: 6...f6 (Game 20 and 31) and 5...d6 (Games 32-34).

Both moves pursue similar objectives: to eliminate the white pawn on e5 and to develop the black queen to f6. This square is very good for the queen, because there it controls the long diagonal, attacks the pawn on b2 and the bishop on f4, and it indirectly threatens the point f2. In many BG games the black queen ends up on f6.

The move ...f6 is more coherent with this idea than ...d6, because the black queen can recapture the white pawn on f6, whereas the white pawn on d6 would stay alive. But the unique advantage of ...d6 is the simultaneous opening of the diagonal for the light-squared bishop.

If Black goes for the immediate 4...♗b4+!?, after 5.♘d2, the break 5...d6!? continues in the spirit of the gambit, risking a lot, but with good chances of wresting the initiative. This type of unbalanced game is quite like a roller coaster.

Games 32-34
after 5...d6

The presented games are very illustrative. White makes simple and good moves, and wins without trouble.

- With the modern 6...f6, Touzane with black, out of three games in the database, loses two and draws the third. In spite of his knowledge of the variation he has the inferior game by move 13.
- With regard to 5...d6, the best thing that can happen to Black is the refusal of the gambit, which, however, allowed Sadler to draw with Rogers (Game 32). The other two games are short and sweet; White punishes Black very severely. If a player chooses the BG because he is aggressive, any one of these two moves is very logical: instead of recovering the e5 pawn, wasting time, Black turns it into a real sacrifice to advance his development. In spite of this logic, the result for our aggressive black player is that White is offered the possibility to create a sparkling miniature and gain brilliancy prizes. Not very encouraging. If Black looks for a surprise, it seems that here it is he who ends up being surprised.

Even though the surprise factor is very important, White succeeds in winning many games. The points gained by Black are:
- 6...f6, 57 games = 33% victories
- 5...d6, 199 games = 40% victories
  The average in the BG is about 41% of the games won by Black.

Let's see the games, gentlemen!

The Solid ♘bd2 – Games

GAME 19
□ **Akiba Rubinstein**
■ **Dawid Daniuszewski**
Lodz ch-POL 1927

Rubinstein eventually changed his strategy. Instead of 5.♘c3 he started to play 5.♘d2 in reply to the check on b4.

1.d4 ♘f6 2.c4 e5 3.dxe5 ♘g4 4.♗f4 ♗b4+ 5.♘d2!? ♘c6 6.♘f3 ♕e7 7.a3!?

This is the most ambitious option (see also Games 21-24). Other plans are 7.e3!?, which we shall analyse in Games 25-30, and 7.♗g5?! ♕c5!, attacking the pawns on f2 and e5.

7...♗xd2+?

This is a historic moment for the Budapest Gambit! Black had a hidden tactical idea; 7...♘gxe5! (see Games 21-23) 8.axb4?? ♘d3 mate.

There are many games with this finish, improving the statistics of the BG! After 8.♘xe5 there follows 8...♘xe5 9.e3 (obligatory; 9.axb4?? ♘d3 mate!) 9...♗xd2+ 10.♕xd2 d6!. The key of this typical variation with ♘bd2 is to try to advance the c-pawn to c5, but it isn't possible now. For 10...0-0? 11.c5! see Game 24.

8.♕xd2 ♘gxe5 9.♘xe5 ♘xe5

10.c5!

Here is the difference. Only now can White play the positional advance that fixes Black's structure. If 10.e3 d6!.

10...0-0

In case of 10...♕xc5 11.♖c1 ♕d6 (11...♕e7 12.♖xc7±) 12.♕xd6 cxd6 13.g3 White obtains a clear advantage.

11.e3! ♖e8

Black doesn't decide on ...d6 or ...b6 yet. 11...d6 12.cxd6 cxd6 13.♗e2±; 11...b6?? 12.♕d5+−.

12.♖c1!± a5?!

Daniuszewski cannot find anything attractive and continues without a clear plan. Soon he will pay for this! 12...b6 13.cxb6±.

13.♗e2 ♕f6 14.0-0 b6

Too late.

15.cxb6 ♕xb6 16.♕c3 ♘c6 17.♖fd1 ♖b8 18.♖d2 h6 19.h3

No rush, White's advantage is very solid.

19...♖e7 20.♗g4 f6 21.♗f5 ♔f7 22.h4+− g6 23.♗b1 h5 24.♕c2 f5 25.♗a2+ ♔g7 26.♕c3+ 1-0

26...♔h7 27.♕f6! ♖g7 28.♕g5.

After this important game the plan of 5.♘bd2 against 4...♗b4+ became popular and quite respected.

GAME 20
□ Akiba Rubinstein
■ Savielly Tartakower

Bad Kissingen 1928 (10)

This chapter would be incomplete without this game.

1.d4 ♘f6 2.c4 e5 3.dxe5 ♘g4 4.♗f4 ♗b4+ 5.♘d2 ♘c6 6.♘f3 f6!?

Tactics! The motif of this move is to solve the problem with a traditional BG method. 6...♕e7 is the classical option.

7.exf6 ♕xf6 8.g3!?

Although still a solid answer, surprisingly this move is not as popular as 8.e3!?, the modern way of playing that will be analysed in Game 31 (Lazarev-Touzane). Dangerous seems 8.♗xc7?! ♕xb2 (△ 9...♘d4!), for example: 9.e3 (9.♖b1 ♕xa2⇄; 9.♗f4 0-0 10.e3 ♘ge5!→) 9...0-0!? (another resource is 9...♘ge5!? 10.♘xe5 ♗xd2+ 11.♕xd2 ♕xa1+ 12.♕d1 ♕xa2) 10.c5? (better is 10.♖c1, also with unclear play)

10...♗xd2+? Vareille-Anagnostopoulos, London 1994; 10...d5!↑.

8...♕xb2 9.♗g2 d6 10.0-0 0-0

After the game Tartakower recommended 10...♗f5 as an improvement, which has been tried several times without success: 11.♘b3! ♗e4 (11...0-0 12.♘fd4!±; 11...♕f6 12.♘fd4↑) 12.♘g5! ♗xg2 13.♔xg2±. The alternative 10...h6!?, suggested by Tseitlin, may be interesting after 11.a3!? (11.♘e4!?) 11...♗xd2 (11...♗c5 12.♘e4!±) 12.♗xd2 (12.♕xd2!?). White must be slightly better, but there are no practical examples to confirm this assessment.

11.♘b3! ♕f6!

A critical moment in the game. If 11...h6?! (Tartakower) then White has 12.a3! ♗c5 13.♘xc5 dxc5 14.♕d5+.

12.♘g5!

A very strong practical move which will annoy your opponent. As always, 12.c5!? was interesting: 12...♗c3 (12...♔h8!?) 13.♖c1 ♗e5 with a complex position.

12...h6?

Handing White the initiative. Better was 12...♕g6! 13.♕d3 (13.c5!?) 13...♕xd3!? (13...♕h5?! 14.h3 ♘ge5 15.♗xe5! dxe5 16.f4!↑) 14.exd3 ♘f6 with a more or less equal ending.

13.♘e4± ♕f7 14.a3!

The bishop doesn't have any decent squares to retreat to.

14...♗a5 15.♘xa5 ♘xa5 16.h3 ♘e5 17.c5!

17...g5

17...♘g6 18.cxd6 ♘xf4 19.gxf4±.

18.♗d2 d5

The complications favour White.

19.♘xg5

19.f4! is even more clear-cut.

19...hxg5 20.♗xa5+– ♗e6 21.♗c3 ♘c6 22.♕d2 ♕f5 23.g4 ♕f4 24.♗xd5! ♗xd5 25.♕xd5+ ♔h7 26.e3 ♕f3 27.♕xg5 ♕xh3 28.♕g7

Mate. A great game by Akiba Rubinstein.

Conclusion: White has discovered certain weaknesses in the sub-variation 6...f6, such as the bad placement of the bishop on b4 and the tempo-losing capture of the b2 pawn, that allow him to obtain the initiative. Black must play energetically during moves 10-12, which is the decisive phase of the game.

GAME 21
□ **Walter Browne**
■ **Jonathan Speelman**
Taxco izt 1985 (6)

In this game, GM Speelman demonstrates some excellent strategic and tactical ideas against the 6.♘bd2 plan. The level of his play throughout the game is very high.

1.d4 ♘f6 2.c4 e5 3.dxe5 ♘g4 4.♗f4 ♘c6 5.♘f3 ♗b4+ 6.♘bd2 ♕e7 7.a3 ♘gxe5!

8.♘xe5

An alternative is 8.e3 ♗xd2+ (8...♗d6!?) 9.♕xd2 d6=.

8...♘xe5 9.e3 ♗xd2+

Forced: 9...♗d6?! 10.♘e4! (10.♗e2?! ♘d3+! 11.♗xd3 ♗xf4⇄) 10...♘xc4 11.♘xd6+ ♘xd6 12.♖c1!.

10.♕xd2 d6!

We are going to study this important position thoroughly in Games 21-23. We already know that 10...0-0?! is met by 11.c5!, see Game 24.

11.♗e2

11...b6!?

Preparing 12...♗b7. The text is very useful, since it defends against the c4-c5 advance, as well as permitting counterplay along the a8-h1 diagonal and preparing queenside castling.

A good alternative is 11...0-0 12.0-0 b6 13.f3 (13.b4 ♗b7=) 13...f6 14.e4 ♗e6 15.b3 a5 16.a4 ♘d7⇄ ½-½ Skripchenko-Moskalenko (CapNemo) Blitz playchess. com 2006.

12.e4

Strangely enough, in these positions e2-e4 almost never gives White an advantage. Black has good statistics in this position. Why? Because of White's passive light-squared bishop. Also, Black has ...f5 in reserve. Not dangerous is 12.♗xe5 dxe5 13.♗f3 ♖b8 14.♗c6+ ♗d7 15.♕d5 ♗xc6 16.♕xc6+ ♕d7 17.♕e4 ♕e6 18.0-0-0 f5 19.♕d5 ♔e7! ½-½ Rodriguez Vargas-Alonso Rosell, Catalonia tt 2007.

12...♗b7 13.f3 0-0-0!?

Black prefers to complicate. Safer was 13...0-0 and if 14.0-0 ♖ae8!? with excellent play (14...♕e6!?; 14...f5?! 15.exf5 ♖xf5 16.♗g3±).

14.0-0-0

To the same side. Better was 14.a4!? with the idea of 15.a5, taking advantage of the unstable position of Black's king. But Black has 14...♖hg8! intending ...g4 and ...f5!.

14...f6 15.h4 h5! 16.♖he1

The position seems equal, but White cannot carry out any of his typical plans, such as c4-c5, and also his king is worse.

16...♖hg8!

On the other hand, Black can improve his position, thanks to White's many weaknesses.

17.♕c3 g5 18.hxg5 fxg5 19.♗h2 g4!

Black has the initiative. Here, White's bishops do not help him much.

20.f4 ♘d7 21.♗d3 h4 22.b4

Defending against the knight jump to c5, but creating more weaknesses in his king's position.

22...♕f7 23.♖f1 ♖de8 24.♖de1 g3 25.♗g1 h3 26.gxh3 g2 27.♖f3 27.♖f2 ♖g3!.

27...♘e5! 28.♖f2 ♘xd3+ 29.♕xd3

29...♕f6

White's position is difficult. Here we have a typical opposite-coloured bishops' attack. Also possible was 29...♕f5!? 30.exf5 ♖xe1+ 31.♕d1 ♖xd1+ 32.♔xd1 ♔d7∓.

30.♔b1 ♕h4 31.e5 dxe5 32.fxe5 ♖g3 33.♕f5+ ♔b8 34.♕c2

White's king is too exposed.

34...♕xh3 35.♔b2 a6 36.♖d2 ♗c8 37.♖f2 ♖d8 38.e6 ♗xe6 39.♖f6 ♗xc4! 40.♕xc4 ♖d2+ 41.♔b1 ♖b3+ 0-1 42.♔a1 ♖xa3+ 43.♔b1 ♖a1+! 44.♔xa1 ♕a3+ 45.♔b1 ♕b2 mate.

GAME 22
□ **Evgeny Bareev**
■ **Georg Mohr**
Ljubljana/Portoroz 1989 (12)

1.d4 ♘f6 2.c4 e5 3.dxe5 ♘g4 4.♗f4 ♘c6 5.♘f3 ♗b4+ 6.♘bd2 ♕e7 7.a3 ♘gxe5 8.♘xe5 ♘xe5 9.e3 ♗xd2+ 10.♕xd2 d6!

We have arrived at the key position of the sub-variation 6.♘bd2 and 7.a3.

11.♗e2

The alternatives are:

A) 11.b4 0-0 (11...a5!?; 11...♗e6 12.c5 0-0-0) 12.♗e2 b6!? (12...♖e8 13.0-0 ♗f5 14.♖fd1 ♖ad8 15.♕c3 f6 16.c5!? d5 17.b5 c6 18.a4± Nybäck-Summerscale, England tt-2 2004/05) 13.c5 dxc5 (13...♘g6!? with the idea of 14.cxd6 ♕f6!⇄) 14.♕d5 ♘g6! 15.♗g5 ♕e5 16.♕xe5 ♘xe5= 17.bxc5 ♗f5 18.0-0 ♗d3 19.♗xd3 ♘xd3 20.♖fd1 ♘xc5 21.♗e7 ♖fb8 22.♗xc5 bxc5 23.♖d5 ½-½ Kouatly-Illescas Cordoba, France tt 1989;

B) 11.c5 dxc5 12.♕d5 (12.♕c3 f6) 12...♘g6!? (12...f6 13.♖c1 c6=) 13.♗b5+ c6? (13...♔f8∞) 14.♗xc6+ bxc6 15.♕xc6+ ♕d7 16.♕e4+? (16.♕xa8 ♘xf4 17.♖d1! ♕e6 18.0-0-0±) 16...♕e6 17.♕xa8 ♘xf4 18.0-0 ♘d3 19.♕xa7 0-0⇄ 20.b4

cxb4 (20...c4!?) 21.axb4 ♘xb4 22.♖ab1 ♘c6 ½-½ Avshalumov-A. Kovacevic, Belgrade 1989;

C) 11.♖c1 – see Game 23.

11...b6 12.b4!?

This seems logical, preparing c4-c5!; 12.0-0 ♗b7 13.♕c3!? 0-0 14.♖fd1 (14.c5!?) 14...♘g6!? 15.♗g3 f5 (15...a5!?) 16.♗f1 h5 17.h3 h4 18.♗h2 f4 19.exf4 ♘xf4 20.♖d4 ♘e2+ 21.♗xe2 ♕xe2 22.f3 ♖ae8⇄ Hernandez Holden-Moskalenko, Tamarite rapid 2007.

12...♗b7 13.0-0 ♘g6!?

The start of an interesting plan, but the knight leaves the centre. 13...0-0!? 14.♕c3 ♘g6 (14...♕f6!? △ 15...♘f3+) 15.♗g3 f5! (15...a5!?) 16.♖fe1 ♕g5? (16...a5!) 17.c5!↑ Iliushin-B. Savchenko, Krasnodar 2002.

14.♗g3

14...h5!

This aggressive move initiates Black's counterplay on the kingside, thus balancing the white threat of c4-c5.

15.f3

15.h3!? h4 (15...♕g5 16.♕d1□ h4 17.♗f3∞) 16.♗h2 ♕g5 (16...0-0!? intending ...a5 or ...♖ae8, ...f5) 17.f3 0-0∞; 15.c5 h4 (15...dxc5!? 16.bxc5 h4⇄) 16.cxd6 ♕d7 17.♗f4 ♘xf4 18.exf4 0-0 (18...0-0-0!?) 19.♖fd1

♖ad8 20.♖ac1 cxd6= ½-½ Beltran Rueda-Moskalenko, Barcelona 2007.

15...h4 16.♗f2 h3! 17.g4

17.g3 f5! with the idea ...♘e5xf3.

17...f5!?

Maybe attacking too hastily. 17...0-0!? 18.♗g3 ♖fe8 (18...a5!?) 19.e4 a5⇄.

18.gxf5

18.♗g3!? with the idea 18...fxg4 19.c5! with an unclear game.

18...♕g5+ 19.♗g3 ♘h4 20.♖ad1

The critical moment of the game.

20...♕xf5??

He should have captured with the knight: 20...♘xf5! 21.e4□ ♕xd2 (21...♘e3 22.♖b1 ♕h6 23.♖fc1±) 22.♖xd2 ♘xg3 23.hxg3 a5! 24.♔h2 with equal chances.

21.e4!±

Now White is very solid.

21...♕h5 22.c5!

At last this powerful advance.

22...0-0 23.c6!? ♗xc6 24.♖c1 ♗b7 25.♖xc7 ♘xf3+ 26.♖xf3 ♖xf3 27.♖xb7 ♖af8 28.♖c7 ♕g4 29.♖c3?!

Better was 29.♗xf3 ♕xf3 30.♖c1+−.

29...♖f2! 30.♗c4+ ♔h8 31.♕xf2 ♖xf2 32.♔xf2 ♕xe4 33.♗f1 ♕d4+ 34.♖e3 ♕d2+ 35.♗e2 ♕d4 36.♗f1 ♕d2+ 37.♔f3 ♕d5+ 38.♔g4 ♕f7 39.♗d3 d5 40.♖f3 ♕e6+ 41.♗f5 ♕e2 42.♗f2

g5 43.♔g3 ♔g7 44.♗xh3 ♕e5+ 45.♔g2 d4 46.♔g1 ♕e2 47.♖g3 ♔g6 48.♗f1 ♕d1 49.♖d3 ♕g4+ 50.♗g2

1-0

GAME 23
□ **Alexandre Lesiège**
■ **Peter Svidler**
Oakham 1992 (2)

In a dynamic game, Svidler risks too much, but he manages to save the day at the last moment.

After 14...♗b7 the position is equal.

1.d4 ♘f6 2.c4 e5 3.dxe5 ♘g4 4.♗f4 ♘c6 5.♘f3 ♗b4+ 6.♘bd2 ♕e7 7.a3 ♘gxe5 8.♘xe5 ♘xe5 9.e3 ♗xd2+ 10.♕xd2 d6! 11.♖c1!?

White wants to play c4-c5 quickly, before castling. 11.♕c3!? has the same idea: 11...f6 (11...0-0!? 12.c5 ♗g4⇄; 11...b6!? 12.c5!? bxc5 13.♗b5+ c6∞) 12.♗e2 0-0 13.b4 (13.0-0 a5 14.b4 ♗e6⇄) 13...♘g6!? 14.♗g3 f5! 15.♕d2 f4 Rowson-Wippermann, Gibraltar 2004. Safer is 11.♗e2, see Games 21 and 22.

11...b6!?

Controlling the c5-square. But also good was 11...♘g6!? 12.♗g3 0-0 and if 13.c5!? dxc5 14.♕d5 ♖d8 15.♕xc5 ♕xc5 16.♖xc5 c6 17.♗e2 ♗e6 with a balanced ending, Lesiège-St Amand, Quebec 1990.

12.c5!? bxc5 13.b4!

Before, 13.♗xe5 was played: 13...♛xe5 14.♗b5+ ♚f8! (14...♗d7?! 15.♗xd7+ ♚xd7 16.b4↑) 15.♗c6 ♖b8 16.b4 ♗a6 (better chances are offered by 16...cxb4 17.axb4 ♗a6) 17.f4 (17.b5!?) 17...♛f6 18.♚f2 g6 19.bxc5 ♚g7 20.cxd6 ♖b2 21.♖c2= ½-½ Kiriakov-Svidler, Alma-Ata ch-URS U18, 1991.

13...0-0 14.bxc5 ♗b7!

A critical position. White has the two bishops and the better pawn structure, but he is badly developed. For the moment chances are equal.

15.f3

The only move.

15...dxc5 16.♛c3 ♘g6?!

An impulsive reply. Now that the knight leaves the centre, White is better. 16...♖fe8!? 17.♛xc5 (17.♚f2 ♛h4+ 18.♗g3 ♛f6↑) 17...♛f6!? (17...♛xc5 18.♖xc5 ♘g6 19.♚f2 ♘xf4 20.exf4±) 18.♚f2 ♖ad8 was a better shot at counterplay.

17.♗g3± ♖fe8

Black understands the idea too late.

18.♚f2

18.e4!? f5?? 19.♛b3++−.

18...h5

18...♖ad8 19.♗e2±; 18...♘e5!? 19.♛xc5 ♛f6⇄.

19.h4

An automatic answer. Too risky was 19.♛xc5!? h4 20.♗xc7 ♖ac8⊖, for example: 21.♖c3 ♛d7!? (21...♛xc5!? 22.♖xc5 ♖e7 23.♗d6 ♖xc5 24.♗xc5 ♖c7⊖) 22.♗e2 ♘f4!?.

19...♖ad8 20.♗b5 ♖f8

20...c6 21.♗e2±.

21.♗e2 ♖fe8 22.♛xc5 ♖d2 23.♖he1?!

Too passive. After 23.♛xe7!? ♖xe7 24.♖hd1! ♖a2 25.♖d8+ (25.♖a1!?) 25...♘f8 (25...♚h7 26.♖c5!+−) 26.♖xc7 ♖xc7 27.♗xc7 ♗a6 28.♗d6 White is better.

23...♗a6

23...♛e6!?.

24.♛xe7 ♘xe7! 25.e4

25.♖xc7 ♘f5 26.♗f4 ♘xh4⇄.

25...♘f5! 26.exf5 ♗xe2

26...♖exe2+!? 27.♖xe2 ♖xe2+ 28.♚g1 ♖a2 gave chances of a draw.

27.♖xc7 ♗d3+ 28.♚g1 ♖xe1+ 29.♗xe1 ♖d1 30.♚f2 ♗xf5

30...a6 31.g4±.

31.♖xa7 ♖a1 32.♖a5?

With 32.a4!? White might still win.

32...♖a2+ 33.♚e3 ♗c2 34.♗c3 f6 35.g3 ♗d1 36.♗d2? ♗xf3= 37.♚xf3 ♖xd2 38.♖xh5 ½-½

GAME 24
□ **Mikhail Gurevich**
■ **Normunds Miezis**
Bonn 1996

This example proves that the majority of the BG endings favour White.

1.d4 ♘f6 2.c4 e5 3.dxe5 ♘g4 4.♗f4 ♘c6 5.♘f3 ♗b4+ 6.♘bd2 ♕e7 7.a3 ♘cxe5 8.♘xe5 ♘xe5 9.e3 ♗xd2+ 10.♕xd2 0-0?

Although grandmaster Miezis is a Budapest specialist, he falls into a well-known trap.

11.c5!

Fixing the centre and the queenside.

11...♖e8

A) 11...♕xc5?! 12.♖c1 ♕d6 (12...♕e7 13.♖xc7±) 13.♕xd6 cxd6 14.♖d1±;

B) 11...b6?! 12.♕d5 ♘c6 13.♗xc7±;

C) 11...d6 12.cxd6 cxd6 13.♗e2 ♗f5 14.0-0 ♖ad8 15.♖ac1 ♗e4 16.b4 a6 17.a4 ♖fe8 18.b5 axb5 19.f3 ♗c6 20.axb5 ♗d7 21.e4 ♗e6 22.b6 ♖c8 23.♗b5± Kakhiani-Ioseliani, Tbilisi 1991.

12.♖c1 d6

Black must allow the pawn to be isolated – it is the only way to stay in the game. 12...b6 13.cxb6 cxb6 14.♗e2

(14.♕d5!? ♖b8 15.♖c7) 14...♗b7 15.0-0±.

13.cxd6 cxd6±

White's advantage is stable. 13...♕xd6?! 14.♕xd6 cxd6 15.♖d1±.

14.♗e2 ♗e6 15.0-0 ♖ac8 16.♕d4

16.♕b4!? ♘c6 17.♗xd6 ♘xb4 18.♗xe7±.

16...♘c6!? 17.♕d2

17.♕xd6!? ♕f6 (intending 18...♖ed8) 18.♕d3!.

17...♘e5

17...d5 18.b4!?±.

18.♖xc8 ♖xc8 19.♖c1 ♖c7 20.♖c3 f6 21.e4 a6 22.♗e3 b5

22...♘c4? 23.♕c1 △ 24.b3+−.

23.♕c1 ♖xc3 24.♕xc3 ♕b7 25.f3 ♗c4

25...d5 26.exd5 ♕xd5 27.♕d4±.

26.♗d1!

White must hold on to the key to his advantage: the bishop pair.

26...♗e6 27.♗d4 ♘c6 28.♗f2 ♕d7 29.h3 d5 30.exd5 ♗xd5 31.♗c2 ♕e6 32.♕d3 g6 33.♕e3

33.♕d2, with initiative, was better.

33...♕xe3 34.♗xe3

White couldn't find anything better than to exchange all the pieces and enter the classical ending with the advantage of the bishop pair.

34...♔f7 35.♔f2 ♔e6 36.♗b6 f5 37.♗e3!?

37.g4 was preferable.

37...♗c4

37...♘e5!?.

38.g4! ♘e5 39.♔g3 ♗e2 40.♔f4 ♗d3?

40...♘d3+! 41.♔g5 fxg4 42.fxg4 ♘xb2 43.♔h6 ♗d3!=.

41.♗d1 ♗f1 42.♗d4 ♘c6 43.gxf5+ gxf5 44.♗g7±

The pawns on f5 and h7 are weak.

44...♘e7

44...♗xh3? 45.♗e2! △ 46.♔g3+−.

45.♔g3

45.h4!?.

45...♘g6 46.h4 ♗c4 47.♗c2! ♗e2?
48.h5 ♘e5 49.♔f4 ♗d3 50.♗d1 ♘c4
51.♗c3 ♘d6 52.♔e3 ♗c4 53.♗c2 ♗f1
54.♔f4 ♗h3 55.♗d3 ♗g2 56.♗b4+−

56...h6 57.♔g3 ♗h1 58.♗e2 f4+
59.♔xf4 ♘f5 60.♗c3 ♘e7 61.♔g3
♘d5 62.♗d2 ♘f6 63.♔h2 ♘xh5
64.♗d1   1-0

Because of his weak opening play (10...0-0?), Black found himself in a difficult position. In the rest of the game he could only fight for the draw, but White made good use of his bishop pair.

GAME 25
□ **Evgeny Solozhenkin**
■ **Normunds Miezis**
Gausdal 2001 (5)

1.d4 ♘f6 2.c4 e5 3.dxe5 ♘g4 4.♗f4
♘c6 5.♘f3 ♗b4+ 6.♘bd2 ♕e7 7.e3!?

In this game we start with the study of the line with 7.e3. The idea of this natural move, as opposed to 7.a3, is to try and finish development and win a tempo when the bishop on b4 has to move.

7...♘cxe5 8.♘xe5 ♘xe5 9.♗e2

From now on Black has several alternatives and he has to decide on his future plans.

9...0-0!?

The first critical moment of this sub-variation. The position contains several original ideas, such as 9/10...a5 (Game 29) or the interesting 9...d6!? (Game 28).

10.0-0

Another important moment. A decision must be made.

10...♗xd2

A simple method that solves the problem of the ♗b4, although White has won a tempo by saving out on a3. The alternatives are 9/10...a5!? (Game 29); 10...♘g6 (Game 30); 10...d6?! (Game 27).

11.♕xd2 d6 12.♖ac1

White starts his thematic plan of advancing c4-c5. Another game by Miezis continued: 12.b4!? (with the same idea of preparing c4-c5) 12...f6 (12...♖e8!?; 12...♗f5!?) 13.♕c3. But on this occasion Miezis couldn't find a good plan and soon got into trouble: 13...♗d7?! (13...♗e6) 14.♗g3 ♖ae8 15.♖ac1 ♗e6 16.a3 ♗f7 17.c5 d5?! (17...dxc5 18.♕xc5 (18.bxc5±) 18...♕xc5 19.♖xc5 c6 20.♖d1±) 18.c6!

analysis diagram

The c-pawn is very strong. It breaks open the position. 18...b6 19.♖fd1 ♖d8 20.♖d4 ♖d6 21.b5 a6 22.a4 axb5? (22...a5 23.♗d1!?± and 24.♘b3) 23.axb5 ♖a8 24.♖a1 ♖xa1+ 25.♕xa1 ♖d8 26.♖a4 (strategically Black is lost) 26...g6 27.♕d4 ♘c4 28.♖a7 ♖c8 29.h4 ♔g7 30.♗g4 ♖e8 31.♖xc7 ♕b4 32.♕xd5 ♖e7 33.♖xe7 ♕xe7 34.♕d7 ♕e4 35.c7 ♘d2 36.c8♕ ♕b1+ 37.♔h2 ♘f1+ 38.♔h3 1-0 V. Mikhalevski-Miezis, Dieren 1997.

12...♗e6!?

In this game Miezis improves the placement of his pieces. 12...b6!?.

13.♖fd1 f6!? 14.♕c3 ♕f7 15.♗g3 b6!

Now chances are equal because of Black's strong pawn structure.

16.f4?!

White unnecessarily changes plans. Preferable was 16.b4!? a5! 17.a3 axb4 18.axb4 ♖a2 19.♗f1 ♖fa8 20.c5!⇄.

16...♘d7 17.♗f3 ♖ae8 18.b4 f5!

Fixing the e3-f4 pawn formation.

19.♗c6 ♖e7 20.♗h4 ♘f6 21.♕a3

Attacking a7.

21...♕h5!

Black finds counterplay on the kingside and against the e3-pawn.

22.♗xf6 ♖xf6 23.♗f3

23.c5!?

23...♕e8

The position is equal, but in practice it is easier to play Black here.

24.♕xa7 ♗f7 25.c5!

Best; 25.a4 ♖xe3 26.♖f1 (26.a5?? ♖xf3 27.gxf3 ♕e3+−+) 26...♖b3⇄.

25...bxc5 26.bxc5 c6 27.♕a5 d5 28.a4 ♖xe3 29.♖e1 ♖fe6 30.♔f2

Exchanging rooks was better: 30.♖xe3 ♖xe3 31.♕d2 with a safe position.

30...d4!?

30...♕e7!?.

31.♖xe3

31.♖cd1!? ♕e7 32.♖xe3 dxe3+ 33.♔g1 g5 34.♕d8+ ♕xd8 35.♖xd8+ ♔g7 36.♖d6 ♖e7 37.♔f1 gxf4⇄.

31...dxe3+ 32.♔g1 ♕b8!

A very annoying move. The queen threatens to penetrate along various files and diagonals.

33.♕c3?

A mistake in time-trouble. The only move was 33.♖f1 h6 △ ...e2, ...♕xf4.

33...♕xf4 34.a5 g5?

Returning the favour. After 34...♖h6! 35.h3 ♖xh3! 36.gxh3 ♕xf3 37.♕b2 ♗d5! there are too many threats.

35.a6!

This pawn is a constant worry for Black.

35...e2 36.♖e1 ♖e3 37.♕d2??

The final mistake. 37.♕c1! ♕d4 38.♔h1 f4 39.♗xc6 ♖e7 was still unclear.

37...♖xf3! 38.♕d8+ ♔g7 39.gxf3 ♕e3+ 40.♔g2 g4   **0-1**

This was a typical BG game. Possibly White was better after the opening, but the position is very sharp. After 11...d6 Black has no structural weaknesses but he does have a passive position.

GAME 26
□ **Carlos Garcia Palermo**
■ **Ian Rogers**
Reggio Emilia 1984/85 (2)

1.d4 ♘f6 2.c4 e5 3.dxe5 ♘g4 4.♗f4 ♘c6 5.♘f3 ♗b4+ 6.♘bd2 ♕e7 7.e3 ♘gxe5 8.♘xe5 ♘xe5 9.♗e2 0-0 10.0-0 ♗xd2 11.♕xd2 d6 12.♖fd1

12.b4!?.

12...b6 13.b4 ♗b7

14.c5!

The best option for White in this line.

14...dxc5 15.bxc5 ♘g6?!

15...♖ad8!?.

16.♕d7!

Arriving on the seventh rank. 16.♗g3 ♖ad8 17.♕c3±.

16...♕xd7

16...♕xc5 17.♖ac1 ♕a5 18.♗xc7±.

17.♖xd7 ♘xf4 18.exf4 ♖ac8

This is an important and peculiar moment.

19.♗c4?!

In a later game, as White, Rogers played 19.cxb6! axb6 20.♖c1± ♖a8 21.♗c4↑ ♗a6 22.♗d5 c6 23.♗xc6 ♖fc8 24.♖cd1 ♖ab8 25.♗d5 ♖f8 26.h3 g6 27.a4 ♔g7 28.♖a7 ♗e2 29.♖b1 ♖bd8 30.♗c6 ♖d6 31.♖c7 ♖b8 32.a5 b5 33.a6 1-0 Rogers-Dreyer, Auckland 1992.

19...♗c6 20.♖e7 b5! 21.♗b3 a5

For the moment White has the initiative. But Black has good chances in the endgame thanks to his superior pawn structure. He just has to find a way to exchange rooks.

22.a3 a4 23.♗a2 ♖fd8!

A strong defensive resource.

24.♗xf7+?

Preferable is 24.♖ae1 ♗e8 25.♗b1 (25.♗d5 c6⇄) 25...g6 26.♗e4 ♖d7=.

24...♔f8 25.♖ae1 ♖d1!

This is the way. 25...♗d5 is only equal.

26.♖xd1 ♚xe7 27.♗a2

27...♖b8! 28.♖d4 ♖f8!
Heading for f5; 28...♖d8? 29.♖xd8 ♚xd8 30.f3±.
29.♗b1
To prevent 29...♖f5.
29...♖d8! 30.♖xd8 ♚xd8
As a result of an excellent strategy and an acute tactical execution of his plan, Black has obtained a superior ending.
31.♗a2
Forced; 31.♗xh7 ♗d5 32.f3 ♚d7 33.♚f2 ♚c6 loses.
31...♚d7 32.f3 ♗b7!–+
The idea is 33...♚c6.
33.♚f2 ♚c6 34.♗b1 ♚xc5 35.♗xh7 b4 36.axb4+ ♚xb4 37.♗g8 a3 38.f5 ♗a6
White resigned in view of 39...♗c4.

GAME 27
□ **Anatoly Karpov**
■ **Nigel Short**
Linares m 1992 (1)

This is an extraordinary game in which GM Nigel Short wants to surprise his opponent Karpov, who then demonstrates a great understanding of the position and plays like a machine. Nowadays it's not easy to find a battle on such a high level in the BG.

Nigel Short surprised Anatoly Karpov in their 1992 Candidates' match with a Budapest Gambit, but Karpov proved up to the task.

1.d4 ♘f6 2.c4 e5 3.dxe5 ♘g4 4.♗f4 ♘c6 5.♘f3 ♗b4+ 6.♘bd2
A typical Karpov move in many openings!
6...♕e7 7.e3 ♘gxe5 8.♘xe5 ♘xe5 9.♗e2 0-0
Let's look at an alternative: 9...b6?! 10.0-0 ♗xd2 (10...♗b7 11.♘f3±) 11.♕xd2 ♗b7 (11...d6 12.b4 ♗b7 13.c5!↑) 12.c5! bxc5? (≥ 12...0-0 13.b4!?±) 13.♕a5! d6 14.♗xe5! dxe5 15.♖fc1± Solozhenkin-Stiazhkin, Leningrad 1990.
Maybe the most interesting plan for Black is 9...d6!?, as in Game 28, Ivanchuk-Epishin.
10.0-0 d6?!
Allowing White to obtain a small but stable edge. 10...♖e8!? 11.♘b3 d6 (11...♗d6!?) 12.a3 ♗c5 13.♘xc5 dxc5 14.♕d5 ♘g6 15.♕f3 (15.♗g3!?) 15...a5 16.♖ad1 ♘xf4 led to a draw in Riazantsev-Kortchnoi, Cheliabinsk 2007.

11.♘b3!

The knight controls the retreat squares of the ♗b4.

11...b6 12.a3!

12.♘d4?! ♗c5 13.a3 a5 14.b3 ♗b7 15.♕d2 ♘g6 16.♗g3 d5?! (≥ 16...f5!?⇄) 17.♗f3 ♖ad8 (Bellon Lopez-Illescas Cordoba, Alicante 1989) 18.b4! axb4 19.axb4 ♗xb4 20.♕b2↑.

12...♗c5 13.♘xc5 bxc5

13...dxc5? loses to 14.♕d5 ♘g6 15.♕xa8 ♘xf4 16.♕f3!?.

14.b4! ♘d7

14...cxb4 15.axb4 ♗b7 16.♕d4±; 14...♗b7 15.bxc5 dxc5 16.♕c2±; 14...♗f5!?.

15.♗g4!?

White achieves a favourable position. 15.♕c2!? ♗b7 16.♗d3 also yields a useful initiative.

15...a5

A year later, 15...♖e8!? 16.♖c1 (16.♕f3!?) 16...a5 17.♗xd7 ♗xd7 18.bxc5 dxc5 19.♕d5 ♖a6 20.♗g5 ♕d6 21.♗f4 ♕e7 22.♗g5 ½-½ happened in Ivanchuk-Short, Monaco blind 1993. Not good is 15...♗b7?! 16.♗xd7 ♕xd7 17.bxc5 ♕c6 18.♕d5!±.

16.♗xd7!

The simplest. Karpov wants to control the position.

16...♗xd7 17.bxc5 dxc5 18.♕d5!?

18.♗xc7!?.

18...♖a6!?

Finally an active move! 18...♗e6 19.♕e5±.

19.♕e5?!

Suddenly getting scared! 19.♕b7! ♖g6 20.♕xc7 picks up a pawn.

19...♖e6

Short sacrifices the pawn to activate his pieces and stop defending passively. Karpov must now calculate accurately and the game enters a phase of complications. Although Black is passive, he has saving chances because of the opposite-coloured bishops.

Maybe 19...♕xe5!? was better: 20.♗xe5 ♖c8 21.♖ab1 f6 22.♗f4 ♖b6! with equality.

20.♕xc7 ♖c8 21.♕b7

Why not 21.♕xa5 ♗c6 22.♕c3+−?

21...♛e8 22.♖ab1 h5

22...♗c6 23.♛xc8!? ♛xc8 24.♖b8±.

23.f3 ♗c6 24.♛b2 h4 25.h3!

A typical Karpov-Nimzowitschian block; 25.e4 f5! would allow counterplay.

25...f5!

As he doesn't have any escape route because of the blockade of the a8-h1 diagonal, Short must attack, and try to put his opponent in danger. Meanwhile, Karpov keeps control.

26.♛c2 ♛g6 27.♛c3 a4 28.♖f2 ♖ce8 29.♖d1 ♛h5 30.♛c2 ♛g6 31.♔h1 ♛f6 32.♛b2 ♛e7 33.♖fd2 g5!? 34.♗d6 ♛f7 35.♗xc5 g4! 36.fxg4 fxg4 37.♖f2! ♛h5!?

37...♛g6 38.♖df1! gh3 39.♖f8+−.

Black has created two simultaneous threats: 38...♛xc5 and 38...gxh3. But Karpov now takes advantage of Black's bad king to press the advantage home.

38.♛e2!

The solution.

38...♖g6

Of course not 38...♛xc5 39.♛xg4+ and the attack is unstoppable: 39...♔h8 40.♛xh4+ ♔g8 (40...♔g7 41.♖f7+! ♔xf7 42.♛h7+ ♔f6 43.♖f1+ ♔e5 44.♛f5+ ♔d6 45.♖d1+) 41.♛g4+ ♔h8 42.♖f5. But a good practical chance

may have been 38...♖e5!? 39.hxg4 (39.♗d4 gxh3⇄) 39...♛h7 40.♗d4 h3! 41.♔g1 hxg2 42.♖xg2□ ♗xg2 43.♗xe5 ♗c6 44.♛h2 ♛xh2+ 45.♗xh2 ♖xe3 with some chances to escape.

39.♖d6! ♖e4??

This loses immediately. Black would still be alive after 39...♖xd6 40.♗xd6 ♛g6! 41.♛xg4 ♛xg4 42.hxg4 h3.

40.♖d8+ ♔h7 41.♖f7+ ♖g7 42.♖xg7+ ♔xg7 43.♛b2+ 1-0

Karpov laid bare the disadvantages of 10...d6 with his reply 11.♘b3!, isolating the bishop on b4. After the exchange on c5 he gradually increased his advantage.

GAME 28
□ **Vasily Ivanchuk**
■ **Vladimir Epishin**
Terrassa 1991 (4)

1.d4 ♘f6 2.c4 e5 3.dxe5 ♘g4 4.♗f4 ♗b4+ 5.♘d2 ♘c6 6.♘f3 ♛e7 7.e3 ♘gxe5 8.♘xe5 ♘xe5 9.♗e2 d6!?

Perhaps the most interesting move.

10.0-0

10.♛a4+?! ♘c6.

10...♗d7!?

Personally I like the idea 10...a5!?. After 11.♘b3 (11.a3!? ♗c5 (11...♗xd2!? 12.♛xd2 a4!?⇄) 12.♘e4 ♗b6

13.♕d5 ♘g6? (13...♗e6!? 14.♕xb7 0-0♔) 14.♗g3 (14.♘xd6+!) 14...0-0 15.b4? ♖e8 (15...c6! 16.♕d3 ♗f5∓) 16.♗f3= Epishin-Thielemann, Kiel 2004) 11...a4! we have reached a difficult position.

analysis diagram

12.a3!? (12.♘d4 a3! 13.b3 0-0 14.♖c1 ♖e8 15.♘f3 b6 16.♕d5?! ♖a5 17.♕d4 ♗b7 18.♗xe5 dxe5 19.♕d1 ♗e4!–+ Diggory-Moskalenko (CapNemo) Blitz playchess.com 2007) 12...♗c3!?N – the author learns as well! (also interesting is 12...♗a5!? 13.♘xa5 ♖xa5) 13.bxc3 (13.♕c2 ♗xb2 14.♕xb2 axb3 15.c5 ♗e6∞) 13...axb3 14.♗xe5!? (14.♕xb3 ♘d7! and 15...♘c5 – the Schlechter Knight!; 14.c5 b2!⇄) 14...b2! 15.♖a2! ♕xe5?! (15...dxe5! 16.♕b3 0-0 17.♕xb2 ♖a6!?⇄) 16.♕d4! 0-0= Narciso Dublan-Moskalenko, Catalonia tt 2007.

11.a3

If 11.♘b3 ♗a4! 12.♕d4 ♗xb3 13.axb3 a5 gives Black counterplay. In a recent simultaneous game Anatoly Karpov tried 11.♘f3!? ♗c5 (11...♘g6!? 12.♗g3 a5?! 13.a3 ♗c5 14.b4! ♗b6 15.♖c1 axb4 16.axb4 0-0 17.c5! dxc5 18.bxc5 ♗a5 19.♕b3± Epishin-Bohigas Santasusagna, Badalona 2005)

12.♗xe5?! (12.a3!?) 12...dxe5 13.♕d5 e4 (13...♗g4!?) 14.♕xb7 0-0 15.♘d2 ♖ab8 (15...♗f5!?) 16.♕xe4 ♖xb2 17.♕d3? (17.♗d3!±) 17...♗a4 18.♖ab1 ♖xa2 19.♕c3 ♖d8 20.♖b2 ♖xb2 21.♕xb2 ♗xe3! 22.♘f3 ♗c5–+ and eventually lost the game, Karpov (2668)-Barlag (2093), Wolfsburg simul 2007.

11...♗xd2

11...♗c5!? 12.♘e4 (12.b4 ♗b6∞) 12...♘g6 13.♘xc5 ♘xf4 14.♘xb7 ♘xe2+ 15.♕xe2 ♗c6 16.♘a5 ♗xg2! 17.♔xg2 ♕g5+=.

12.♕xd2

12...f6

There are more interesting plans:

A) 12...♘g6!? 13.♗g3 h5!⇄ 14.c5! (14.f3 h4 15.♗f2 h3⇄) 14...h4 15.cxd6 ♕e6 16.♗f4 ♘xf4 17.exf4 ♕xd6 18.♕xd6 cxd6 19.♖ad1 ♖h6= S. Mohr-Forintos, Berlin West 1988;

B) 12...♗c6!? 13.♕d4 ♘g6!? △ 14.♗g3 (14.♕xg7 0-0-0♔) 14...0-0 15.b4 b6 16.♖ac1 ♖ad8 (16...f5!? 17.♖fe1 ♕g5⇄) 17.♖fe1 ♖fe8 18.♗d3 ♕e6 19.♕c3 ♘e5 20.♗f1 h5 21.♖ed1 ♕f6 (intending 22...h4) 22.c5 bxc5 23.bxc5 ½-½ Mora-C. Flear, France tt 1993.

13.b4 ♖d8?

This is too passive. Preferable was 13...0-0-0!? or 13...h5!?.

14.♗h5+!

White is better, and with this check he starts a dangerous attack.

14...♘f7 15.c5!

Now Epishin has problems.

15...♗b5 16.♖fd1 d5

16...♗a4!?.

17.e4!

17...♗a4!

The best practical chance; 17...g6 18.exd5! gxh5 19.d6!.

18.exd5! ♗xd1 19.♖xd1 0-0 20.d6

20.h3!? would keep the advantage.

20...cxd6 21.cxd6 ♕e6 22.♗f3 ♔h8 23.d7

23.♗xb7 ♘xd6! 24.♗xd6 f5! and 25...♖f6! is unclear.

23...b6 24.♗c7 ♘e5□ 25.♗xd8 ♖xd8 26.♕c2 ♖xd7 27.♕c8+ ♕g8 28.♕xg8+ ♔xg8 29.♖xd7 ♘xd7 30.♗d5+ ♔f8 31.f4 ♔e7 32.♔f2 f5 33.♔e3 ♔d6 34.♔d4 ♘f6 35.♗f3 ♘e8 36.♔c4 ♘c7 37.g3 ♔e6 38.♗e2 ♔d6 39.♗d3 ♔e6 40.♔d4 g6 41.♗c4+ ♔f6 42.a4 h6 43.h3 g5 44.h4 gxf4 45.gxf4 ♘e6+ 46.♗xe6 ♔xe6 47.♔c4 a6= ½-½

A great game that shows perfectly the best resources in the variation with 6.♘bd2 and 7.e3, for both colours.

GAME 29

□ Victor Mikhalevski

■ Jean-Luc Chabanon

Bad Endbach 1995

1.d4 ♘f6 2.c4 e5 3.dxe5 ♘g4 4.♗f4 ♘c6 5.♘f3 ♗b4+ 6.♘bd2 ♕e7 7.e3 ♘gxe5 8.♘xe5 ♘xe5 9.♗e2 0-0 10.0-0 a5!?

To fix the queenside and support the bishop on b4.

11.♘b3

Another possibility is 11.a3!? ♗xd2 (11...♗c5 12.♘b3!?) 12.♕xd2 d6 13.b4 axb4?! (better is 13...♖d8!? temporarily preventing c4-c5; 14.♕c3 ♕f6⇄) 14.axb4 ♖xa1 15.♖xa1↑ b6 16.♗g3 f6 17.h3 ♗e6 18.♕c3 c5?! 19.♖a6 ♕b7?! 20.b5 (Black's position is not to be envied) 20...♕c7 21.♕c2 g6 22.♕a4 ♖b8 23.f4!+− Gyimesi-Nevednichy, Nagykanizsa 2003.

11...a4 12.a3

12...♗d6!

An interesting fight between knight and bishop (we are still in the Bishops vs Knights Chapter). There are more options here:

A) 12...♗a5!? 13.♘d4 (13.♘xa5 ♖xa5=) 13...♗b6 14.♘b5 d6 15.♘c3 ♕e8! (15...♕d7!?) 16.♘d5 ♗a5 (saving the bishop) 17.♕d4 (17.♖c1 f6!? 18.c5!? dxc5 19.♖xc5 c6⇄) 17...♘d7!? (planning 18...♘c5) ½-½ Rogozenko-Moldovan, Bucharest 2000;

B) 12...♗c3!? 13.bxc3 axb3 14.♕xb3 d6 (14...b6!?) 15.c5!?∞;

C) 12...axb3?! 13.axb4 ♖xa1 14.♕xa1±.

13.♘d4

It is always necessary to look for important resources like 13.c5!? ♗xc5 (13...♘f3+? 14.♗xf3 ♗xf4 15.exf4 axb3 16.♖c1±) 14.♘xc5 ♕xc5 15.♖c1 ♕a5□ 16.♕e1 c6 and it seems that Black is OK.

13...♗c5 14.♘b5 d6 15.♘c3 ♘g6

15...♘d7!? 16.♘d5 ♕d8 17.♕c2 ♖e8⇄.

16.♗g3 f5!? 17.♗f3

17.♘xa4? ♖xa4! 18.♕xa4 f4∓.

17...♕e8 18.♕c2 ♘e5! 19.♗e2 ♗e6

At the end of an original opening phase Black has the advantage.

20.♘b5 ♕f7↑ 21.♗xe5 dxe5 22.♕c3 ♖ae8! 23.♕xe5 ♗xc4 24.♕xc5 ♗xe2 25.♖fe1 b6! 26.♕c6??

A mistake that loses the game. The only move was 26.♕b4 ♖e4 27.♘d4 c5 28.♕xb6 cxd4 29.♖xe2 f4! and Black has the initiative.

26...♖e6!–+

Instead of worrying about the bishop, Black plays three intermediate moves and wins material.

27.♕d5 c6! 28.♘d6 ♕g6! 29.♕xf5 ♖xf5 30.♘xf5 ♕xf5

The rest is simple.

31.♖xe2 ♕d3 32.♖ae1 c5 33.e4 b5 34.e5 g5 35.♖e3 ♕d4 36.♖3e2 b4 37.axb4 cxb4 38.h3 b3 39.♔f1 ♔g7 40.♔g1 ♔g6 41.g4 h5 42.gxh5+ ♔xh5 43.♔h2 ♔g6 44.♔g2 ♔f5 45.♔g3 a3 46.bxa3 b2 47.♖b1 ♕d3+ 0-1

In this game Black found an interesting plan to solve the general problem of the bishop on b4. Possibly the move 11.♘b3 just isn't good enough.

GAME 30
□ **Igor Stohl**
■ **Pavel Blatny**
Prague 1996 (1)

1.d4 ♘f6 2.c4 e5 3.dxe5 ♘g4 4.♗f4 ♘c6 5.♘f3 ♗b4+ 6.♘bd2 ♕e7 7.e3

♘gxe5 8.♘xe5 ♘xe5 9.♗e2 0-0
10.0-0 ♘g6!?

Another well-known plan.

11.♗g3

Not 11.♗xc7?? d6−+.

11...♗d6!?

Trying to solve the problem of the bishop on b4 by exchanging it for Rubinstein's bishop on f4.

12.♗xd6 ♕xd6 13.♘e4!?

Taking the knight to the squares c3 and d5. Other experiments have been:

A) 13.♕c2!? ♕e7 14.c5 d6 15.cxd6 ♕xd6 16.♖fd1 ♕e7 (16...c6 17.♘c4 ♕c5 18.♖d2 ♗e6 19.♖ad1 ♕e7 20.♘d6 ♗d5 21.♘f5 ♕e5 22.♘g3 ♖fe8 23.♗c4± Blagojevic-Miljanic, Kladovo ch-YUG 1991) 17.♘b3!? ♗e6 18.♘c5 c6 19.♘xe6 ♕xe6 20.♖d4 ♖fd8 21.♕d2 ♖xd4 22.♕xd4 b6 23.♗c4 c5 24.♕d3 ♕f6 25.♖d1± Korotylev-Pankratov, Moscow-ch 1995;

B) 13.♘b3!? ♕e7 (13...♕xd1 14.♖fxd1 d6 15.c5±; 13...♕e5!?) 14.c5 ♖d8 15.♖c1 d6 16.c6 b6 17.♘d4 ♖f8 18.♖c3 ♘h4 19.f4 a5 20.♕d2 g6 21.♗d3 ♔h8 22.♕f2 a4 23.♘b5 ♘f5 24.e4 ♘g7 25.f5± Belakovskaia-Blatny, New York Open, Newark 1996.

13...♕e5

If 13...♕xd1 14.♖fxd1 d6 15.c5!±; or 13...♕e7 14.♘c3 d6 15.♘d5 ♕d8 16.♕d4±.

14.♘c3±

14...b6?!

A better option was 14...d6 15.♕d5!?±.

15.♕d5!

15.♕d2 ♖e8 16.♖ae1 ♗b7 17.♗d3 (17.♕xd7 ♖ad8⇄) 17...♖ad8 18.♗xg6 hxg6 19.e4 g5 (19...♕c5=) 20.♖e3 g6?! (20...♖e6!?) 21.♖d1± V. Milov-Bellon Lopez, Gibraltar 2007.

15...♗a6!?

15...♕xd5 16.♘xd5 c6 17.♘c3 (△ ♘e4-d6) 17...♖e8 18.♖fd1± and White has good play along the d-file.

16.♕xe5

16.♕xd7!? ♖ad8 17.♕c6 ♖d2 18.♖ab1±.

16...♘xe5

17.♘d5?!

With this move White loses the advantage. Better was the tactical solution 17.f4! ♘xc4 18.♔f2! (18.b3?! ♘xe3∞) 18...♖ae8!? (18...b5 19.♘d5±) 19.♖fd1!?±.

17...c6! 18.♘c7 ♗xc4 19.♗xc4

19.♘xa8?! ♗xe2 20.♖fe1 ♗c4∓.

19...♖ac8! 20.♘d5! cxd5

20...♖fe8? 21.♗a6+−.

21.♗xd5 ♖c2 22.♖ab1 ♖fc8

Black has compensation for the disadvantage of the isolated pawn with his control of the c-file.

23.♖fd1 ♔f8

23...♖e2? 24.♗b3 and 25.♔f1+−.

24.♗b3 ♖2c7 25.♔f1 ♔e7 26.♔e2 ♘c6 27.♖d2 ♘a5   ½-½

Summary of the plan with 10...♘g6 and 11...♗d6: the exchange of the dark-squared bishops reduces White's strategic advantage and allows Black to approach equality. But he hardly has any active counterplay.

GAME 31
□ **Vladimir Lazarev**
■ **Olivier Touzane**
France tt-2 2002 (8)

This game puts White's 8th move in doubt. Which is the best plan? g3 or e3?!

1.d4 ♘f6 2.c4 e5 3.dxe5 ♘g4 4.♗f4 ♘c6 5.♘f3 ♗b4+ 6.♘bd2 f6 7.exf6

7.a3 has been tried, with the same idea as after 6...♕e7. But Black is OK after 7...fxe5! (7...♗xd2+ 8.♕xd2±) 8.♗g3 (8.h3!?) 8...♗xd2+ 9.♕xd2 ♕e7 10.e3 d6 11.♗e2 0-0 12.0-0= (Mirzoev-Bestard Borras, Capdepera 2004) 12...♘f6!?⇄; 7.h3?! ♘gxe5=.

7...♕xf6

8.e3!?

The aim of this move is to finish development quickly and without surprises, and carry on searching for chinks in Black's armour.

For 8.g3, see Game 20.

8...♕xb2 9.♗e2

An interesting option is 9.a3!? ♗c3 10.♖b1 ♕xa3 11.♗xc7 (11.♖b3!?) 11...♕e7 12.♗g3± Kilgus-Chulis, Vienna 2003.

9...0-0 10.0-0 d6

One of the critical positions of the variation with 6...f6 and 8.e3.

11.♘b3

The following continuations deserve attention:

A) 11.c5!? ♗xc5 (11...dxc5 12.♖b1 ♕f6 13.a3↑) 12.♖b1 (12.♘g5!?) 12...♕f6 13.♘e4 ♕e7 14.♘xc5 dxc5 15.♘g5 ♘ge5 (15...♘f6!?) 16.♕d5+

(16.♗xe5!? ♘xe5 17.f4↑) 16...♔h8 17.♗xe5 ♘xe5 18.f4 ♘c6 19.♗c4! ♘d8?? (19...♕xe3+ 20.♔h1 g6!∞) 20.♘xh7!+− Wiener-Raddatz, Pinneberg 1994;

B) 11.♘e4!? ♘f6!? 12.♗d3 ♗f5 13.♘xf6+ ♕xf6 14.♖b1 ♗c5? (≥ 14...♖ab8) 15.♘g5 (15.♖xb7!? ♗b6 16.c5!±) 15...♘b4 16.♗xf5 ♕xf5, with counterplay in B. Damljanovic-Touzane, Zaragoza 1995.

11...♘ge5!?

Black chooses the latest theoretical recommendation. The plan with 11...♕f6?! is too slow: 12.♘g5! (12.c5!? ♗c3 13.♖c1 ♗e5 14.♘xe5 dxe5 15.♗g3 ♕g6 16.♕c2 ♗f5 17.♕c3 ♖ae8 18.♘a5!± E. Gleizerov-Bosch, Cappelle la Grande 1996) 12...h6 (12...♘ge5 13.a3! ♗c5 14.♘xc5 dxc5 15.♕d5+ ♔h8 16.♘e4± Gyimesi-Prié, Paris 1995) 13.♗xg4 ♗xg4 (13...hxg5 14.♗xc8 ♖axc8 15.♕d5+) 14.♕xg4 hxg5 15.♕xg5± Wastney-Hoskyn, corr ch-NZL 1994.

12.c5!?N

A theoretical novelty, corresponding to a classical resource that is normally problematic for Black. The normal move is 12.♘fd4!?; or 12.♘bd4 ♘xd4

(12...♘xf3+!? 13.♘xf3 ♔h8) 13.♘xd4 ♗c3? (13...♗c5) 14.♖b1± Franco Ocampos-Touzane, Santa Cruz 1995.

12...♘xf3+?!

12...♘g6?! 13.♗g3 dxc5 14.♗xc7 ♔h8 15.♘g5 with initiative; 12...♔h8 and 12...♗f5 are interesting.

13.♗xf3 ♘e5 14.♗e4±

The short opening duel (lasting only 6 moves) has worked out well for White. The rest is just a splendid demonstration of technique.

14...♗e6 15.♗xb7 ♖ae8 16.♗d5 ♗xd5 17.♕xd5+ ♔h8 18.cxd6 ♗xd6 19.♕d2 ♕a3 20.♕a5 ♕b2 21.♕d2 ♕a3 22.♗g3 ♖f6 23.♘d4

23.♖ac1.

23...♕a6 24.♕e2!

White intends to simplify and increase his advantage.

24...♕c8 25.♘b5 ♕a6 26.♖fe1 ♕a4 27.♖ac1 ♕a5 28.♖ed1 a6 29.♘xd6 cxd6 30.h3+− h6 31.♖c2 ♕a3 32.♖dc1 ♖ff8 33.♖c7 ♖b8 34.♔h2 ♖b2 35.♖1c2 ♖fb8 36.♗xe5 dxe5 37.♕g4 ♖g8 38.♖xg7! ♖bb8 39.♖cc7 ♕d3 40.e4!   1-0

It seems that the advance c4-c5! poses some questions to the sub-variation 6...f6. But it is far from easy!

GAME 32
□ **Matthew Sadler**
■ **Ian Rogers**
Hastings 1993/94 (3)

1.d4 ♘f6 2.c4 e5 3.dxe5 ♘g4 4.♗f4 ♗b4+ 5.♘d2 d6!?

The idea of this move is to start an attack on the white queen and minor pieces. Therefore it is necessary to chase the e5 pawn from the centre.

6.♘f3

White continues his development, but this is not the way to fight for an opening advantage. Other options do not satisfy either:

A) 6.a3?! dxe5! 7.♗g3 (7.axb4 exf4∓) 7...♗xd2+ 8.♕xd2 ♕xd2+! 9.♔xd2 ♘c6↑;

B) 6.e6? fxe6∓ with an initiative along the f-file (also good is 6...♗xe6!?∓); 7.e3 0-0 8.a3?

analysis diagram

8...♘xf2!? 9.♔xf2 ♗xd2 10.♕xd2 e5 11.♘f3 exf4 12.exf4 ♘d7 (12...♕f6!?↑) 13.♖e1 ♘f6↑ Dreev-B. Savchenko, Canada de Calatrava rapid 2006.

6...dxe5 7.♗xe5

7.♘xe5 ♗xd2+ (7...♕d4!? 8.♘d3 ♘xf2!↑) 8.♕xd2 ♕xd2+ 9.♔xd2 ♘xf2 10.♖g1 ♘e4+!? (10...♘a6!? 11.♘d3 ♘e4+ 12.♔e3 ♘f6↑ 13.h3 ♗d7 14.♗e5 0-0-0 ½-½ Gomez Esteban-G. Mohr, Maribor 1995) 11.♔e3 ♘c5⇄ Path-Wippermann, Cork 2005.

7...♗xd2+!?

I also like the middlegame for Black after 7...♘xe5!? 8.♘xe5 ♕e7 9.♘d3 ♘c6.

8.♕xd2 ♕xd2+ 9.♔xd2 ♘xf2

It is clear that White does not have an advantage.

10.♖g1 0-0

The position is still full of possibilities. Interesting would be 10...♘e4+!? 11.♔e3 ♘d6=.

11.♗xc7 ♘a6 12.♗e5 ♘e4+

In the classic game Spassky-Szabo, Beverwijk 1967, there followed 12...♖d8+ 13.♗d4 ♘e4+ 14.♔c1 ♗e6 15.e3 ♖ac8 16.b3 b5 17.♔b2 bxc4 18.♖c1 ♘b4 19.♗xc4 ♗xc4 20.♖xc4

♖xc4 21.bxc4 ♖b8 22.a3 ♘c6+
23.♔c2 ♘a5 24.♗xa7 ♖b3 25.♖b1
♖c3+ 26.♔d1 h6 27.♖a1 ♖xc4
28.♗d4 ♘f2+ 29.♔e2 ♖c2+ 30.♔f1
♘e4 31.a4 g5 32.♘e1 ♖f2+ 33.♔g1
♘b3 34.♖d1 ♖a2 ½-½.

13.♔e3 ♗f5?!

Better was 13...♘ec5!?♟.

14.g4 ♗g6 15.♘h4 ♖fe8

15...♘ac5 16.♘xg6 fxg6!? is unclear.

16.♘xg6 ♘ac5 17.♘f4 ♖xe5 18.♗g2 ♖ae8

It seems that Black is active, but he lacks resources for the attack, while White maintains the extra pawn.

19.♗f3 ♘d6+ 20.♔d4 b6 21.♘d3 ♖5e6 22.♗d5

22.♘xc5!? bxc5+ 23.♔xc5 ♖c8+
24.♔d4 ♖xc4+ 25.♔d3±.

22...♖xe2 23.♘xc5 bxc5+ 24.♔xc5

Now White is better, but Rogers defends successfully.

24...♘e4+! 25.♗xe4

25.♔c6!?.

25...♖8xe4 26.b3 h5!?

There are no lost positions! 26...♖xh2
27.♖ge1 ♖xe1 28.♖xe1 ♔f8 29.a4±.

27.gxh5

27.h3!?.

27...♖e5+ 28.♔c6 ♖xh5 29.♖gd1
½-½

GAME 33
□ **Nino Gurieli**
■ **Michael Ponater**
Hamburg 1999 (7)

For a player to enter the line with 6.exd6! ♕f6 7.e3!? it is not essential to know many strategic concepts. It's more important to have good calculating and analytical abilities. The annotations to Games 33 and 34 are important for those who are thinking of playing the Budapest Gambit.

1.d4 ♘f6 2.c4 e5 3.dxe5 ♘g4 4.♗f4 ♗b4+ 5.♘d2 d6!? 6.exd6!

From now on the position gets very complicated.

6...♕f6

If 6...♗xd6 7.♗xd6 ♕xd6 8.h3
(8.♕c2!? defends everything) 8...♘f6
(8...♘e3?! 9.♕b3±) 9.♘gf3. White maintains the extra pawn.

7.e3!

The safest and most solid answer. After 7.♘h3!? ♘xf2! the position is highly unclear (see Game 34); 7.♗g3?! ♗xd6 8.♘gf3 ♗xg3 9.hxg3 ♕xb2⇄.

7...♘xf2

An important moment in the 5...d6 line. Let's look at alternatives:

A) 7...♕xb2 8.♘f3 ♗xd6 (8...cxd6
9.♖b1±) 9.♗xd6 cxd6 10.♗e2 0-0

11.0-0± with the idea 12.♘e4! with a clear advantage;

B) 7...♗xd6 8.♗e2! h5 (8...♘xf2? 9.♔xf2 g5 10.♘e4+−) 9.♗xg4?! (9.♘e4! ♗b4+ 10.♔f1±; 9.♗h3!?) 9...♗xg4 10.f3 (10.♕b3 ♗xf4∞) 10...♗xf4 11.exf4 ♗e6 12.♘e2 ♘c6 13.♕b3 0-0-0↑ Volkov-B. Savchenko, Internet Chess Club 2005;

C) 7...g5 8.♗g3 h5 9.dxc7! ♘c6 10.h4! ♕xb2 11.♘f3 ♗f5 (11...♘ge5!?) 12.♗e2 ♗c2 13.♕c1 ♗a3 14.0-0! ♕xc1 15.♖axc1 ♗xc1 16.♖xc1+− Kachiani Gersinska-Vianin, Crans Montana 2000.

8.♔xf2 g5 9.♘e4!

9.♘gf3?! gxf4 10.♘e4 ♕xb2+ 11.♗e2 fxe3+ 12.♔xe3 ♘c6 13.dxc7 f5, unclear.

9...♕xb2+

The critical position.

10.♗e2!?

For players with a good nervous system the following variations are well worth studying: 10.♘e2!? gxf4 11.♖b1! (11.♕d4? fxe3+ 12.♔xe3 ♕xd4+ 13.♔xd4 ♘c6+↑) 11...fxe3+ 12.♔f3 ♕g7! (12...♕e5 13.♖xb4 f5!?) 13.♖xb4 f5 (13...♘c6!? 14.dxc7! 0-0 15.♖b5! f5 16.♘d6∞) with a complicated position in which the black queen and pawns attack the white king.

analysis diagram

14.♘c5!?. If there is no mate, White is better! For example: 14...f4!? (14...♘c6 15.♖b3 ♘e5+ 16.♔xe3 cxd6 17.♘a4±) 15.♕d5! ♕g4+ 16.♔e4 ♘c6!? 17.♖b3! (cold-blooded) 17...♖f8 18.d7+! ♗xd7 19.♕xd7+ ♕xd7 20.♘xd7 ♔xd7 21.♖d3+!+−.

10...gxf4 11.exf4

11...♗f5?

This loses immediately. The players make tactical mistakes because it's very difficult to calculate all the moves – nobody is perfect. Black could have put up more resistance with 11...♘a6 12.♘f3! and his position is still playable. Another possibility was 11...♘c6!? 12.♖b1 ♕g7 13.c5!? (13.♖b3 f5!? 14.♗h5+ ♔f8∞; 13.♘f3?! f5!⇄; 13.dxc7!? 0-0 14.♘f3±) 13...♗f5 14.♖xb4! ♘xb4 15.♘g3 with a white initiative.

12.♖b1 ♗c5+

12...♕a3   13.♕d4+−;   12...♕g7
13.♕d5!+−.

13.♔f1! ♕d4 14.♕xd4 ♗xd4 15.dxc7!
1-0

GAME 34
□ **Günther Beikert**
■ **Boris Chatalbashev**
Sofia Wch U26 1994 (2)

1.d4 ♘f6 2.c4 e5 3.dxe5 ♘g4 4.♗f4
♗b4+ 5.♘d2 d6 6.exd6 ♕f6 7.♘h3!?

7...♘xf2!

7...♗xd6 8.♗xd6 ♕xd6 9.e3±.

8.♔xf2!

The king leaves the stage! Clearly worse is
8.♘xf2? ♕xf4 9.dxc7 ♘c6 (9...♕xc7!?)
10.a3?! (10.♘d3∞)   10...♗a5   11.g3
♕e3 12.♗g2 0-0 13.b4 ♗xc7 14.♗xc6
bxc6 15.♕b3 ♕h6↑ Shulman-Gossell,
Sioux Falls Cup, USA 2004.

8...♗xh3 9.g3! ♗c5+!?

Black has a super-ambitious idea – never
forsake a check in the opening!. More
popular is 9...♗xf1?! and now every-
body continues 10.♖xf1 ♕d4+ 11.♔g2
(11.♔f3   ♗xd6   12.♘e4   ♕xd1
13.♖axd1 ♗xf4 14.gxf4 ♘d7 15.♖g1
g6   16.h4± Scherbakov-Chatalbashev,
Anapa   1991)   11...♗xd6   12.♕b3!
(12.♘f3 ♕xd1 13.♖axd1 ♗xf4 14.gxf4
♘d7= Neuman-Rivera Kuzawka,
Pardubice 2005) 12...♘d7? (12...0-0;

12...♗xf4? 13.♖xf4±) 13.♗e3 ♕e5
14.c5! ♘xc5 15.♕xf7+ ♔d8 16.♘c4
♕e4+   17.♖f3   ♘e6   18.♘xd6 cxd6
19.♖d1 1-0 Komarov-Chatalbashev, St
Raphael 1998.

Surprisingly, 10.dxc7! has so far been
played in one single game (from 21)
only. There followed 10...♘c6 11.♖xf1
♗xd2? (11...0-0 12.♘e4±) 12.♕xd2
g5   13.♕e3+! ♘e7   14.♕e5   ♕xe5
15.♗xe5 ♖g8 16.♔g2 ♖c8 17.♖f6 ♘c6
18.♗d6 ♘d4 19.♖af1 ♖g6 20.♖xf7 1-0
Dumitrache-Biti, Zagreb 1997.

10.e3!?

Or 10.♔e1 ♗f5! (10...♗xf1?? 11.♘e4!
♕xb2 12.♔xf1 ♘d7 13.dxc7 0-0
14.♖c1+− Radziewicz-Gara, Budapest
2002) 11.dxc7 ♘a6!? and things are
very complicated.

10...g5!?

10...♗f5!? 11.dxc7 ♘c6 12.♘f3 0-0
13.♕d5!±.

11.♘e4!

Suddenly, White starts to make incredible moves... winning the game!

11...♕xb2+ 12.♕e2! ♕xa1

12...♕xe2+ 13.♗xe2 gxf4 14.♘xc5±.

13.♗xh3!

13.♘xc5?!   gxf4!   14.exf4+   ♔f8
15.♕e7+ ♔g7 16.♕g5+=.

13...♕xh1

14.♕b2!
Worse was 14.♕g4 ♕xh2+ 15.♔f3 ♕h1+ with no more than a draw.
14...0-0 15.♘f6+ ♔h8 16.♗xg5+– c6
Or 16...♗a3 17.♕xa3+–.
17.♘g4+   **1-0**
With mate in 3 after every defence.
A very complicated game. Black must look for still more complicating moves.

Summary of ♘bd2
White prefers a quiet game, trying to reduce the activity of Black's pieces and to obtain some positional advantage with his bishop pair and better pawn structure. He aims to develop quietly and naturally (Games 19 and 21-30), if possible ignoring the bishop on b4 (Games 25-30) and trying to fix Black's structure with c4-c5!, which is his main resource.

Nevertheless, Black has interesting possibilities in all lines against ♘bd2 and can continue fighting for counterplay. White has to watch out for the well-known mate trap on d3 (Game 19), Black also has the option to castle queenside (Game 21), or fix White's queenside (Game 29). Typical breaks to try and wrest the initiative are 6...f6 (Games 20 and 31) and 5...d6 (Game 32).

In the line with 4...♘c6 5.♘f3 ♗b4 6.♘bd2, if Black recaptures the e5 pawn with 6...♕e7, 7.a3 is the most ambitious option, but I believe that chances are equal here. 7.e3 is more natural, but I do not see anything special for White here either.

In the variation 4...♗b4+ 5.♘d2 d6, most of the games finish quickly in White's favour, but during these first 15 or 20 moves you cannot relax; it's quite as if you're in a roller coaster fairground attraction!

Part III – Black Jet or The Fianchetto

1.d4 ♘f6 2.c4 e5 3.dxe5 ♘g4 4.♗f4 g5

Introduction

The thrust with the 'Black Jet', 4...g5, is a creative move which attacks White's queen's bishop and aims to fianchetto the bishop on f8 at the same time. The stem game is Skalicka-Vecsey, Prague-ch 1930, see the comments in Game 37 Tunik-Tiurin.

Without doubt, 4...g5 is an extravagant reply that never fails to surprise the opponent. Black's intention is to fianchetto his bishop on g7 and recover the e5 pawn. The disadvantage of this aggressive move consists in the many weaknesses that arise in Black's kingside pawn structure, forcing him to play as actively as possible. However, it is a very interesting possibility about which there is hardly any theoretical analysis.

The key of this line is the development of the black bishop to g7 instead of b4. The bishop is much more powerful on this square, dominating the long a1-h8 diagonal, controlling key squares in the centre and threatening the b2 pawn.

The determining move of the Budapest Gambit is 2...e5, which opens the f8-a3 diagonal for the development of the dark-squared bishop. So, why is it necessary to play a second move such as 4...g5, opening a second diagonal, with all the weaknesses that this move creates? Simply because it attacks Rubinstein's bishop on f4 and thus forces White to choose between two alternatives:

  1. Abandon the defence of the e5 pawn, which is the key of Rubinstein's plan, and move it to d2;

  2. Maintain the support of the pawn, but from the less active square g3.

Directions

What is the best plan for White, 5.♗g3 or 5.♗d2? And does an effective refutation of the aggressive 4...g5 advance exist?

A) 5.♗g3

The most common reply. Now there are many options for both sides.

After 5...♗g7 6.♘f3! ♘c6 it seems that White's best alternatives are:

A1) 7.♘c3. A natural move; see Games 36-38. The best examples are: Kortchnoi-Yukhtman (Game 36) 7...♘gxe5 8.♘xe5 ♘xe5 9.e3 d6 10.h4! and Tunik-Tiurin (Game 37), which features another crazy advance: 9...h5!?.

A2) 7.h4!?

A dangerous break which may be a good attempt to quickly refute 4...g5, see Games 39-41. In my opinion, Kouatly-Preissmann (Game 39) contains a strong plan to seek an advantage with this break.

The basic plan for Black is to attack the white king's pawn with the bishop on g7 and the knight on c6, and generally to capture it. The rest of the pieces are developed as follows: the c8 bishop goes to e6, the queen goes to d7 and the king castles queenside. Once he has completed development, Black proceeds to attack the white kingside, taking advantage of his g- and h-pawns (see Game 35 Van Wely-Mamedyarov).

The basic plan for White is to develop his g1 knight to f3 and exchange it on e5. The f1 bishop goes to e2, and the b1 knight to c3. The key to his strategy is the move h2-h4!?, with which White tries to attack the dark-square weaknesses, opening the h-file, and in some lines the rook enables Rubinstein's bishop on g3 to move to h4.

What does Black play to counter White's h2-h4? Generally, he either waits until White captures the g-pawn or advances it to keep the h-file closed.

In Game 37 (Tunik-Tiurin), Black played 9...h5!? and it worked for him, because White replied 10.h3?! instead of 10.h4! as suggested in the annotations. Of the three games in which White plays 7.h4, in two of them White wins and the other ends in a draw. Really incredible is Game 39 (Kouatly-Preissmann), won by White. Black only tried to avoid the opening of the g-file in Game 41 (Simacek-Tiurin), which was drawn. In the games in which White didn't play h4 or postponed it, Black achieved three wins and one draw.

White's attack is conducted by two typical Budapest Gambit moves: c4-c5 and ♘c3-d5, as well as different attacks by the white queen on the light-squared diagonals. The movement of the pawn to c5 was analysed in Part I. In fact, Rubinstein's bishop stays on the h2-b8 diagonal and therefore all that has been said there applies also here. The queenside knight has an excellent square on d5 from which it attacks both the queenside and the weak squares on the kingside;

The white queen is an important piece in this variation. It is much more active here than in other lines of the Rubinstein Variation. Here, it moves along the light-squared diagonals d1-a4, d1-h5 and c2-h7 and can attack both the kingside light-squared weaknesses and the b7 or c6 squares.

Advance e2-e4

White's move e2-e4 (see Games 38, 43) is not very successful here. In fact, it almost never is in the Rubinstein Variation. The pawn is better placed on e3, where it does not obstruct the b1-h7 and h1-a8 diagonals and where it also facilitates a possible f2-f4 break.

B) 5.♗d2

5.♗d2!? is a strong and solid counterplan.

The Rubinstein bishop will move to c3 and attack on the long diagonal a1-h8, which is severely weakened. In the clash between the two bishops, White's is defended, so Black must pay attention to the pin on his knight after capturing on e5. This is what happened in Game 42 (Gligoric-Fuderer).

One way to avoid this pin is to capture the white knight with the bishop after the exchange on e5. If the white bishop attacks the black bishop on e5 it can be defended with either the knight on c6, the d-pawn or the queen on f6. It seems to me that the queen will be well-placed on e5 or on the diagonal a1-h8 (see Game 46 Candela-Campora). On the other hand, the black knight will be well placed on c5, where it defends the queenside, especially square b7, and also controls some central squares. The c8 bishop nearly always goes to e6.

In this variation, the h-pawn was only advanced on one occasion (Game 43 Dreev-Topalov), and therefore Black castles kingside more often than in the case of 5.♗g3. By castling kingside Black defends some of the weaknesses created by 4...g5. If White also castles kingside, Black's dark-square weaknesses on this flank are even more glaring.

The white queen keeps playing on the light squares, but in the examples with 5.♗d2 its attack is not so strong as with 5.♗g3. For example, in Game 47 (Streitberg-Choleva) the white queen captured all the black queenside pawns, but Black still managed to draw.

Black Jet – Games

GAME 35
□ **Loek van Wely**
■ **Shakhriyar Mamedyarov**
Ciudad Real tt 2004 (4)

1.d4 ♘f6 2.c4 e5

Once again, young GM Mamedyarov opts for the BG, as he already did in his game against Nybäck in the European Championship 2004 (see Chapter Three).

3.dxe5 ♘g4 4.♗f4

Before this game, Van Wely had only faced the Gambit in four serious games and had always chosen 4.♗f4.

4...g5!?

The idea of Zoltan Vecsey, see Game 37.

5.♗g3 ♗g7

6.e3

An unusual move, but White wants to try out a new plan, developing his knight on e2. 6.♘f3 may be preferable.

6...♘xe5 7.♘c3 d6 8.h4 g4!

I think that this is the best option for Black against the h2-h4 thrust. The kingside is temporarily fixed, giving Black time to breathe and finish his development. The h-pawn will be weak if White decides to castle kingside.

But never 8...h6?! 9.hxg5 hxg5 10.♖xh8+ ♗xh8 11.♕h5 with a strong initiative for White.

Of the youngest generation, Shakhriyar Mamedyarov is one of the few supporters of the Budapest Gambit.

9.♘ge2 ♘bc6

Black prepares an ambitious plan involving queenside castling. 9...0-0 looks more solid, though.

10.♘f4

With the idea of ♘h5.

10...h5!?

11.♘cd5

Occupying the d5-square. This may be Black's weakest square in the BG, but there are many more important squares on the board!

Another plan is 11.♕c2!? with the idea of 0-0-0, c5.

11...♘e7

11...♗f5!?.

12.♘xe7 ♕xe7 13.♕c2 ♗e6 14.♖c1

A very discreet try to attack with c4-c5. Better was 14.0-0-0 0-0-0.

14...0-0-0!

Black rounds off the opening phase successfully and is ready for central action. Meanwhile, the white king isn't safe.

15.♗e2 ♔b8!? 16.b4

The critical middlegame moment. The position is balanced – however, both armies will be shedding blood...

16...♘g6!? 17.♘xg6 fxg6 18.♕xg6 ♗e5

Interesting was 18...♗b2!? 19.♖c2 ♗e5, when the queen cannot return to c2.

19.♗xe5

Safer is 19.0-0!?=.

19...dxe5 20.a3 ♖hg8! 21.♕c2 g3!

Such moves never fail to annoy the opponent.

22.f3 ♕f6 23.♕c3 ♕f5

A natural continuation was 23...♖g4!? 24.♖d1! ♖xd1+ 25.♔xd1 ♖xh4 26.♖xh4 ♕xh4 27.♕xe5 ♗c8 28.♔d2 ♕h2 29.f4 ♕xg2 30.♕xh5 ♕g1 31.♗g4! ♕f2+ 32.♔d3 ♕f1+ 33.♔d2 g2 34.♕e8! ♕e1+ 35.♔d3!=.

24.♕c2 ♕f6

Maybe Van Wely needed the full point, so he continued:

25.♗d3?!

Objectively it would have been better to repeat moves with 25.♕c3!?.

25...♖g4!

Maybe this sacrifice is more powerful now than in the previous note.

26.♕c3?

The most interesting would have been to accept the rook: 26.fxg4!? ♖xd3! 27.♖f1! ♕d8! 28.♖f3 e4! 29.♖xg3 hxg4!? with an attack for Black.

26...♖xh4–+ 27.♖g1 ♖h2 28.♖d1 ♗h3! 29.♖d2 h4 30.♗e4 ♖xd2 31.♕xd2 ♗c8 32.♕d5 ♕h6! 33.♔e2 h3

In this game the g- and h- pawns are the best soldiers in Black's army.

34.♕g8 ♖xg2+ 35.♖xg2 hxg2 36.♗f5 a6! 37.♕xc8+ ♔a7 38.♗e4 ♕b6

38...c6.

39.c5

At last this advance!
39...♕b5+ 40.♗d3 ♕c6 41.♗e4 ♕b5+ 42.♗d3 g1♘+!
First, the h-pawn promotes to a new piece (Bishops against Knights!).
43.♔d2 ♕c6
43...♘xf3+!.
44.♕g4 ♕xf3 45.♕g7 g2 46.♕xc7 ♕c6 47.♕xc6 bxc6 48.♗e4 ♘f3+ 0-1
And on the next move the g-pawn promotes, and the strong 'Black Jet' brings victory.

The next game is from the 1959 USSR Championship, in which the talented young player Yukhtman applied this variation successfully against a stronger opponent.

GAME 36
□ **Viktor Kortchnoi**
■ **Jacob Yukhtman**
Tbilisi ch-URS 1959 (13)

1.d4 ♘f6 2.c4 e5 3.dxe5 ♘g4 4.♗f4 g5 5.♗g3 ♗g7 6.♘f3 ♘c6 7.♘c3
A natural move. A dangerous break is 7.h4!? – Games 39-41. If 7.♕d5?! d6!.
7...♘gxe5 8.♘xe5 ♘xe5 9.e3
9.c5!? or 9.h4!? are always convenient options in this variation.
9...d6 10.h4!

10...h6?!

A normal reaction. After 10...g4!? interesting is 11.c5!? and after, for example, 11...dxc5 (11...0-0!? 12.cxd6±) 12.♕xd8+ ♔xd8 13.h5!? h6 14.0-0-0+ ♗d7 15.♗e2 it seems that Black is not OK.
11.♕b3!?
Kortchnoi wants to play classically with ♖d1 and then c4-c5, but this is too slow here. He could have played the direct 11.c5!? dxc5 12.♕xd8+ ♔xd8 13.0-0-0+ ♗d7 14.♖d5! and White has the initiative. Now 14...♖e8? loses to 15.hxg5 hxg5 16.♖h7.
11...0-0?
An optimistic decision. There were two more useful moves: 11...♘d7!? and 11...♗e6!?.
12.hxg5 hxg5

13.♖d1?!
Leaving his king in the centre. After the more aggressive 13.0-0-0! – which would have been truer to Kortchnoi's style – White would have an advantage in the centre and on the kingside.
13...♗e6 14.♘b5
14.♕c2!? f5 15.c5.
14...f5 15.♗xe5
15.♘d4!?.
15...♗xe5 16.♘d4 ♗xd4 17.♖xd4 b6 18.♗e2 ♕f6 19.♕c2 ♔g7!

89

Black has a good position.

20.♖d1 ♖h8 21.♔d2 f4 22.♕c3 fxe3+ 23.fxe3 ♕xc3+ 24.♔xc3 ♖xh1?!

This exchange was not necessary. 24...♔f6!? 25.♗f3 ♖af8⇄.

25.♖xh1 ♗f5 26.♗d3 ♗xd3 27.♔xd3 ♖f8 28.♔e2=

Now the most probable result is a draw.

28...a5 29.g4 a4 30.♖h2 ♖d8 31.♔d3 d5 32.♖c2 ♔f6 33.♖f2+ ♔e6 34.♔c3 c6 35.♖f5 dxc4 36.♔xc4 ♖d2 37.♔c3 ♖e2 38.♖xg5 ♖xe3+ 39.♔d2 ♖g3 40.a3 b5 41.♔c2 ♔d6 42.♔d2 c5 43.♔c2 b4 44.axb4 cxb4 45.♖a5 ♖xg4?!

45...b3+ 46.♔d2 ♖xg4 47.♔c3=.

46.♖xa4 ♖g2+ 47.♔c1 ♔c5 48.b3

½-½

An interesting game that demonstrates the power of the move 4...g5!?. If Black plays actively and doesn't allow White to consolidate, then chances are equal.

GAME 37
□ **Gennady Tunik**
■ **Alexander Tiurin**
Voronezh Open 2003 (7)

1.d4 ♘f6 2.c4 e5 3.dxe5 ♘g4 4.♗f4 g5 5.♗g3 ♘c6 6.♘f3 ♗g7 7.♘c3 ♘gxe5 8.♘xe5

8.e3 d6 9.c5!? ♘xf3+ (9...0-0 10.cxd6 cxd6±) 10.♕xf3 ♘e5 11.♕e4 0-0 12.h4 g4 13.0-0-0 ♗e6!⇄ 14.♕xb7 ♖b8 15.♕a6 ♕f6 16.♕a3 dxc5 17.♕xc5 ♖b6 (17...♕f5!?) 18.♖d2 ♖fb8 19.♗xe5 ♕xe5 20.♕xe5 ♗xe5 21.♗d3= Khenkin-Cebalo, Bratto 2004; 21...♖c6!? 22.♖c2 ♗xa2! 23.♘xa2 ♖xc2+ 24.♗xc2 ♖xb2 25.♗b1 ♖xf2♔♔

8...♘xe5 9.e3 h5!?

Black has high hopes!

10.h3?!

This move loses an important tempo. The original 4...g5 game went: 10.h4! g4 11.♕c2!? (if 11.c5 b6!? 12.♕d5 c6∞) 11...d6 12.♖d1 (12.c5!?; 12.0-0-0 ♗e6 13.c5 0-0∞) 12...♗e6 (12...b6) 13.c5 0-0 14.cxd6 cxd6 15.♗e2 ♖c8 16.0-0∞

with a complicated position. The d6-pawn is weak but Black's pieces are active, Skalicka-Vecsey, Prague 1930.
De Haan-Moskalenko, Sitges 2007, continued 16...♕b6 (16...♗xa2!?) 17.♖d2 ♗xa2 18.♕e4?! (18.♕f5 ♗b3!? 19.♕xh5 ♖c5⇄) 18...♗e6 19.♘d5 ♗xd5 20.♕xd5 ♖c5! 21.♕e4 d5! 22.♕b1 ♖d8 23.♖fd1 a5∓ 24.b3 ♘c6 25.♗f4 ♘b4 26.♕f5 ♕g6 27.♕xg6 fxg6 28.♗g5? ♖e8-+ 29.♖b1 ♔f7 30.♗f4 ♗e5 31.♗g5 ♖ec8 32.g3 ♖c1+ 33.♖d1 ♖xb1 34.♖xb1 ♖c2 35.♗b5

♞a2 36.♗d3 ♖d2 37.♗f1 ♞c3 38.♖c1 ♖a2 39.♗d8 b5 40.♗c7 ♗f6 41.♖xc3 ♗xc3 42.♗xb5 ♖b2 43.♗a4 ♚e6 44.♚f1 ♚f5 45.♗b6 ♚e4 46.♗e8 ♚f3 47.♗xg6 ♖xf2+ 0-1.

10...d6 11.♗e2 ♗e6 12.♖c1 ♕d7 13.b3 h4 14.♗h2 0-0-0

Black has the initiative. White's king will soon be under attack by ...f5, ...g4.

15.♞b5 ♚b8 16.♞d4 f5!

Starting a classical attack with the kingside pawns.

17.♞xe6 ♕xe6 18.♕d5 ♕g6! 19.♖d1 g4 20.hxg4 fxg4 21.♗f4 c6 22.♕d2 h3 23.gxh3 gxh3

White has no counterplay.

24.♗xe5 ♗xe5 25.♗f1 ♕f6

25...h2! was also winning.

26.♚e2 d5 27.♖xh3 ♖hf8!

This is the second stage of the attack, now with pieces.

28.f4 d4! 29.♕a5 ♖de8

The position is too complex. The best move was 29...♗c7! 30.♕g5 ♕e6−+.

30.fxe5 ♖xe5 31.♕e1 ♖f5?

31...dxe3→.

32.♕g3+?!

With 32.♚d3! dxe3 33.♗e2 White could have put up more resistance.

32...♚a8 33.♕h4?

33.♖xd4 ♖f2+→.

33...d3+! 34.♚xd3 ♖d8+   0-1

35.♚c2 ♖f2+ or 35.♚e2 ♕b2+.

GAME 38
□ **Svetozar Gligoric**
■ **Elek Bakonyi**
Budapest 1948 (4)

1.d4 ♞f6 2.c4 e5 3.dxe5 ♞g4 4.♗f4 g5 5.♗g3 ♗g7 6.♞f3 ♞c6 7.♞c3 ♞gxe5 8.♞xe5 ♞xe5 9.e4

Another complex option, but now Black obtains good counterplay.

9...d6 10.♗e2 ♗e6 11.0-0

11.♕b3!?.

11...♕d7

Intending ...0-0-0. Better is 11...h5! or 11...c6!?.

12.♞d5 0-0-0 13.♕d2 h6 14.♖ad1

A sharp game ensues, full of the tactical mistakes that typically occur in the Budapest Gambit.

14...f5?

14...c6! gave ample counterplay.

15.exf5 ♗xf5 16.c5!↑ dxc5?

16...♔b8!? was better.

17.♕a5 ♞c6? 18.♕xc5 ♗d4

19.♞e7+?

19.♖xd4! ♞xd4 20.♕xd4 ♕xd5
21.♕xa7, with attack.

**19...♕xe7 20.♕xf5+ ♔b8∞ 21.♗b5
♖hf8 22.♕g4?**

22.♕c2 was the better choice.

**22...♕b4 23.♗e2 ♗xb2 24.♕h5 ♖xd1
25.♖xd1 ♕e7 26.♗f3 ♕f6 27.h3 ♗e5
28.♖b1 ♗xg3 29.fxg3 b6 30.♔h2
♞d4–+ 31.♗e4 ♕e6 32.♖e1 c5
33.a4 ♖f2 34.♕d1 ♕d6 35.♕d3
♞f3+ 36.♕xf3 ♖xf3 37.♗xf3 c4
38.♖e8+ ♔c7 39.♗g4 ♕b4 40.♖c8+
♔b7 41.♖h8 c3 42.♖h7+ ♔b8 43.♗f5
♕xa4 44.♖xh6 b5 45.♖c6 ♕d4
46.♖g6 ♕e3   0-1**

As this game shows, in the Rubinstein Variation the quick advance e2-e4 is not the best idea. See for another example Game 43 Dreev-Topalov.

GAME 39
□ **Bachar Kouatly**
■ **Emmanuel Preissmann**
Bagneux Open 1983

**1.d4 ♞f6 2.c4 e5 3.dxe5 ♞g4 4.♗f4
g5 5.♗g3 ♗g7 6.♞f3 ♞c6 7.h4!?**

This seems like the best moment to make this dangerous break.

7...♞gxe5! 8.♞xe5

8.♞xg5?! h6 9.♞e4 ♞xc4⇄.

8...♞xe5 9.hxg5!?

Pursuing the idea behind 7.h4.

9...♞xc4!?

The complications start. The alternative is 9...♕xg5 10.e3 d6 11.♞c3 ♗e6 12.♞d5!± 0-0-0?? (≥ 12...♕d8 13.♗h4 f6 14.♞f4!±) 13.♖h5 winning the black queen, 1-0 Riazantsev-Tiurin, Voronezh 2004.

10.♞c3! c6!?

10...♕xg5 11.♖h4!±; 10...♞xb2?
11.♕c1!? (11.♕c2 ♞a4 12.♞d5!↑)
11...♞c4 12.♞d5! c6 13.♞c7++–.

11.e4!

Maybe now this is the best move.
11.♕c2!? is an alternative.

14...b5?
14...♗g7 15.e5 was more tenacious, or 14...♖g8 15.f4 b5 16.♘c5 b4 17.♔d1!.
15.♘b2!+− ♖g8 16.♖xh7 ♗xb2
16...♗b7 17.g6!?.
17.♕xb2 ♕xg5 18.♖h8!   1-0
Black will be mated in a few moves. An excellent game by White that shows an interesting method to combat the Black Jet.

GAME 40
□ **Zoltan Gyimesi**
■ **Janos Dudas**
Hungary tt 1998/99

1.d4 ♘f6 2.c4 e5 3.dxe5 ♘g4 4.♗f4 g5 5.♗g3 ♗g7 6.♘f3 ♘c6 7.h4 h6?!

This allows White to attack along the h-file.
8.hxg5!?
8.e3 ♘gxe5 9.♘xe5 ♘xe5 10.♘c3 d6 11.♗e2 ♗e6⇄ Fernandez Quintero-Belezky, Coria del Rio 2005; 8.♘c3!? ♘gxe5 9.♘xe5 ♘xe5 10.hxg5 hxg5 11.♖xh8+ ♗xh8 12.♕c2 with the possibilities of ...♕h7, ...0-0-0, and ...c5.
8...hxg5 9.♖xh8+ ♗xh8 10.♕c2
Eyeing the h7-square.
10...♘gxe5 11.♘xe5 ♗xe5
11...♘xe5 12.♘c3↑.
12.♗xe5 ♘xe5 13.♘c3 d6 14.0-0-0

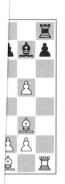

.♕a5 13.♖c1±, is 12...d5!, with ...ation 13.♕xb2 ...♗xc4 dxc4∞) ... 15.♖c1 ♗f8! ...xc3+ 17.♖xc3±) ...ng 17.♗c4) ...g is still unclear.

...ming. Black was ...g 13.♖c1 ♘xc3 ...♘xc3 14.♕xc3

13...♗xa1 14.♗d6!

Now Black is in trouble.

Black has not solved his opening problems. Let's have a look at the punishment.

14...b6 15.e3!?

Intending f2-f4.

15...♗b7 16.♕f5

16.f4!?↑.

16...g4 17.♘d5!+– ♗xd5 18.cxd5 a6 19.♗e2 ♕d7 20.♕f6 ♕e7 21.♕h8+ ♕f8 22.♖h1 0-0-0

22...♔d7 23.♕f6+–.

23.♗xa6+ ♔b8 24.♕f6 ♘d7 25.♕d4 ♘e5 26.♗b5 ♔b7 27.♕a4 ♖a8 28.♗c6+ ♘xc6 29.dxc6+ ♔b8 30.♕d4! f6 31.♕xg4 ♖xa2 32.♖h7 ♖a1+ 33.♔d2! d5 34.♖xc7

34.♔e2!? with the idea 34...♕b4 35.♕c8+!.

34...♖a7 35.♖xa7♔xa7 36.c7   1-0

GAME 41
□ **Pavel Simacek**
■ **Alexander Tiurin**
Pardubice Open 2006 (3)

1.d4 ♘f6 2.c4 e5 3.dxe5 ♘g4 4.♗f4 g5 5.♗g3 ♘c6 6.♘f3 ♗g7 7.h4 ♘gxe5 8.♘xe5 ♘xe5 9.e3

White prefers to play without risk; 9.hxg5!? is interesting.

9...g4!?

It's best to push this pawn. If 9...♘g6!?, interesting is 10.hxg5! with the idea

10...♗xb2 11.♘d2 d6 (11...♗xa1?! 12.♕xa1 ♕xg5 13.♗d3!↑) 12.♖b1 ♗c3 (12...♗g7 13.♘e4±) 13.♕c2 (13.♕a4+!?) 13...♗xd2+ 14.♕xd2 ♕xg5 with a complicated position in Kachiani Gersinska-M. Socko, Gothenburg 2005.

10.h5!? h6

10...d6!? 11.h6 ♗f6.

11.♘c3

This is similar to the plan with 7.♘c3.

11...d6 12.♗h4!?

12.♕c2 ♗e6 13.0-0-0 0-0∞ 14.♘d5 (14.c5 ♕c8!?) 14...f5 (14...♕d7!?⇄ intending ...c6, ...b5) 15.♗e2 ♕d7 16.♔b1 (16.♘f4!?) 16...♕f7! 17.f4 ♘c6 18.♗e1 a5! 19.♗c3 ♘b4 (19...♗xc3 20.♕xc3 b5!) 20.♕d2 ♗xc3 21.♕xc3 b5!→ 22.e4 fxe4 23.♘e3 ♕xf4 24.a3 ♘d3 25.♗xd3 exd3 26.♖xd3 b4 (26...bxc4–+) 27.axb4 axb4–+ Amonatov-Tiurin, St Petersburg 2004; 12.c5!? dxc5 13.♕xd8+ ♔xd8 14.0-0-0+ ♗d7 15.♗e2↑ see also the notes to Game 36.

12...f6

12...♕d7 13.♘d5! 0-0 14.f4!↑.

13.f4

This push is an important resource for White in this variation. The other motif is, as always, 13.c5!?.

13...gxf3 14.gxf3 ♗e6 15.f4

White is better but Black still has many counterchances.

15...♘c6 16.♘d5 ♕d7 17.♘xf6+ ♗xf6 18.♗xf6 ♖g8 19.♕b3 ♕f7!? 20.♕xb7 ♔d7⇄ 21.♗c3 ♗xc4 22.0-0-0

22.♗h3+!? ♗e6 23.f5 ♗d5 24.f6+↑.

22...♗xf1 23.♖hxf1 ♕e6 24.♖fe1 ♖ab8 25.♕a6 ♘b4!? 26.♕a4+ ♔c8 27.♗xb4 ♕c4+ 28.♕c2 ♖xb4 29.b3 ♕xc2+ 30.♔xc2 ♖b5!

Rook endings are almost never won!

31.♖h1 ♖g2+ 32.♔d2 ♖a5 33.a4 ♖c5+ 34.♔d1 ♖g3 35.♔d3 ♖g2 36.♖d2   ½-½

Summary of 5.♗g3

In this line White generally has a suitable pawn structure for an attack with h2-h4 or c4-c5. These moves are always convenient options in this variation; see Games 35-41. In all respects Van Wely-Mamedyarov (Game 35) is the main game and the best example.

As the analysis of the next game shows, after 5.♗d2 ♘xe5 6.♗c3 White doesn't have any important advantage. But he can maintain the tension during the opening and the complicated middlegame.

GAME 42
□ **Svetozar Gligoric**
■ **Andrija Fuderer**
Belgrade ch-YUG 1948 (4)

1.d4 ♘f6 2.c4 e5 3.dxe5 ♘g4 4.♗f4 g5 5.♗d2 ♘xe5 6.♗c3!?

This seems strong, but it may be too hasty. Another strong possibility is 6.♘f3!?, see Games 44-48. The move 6.e4 isn't very successful. After 6...♗g7 Black got a good position in Dreev-Topalov, Arnhem 1989, see Game 43.

6...♘bc6

6...♗g7!? 7.e3 g4 (7...♕e7!?) 8.♘e2 d6 9.♘f4 ♘bc6 10.♘h5 ♗h6 11.♘d2 ♗f5 was unclear in Bronstein-Pangrazzi, Rome 1990.

7.♘f3

Maybe 7.e3!? is more accurate, with the threat of f2-f4. Although 7...♕f6!? (7...g4!? 8.h3 ♕h4!⇄) 8.♘e2 ♗b4!? is unclear.

7...♗g7

Interesting was first 7...d6!? in order to recapture with the pawn on e5, for instance: 8.e3 (8.♘xe5 dxe5!) 8...♗g7 9.♗e2 ♕e7 and now:

A) 10.0-0 0-0 11.♘xe5 dxe5! 12.♘d2 f5! 13.♕c2 ♗e6⇄

analysis diagram

Sakaev-Agamaliev, ICC Internet 2005;

B) 10.♘xe5 dxe5 11.♗g4 ♗xg4
12.♕xg4 h5!⇄ Jauernig-Teske, Regensburg 1998.

8.♘xe5 ♘xe5

8...♗xe5 9.♗xe5 ♘xe5 10.♘c3±.

9.e3

9...d6?!

Better moves are 9...♕e7!? 10.♗e2 0-0
11.h4 gxh4∞ or 9...0-0! with the idea
to give up the Black Jet pawn: 10.h4
(10.f4 gxf4 11.exf4 ♘g6=) 10...g4!
11.♗xe5 ♗xe5 12.♕xg4+ ♔h8♙
13.♘c3 f5! (13...d6!?) 14.♕h5 d6
15.♗d3 ♗e6 16.g4?! ♕d7! 17.gxf5
♗xf5 18.♗xf5 ♖xf5 and Black has a
good position.

analysis diagram

19.♕g4 ♖g8 20.♕e4 ♕f7 21.♖f1 c6!?
22.♖d1 ♖e8 23.♕d3 ♖f4! 24.b3
(24.exf4 ♗xc3 mate) 24...♖xh4

25.♘e2 ♖h2 26.♖d2 ♖f8 (26...a6!? △
...b5) 27.♘d4 d5 28.cxd5 ♕xd5 29.e4
♕a5 30.♘f3? ♖h3 0-1 R.Gonzalez-
Moskalenko, Sabadell 2007.

10.♗e2

Maintaining a small positional advantage, but missing a tactical possibility:
10.f4!? gxf4 11.exf4 ♗g4?? 12.♗e2
and White wins a piece without complications: 12...♕h4+ 13.g3 ♕h3
14.fxe5+— Campero-Llorens, Santiago
1999.

However, this is not so clear if Black
plays 11...♖g8 12.fxe5 ♕h4+ 13.♔d2
♗f5 14.♔c1 0-0-0.

10...♖g8?!

10...0-0 11.0-0 g4!⇄.

11.♕c2 f5

11...♕f6!?.

12.♘d2 ♕e7 13.0-0-0 ♗e6 14.f4!

Fixing the kingside.

**14...♘g6 15.♗xg7 ♖xg7 16.g3 0-0-0
17.♗d3**

White's position is stable. The f5 pawn
is weak and Black has no counterplay.

17...gxf4

17...♕f6 18.♘f3±.

18.exf4 ♕f6 19.♖he1±

From here on Gligoric commits many
inaccuracies, but his advantage remains
big enough to win.

19...♔b8 20.♘f1 ♖e7 21.♘d2 ♖de8 22.♘f3 ♗d7 23.♕f2 ♗c6 24.♖xe7 ♖xe7 25.♕d4 ♕f8 26.♘d2 b6 27.♘b1 ♗f3 28.♖d2 ♖e1+ 29.♔c2 ♗e4?!

29...♖h1 30.♕f2 ♗b7 31.♘c3 ♘e7 was the right defence.

30.♘c3 ♗xd3+ 31.♕xd3 ♘e7 32.♕f3 ♕e8 33.♖e2 ♖xe2+ 34.♕xe2 ♕f7 35.♔d2 ♘c6 36.♘d5 ♕g7 37.♔e1 ♕d4 38.♔f1 ♔b7 39.b3 a5 40.♔g2 b5 41.♔h3 a4 42.♕c2 ♕c5 43.♕d3 ♘d4 44.♘f6 bxc4 45.bxc4 ♘c6 46.♘d5 ♕a5 47.♘e3 ♔c6 48.♔h4!+− ♔d7 49.♔g5 ♔e8 50.a3 c6 51.♕c3 ♔d7 52.♕d3?! ♔e8 53.♔h4 d5 54.cxd5 cxd5 55.♘xd5 ♕f8 56.♕b5+ ♔f7 57.♕d7+ ♔g8 58.♘e7+ ♔h8 59.♕d4+ **1-0**

GAME 43
□ **Alexey Dreev**
■ **Veselin Topalov**
Arnhem Ech-jr 1989

1.d4 ♘f6 2.c4 e5 3.dxe5 ♘g4 4.♗f4 g5 5.♗d2 ♘xe5 6.e4?!

This advance leaves the f1 bishop too passive. Black achieves counterplay easily. Better is 6.♗c3 or 6.♘f3!?.
6...♗g7 7.♘c3 d6 8.♘f3 h6 9.♗e2 ♘bc6 10.h4?! ♘xf3+ 11.♗xf3 ♗e6
11...gxh4!?∓.

12.hxg5 hxg5 13.♖xh8+ ♗xh8 14.♘d5 ♘e5!⇄ 15.♗e2 c6 16.♘e3 ♕b6 17.♕b3 ♘d7!?∓ ½-½

Black is planning ...♘c5. He is still doing very well here.

GAME 44
□ **Martin Mitchell**
■ **Sasha Belezky**
Gibraltar 2005 (10)

1.d4 ♘f6 2.c4 e5 3.dxe5 ♘g4 4.♗f4 g5 5.♗d2 ♘xe5 6.♘f3!?

White prefers to simplify, trying to take advantage of his superior pawn structure.
6...♘xf3+?!
This exchange doesn't seem to favour Black. Better is 6...♗g7!? (Games 45-48) or 6...♘bc6.
7.exf3
With play on the open e-file. Also possible is 7.gxf3!? to play along the g- and h-file, for example: 7...♗g7 8.♗c3 ♗xc3+ 9.♘xc3± ♘c6 10.♕d2 d6 11.f4!? f6 12.♘d5 ♗e6 13.0-0-0→ Prusikin-Eichner, Dortmund 1997.
7...♕e7+
If 7...♗g7 8.♕e2+! ♔f8 9.♘c3 ♘c6 10.♗e3 (10.0-0-0! d6 11.h4±) 10...♗xc3+ 11.bxc3 ♕e7 12.h4!± Blazquez Gomez-Carbonell Bofill, Alicante 1989 or, for example, 7...♘c6

8.♗c3 (8.♕e2+!?) 8...♗b4 9.♗e2 d6 10.0-0 ♗xc3 11.♘xc3 ♗e6 12.♕d2± Peralta-Campora, Ayamonte 2006.

8.♗e2 d6 9.0-0

9.♘c3!?.

9...♘c6 10.♘c3

With an enormous advantage for White. His knight finds a wonderful post on d5.

10...♗e6 11.♘d5!

11...♕d8 12.♗c3 ♘e5 13.f4 gxf4 14.♘xf4 ♖g8 15.♘xe6 fxe6 16.♗xe5 dxe5 17.♗h5+ ♔e7 18.♕f3 ♖g7 19.♖ad1 ♕c8 20.♕e4 ♖g5 21.♕h4 ♗h6 22.f4 exf4 23.♖xf4 e5 24.♖f7+ ♔e6 25.♕h3+

And mate next move. Black resigned.

The next two games are good examples of how Black should fight against the solid 5.♗d2.

GAME 45
□ **Ruben Fernandez Cueto**
■ **Ivan Diaz Fernandez**
Candas Open 1997

1.d4 ♘f6 2.c4 e5 3.dxe5 ♘g4 4.♗f4 g5 5.♗d2 ♗g7!? 6.♘f3 ♘xe5 7.♘xe5 ♗xe5 8.♗c3 ♘c6

8...d6 9.♗xe5 dxe5 10.♕b3!?↑.
For 8...♕f6!? see Game 47.

It is important for Black that the h-file is not opened, as in the 5.♗g3 variation.

9.♗xe5!? ♘xe5 10.e3

Also playable is 10.♕d4!? d6 11.e3 (intending f2-f4) 11...c5!? (11...♗e6!? with the idea 12.f4? gxf4 13.exf4 ♕h4+; 11...0-0!?⇄) 12.♕e4 (12.♕d2!?) 12...♗e6 (12...♕b6!?⇄) 13.♘c3 0-0 14.0-0-0 f5! 15.♕xb7 ♖b8 16.♕a6 ♖b6 17.♕xa7 ♘xc4 18.♗xc4 ♗xc4, with compensation, Cordes-Bartsch, Germany Bundesliga 1980.

10...d6 11.♘c3 ♗e6! 12.b3

The good thing about the 4...g5 variation is that White cannot play passively. For 12.♕d4!? see the analysis of 10.♕d4 in the note to 10.e3.

12...g4!?

12...0-0=.

13.♖c1 c6 14.♗d3 f5

14...h5!?.

15.♗b1

Continuing to play without ideas.

15...♕e7 16.♕d4 0-0

16...b6!? 17.♖d1 0-0-0⇄.

17.0-0 ♖f6!?

Black does find a plan, geometrically pleasing and ending with a great shot. He intends to attack with ...♖h6 and ...♕h4.

18.♘e2 ♗d7 19.♖cd1 ♔h8

Intending ...♖g8.

20.♖fe1 ♖g8

Threatening 21...♘f3+.

21.♘g3 c5!?

Preparing 22. ...♗c6.

22.♕d2 ♖h6 23.e4

23.♗xf5 ♕h4→.

23...♕h4→ 24.♘f1??

Defending the h2-pawn, but...

Necessary was 24.exf5! ♕xh2+ 25.♔f1 ♗c6 26.♗e4.

24...♘f3+! 25.gxf3 gxf3+ 26.♔h1

♕h3   **0-1**

GAME 46

□ **Jose Candela Perez**

■ **Daniel Campora**

Dos Hermanas 2006 (9)

In this game we witness more dynamic play than in the previous one.

1.d4 ♘f6 2.c4 e5 3.dxe5 ♘g4 4.♗f4 g5 5.♗d2 ♘xe5 6.♘f3 ♗g7 7.♘xe5 ♗xe5 8.♗c3 ♘c6 9.e3

9...d6!

Supporting the e5-square and preparing attacking plans. 9...♕e7?! 10.h4 (10.♗xe5!?) 10...d6 11.hxg5 ♕xg5 12.♗xe5 ♕xe5 13.♘c3 ♗e6 14.♕d2 0-0-0 15.0-0-0 h5= Ramon Perez-Ruiz Bravo, Badalona 2000.

10.♗d3

10.♗xe5!?.

10...g4!?

Gaining more space.

11.♕c2 ♗e6 12.♘d2 ♕f6!

With the idea of putting the black queen on g7! The most common move is 12...♕d7 and then ...0-0-0.

13.♘e4 ♕g7 14.0-0-0

Normally in these structures White is afraid to castle kingside; after 14.0-0-0 Black has good attacking chances, as we have seen in the previous game.

14...0-0-0 15.♔b1 ♔b8

A duel of kings. Also good was the direct 15...h5!?.

16.♖c1?!

16...h5!

Symmetrical play has finished. 'Now I'm going to thrash you.'

17.♘g3?!

White loses his way and, consequently, the game.

17...♗xc3 18.♕xc3 ♕xc3 19.♖xc3 ♘e5

Even without queens Black's game is far superior.

20.♔c2 d5!? 21.cxd5?

21.c5 h4 would have been advisable.

21...♗xd5 22.e4 ♗xa2 23.♗b5 c6 24.♗a4 ♗c4 25.♗b3 ♗d3+ 26.♔c1 h4   **0-1**

Statistically in the Budapest, in most of the games in which White castles queenside, Black wins.

GAME 47
□ **Petr Streitberg**
■ **Zdenek Choleva**
Prague Bohemians B 1989

1.d4 ♘f6 2.c4 e5 3.dxe5 ♘g4 4.♗f4 g5 5.♗d2 ♘xe5 6.♘f3 ♗g7 7.♘xe5 ♗xe5 8.♗c3 ♕f6!?N

The idea of this move is to add force to the fight for the dark squares with the queen. The rest is similar to the variation with 5. ♗d2.

9.♗xe5 ♕xe5

The black queen defends and at the same time attacks the dark-square diagonals a1-h8 and h2-b8.

10.♘c3 d6 11.e3

11.g3 ♗d7 (11...♗e6!? 12.♗g2 ♘d7! 13.0-0 0-0-0∞) 12.♗g2 ♗c6 13.♗d5± Narciso Dublan-Belezky, Badalona 2005.

11...♗e6

11...♘a6!?.

12.♕b3!?

Less good is 12.♗e2 ♘c6 13.♕d2 0-0-0 14.0-0 g4 (14...h5!?) 15.♘d5 h5 16.♖ad1 ♔b8 17.♕c3 h4 18.♕xe5 ♘xe5 with an initiative for Black in the ending, O'Kelly de Galway-Drimer, Havana 1968.

12...♘d7!

In the following complications both players can as easily win as they can lose. Not good was 12...b6? 13.♘d5 ♗xd5 14.cxd5± Ivkov-Drimer, Raach Zonal 1969.

13.♕xb7 ♖b8 14.♕xc7 ♖xb2 15.♖c1 0-0

Sufficient was 15...♕c5!? 16.♕xc5 ♘xc5♔.

16.♗e2 ♘c5 17.0-0 ♖b7?!

The rook was OK on the second rank. 17...f5! 18.♕xa7 f4 was preferable.

18.♕a5 f5!?

Trying to change the direction of the attack by ...f5-f4.

19.♗f3 ♖bf7 20.♗d5 f4 21.exf4 ♖xf4 22.♗xe6+ ♕xe6 23.♘d5 ♖e4 24.♖ce1 ♘d3 25.♖xe4 ♕xe4 26.♘e3 h6 27.♕d5+ ♕xd5 28.cxd5±

Up to here White has played well, but things are still not easy.

28...♖b8 29.♖d1 ♘e5 30.♘f5 ♘f7 31.g3 ♖b2 32.♖c1?

32.a4!?.

32...♖xa2 33.♖c6 g4 34.♘xd6 ♘g5 35.♖c8+ ♔h7 36.♖f8??

Incomprehensibly allowing mate.

36...♖d2?

Black could have won with 36...♖a1+! 37.♔g2 ♘h3! and mate in 4.

37.♔g2 ♖xd5 38.♘f5 a5 39.♘e3 ♖d4 40.♖a8 a4 41.♖a7+ ♔g6 42.♖a6+ ♔f7 43.♖xh6 ♘e6 44.♖h7+ ♔g6 45.♖a7 ♘g5 46.♖a6+ ♔f7 47.♖a5 ♔g6 48.♘d5 ♘f3 49.♘c3 ♖c4 50.♘e2 ♘e1+ 51.♔f1 ♘d3 52.♘f4+ ♘xf4 53.gxf4 ♖xf4 54.♔g2 ♔f6 55.h3 gxh3+ 56.♔xh3 ♖f3+ 57.♔g4 ♖a3 58.f4 ♖a1 59.♖a6+ ♔g7 60.♔g5 a3 61.♖a7+ ½-½

Conclusion: After 4...g5, the g-pawn can be an attacker even in the endgame (see the position on move 36).

GAME 48
□ **Stuart Conquest**
■ **Zeinab Mamedyarova**
Pamplona Open 2004 (8)

1.d4 ♘f6 2.c4 e5 3.dxe5 ♘g4 4.♗f4 g5 5.♗d2 ♘xe5 6.♘f3 ♗g7 7.♘xe5 ♗xe5 8.♘c3!?N

A fresh idea from GM Conquest. White mixes up all the possible plans, preferring to play creative chess.

8...d6 9.g3!?

Fianchetto versus fianchetto.

9...♘c6

Interesting is 9...♗e6!? 10.♗g2 ♘d7.

10.♗g2 ♗e6 11.♕a4

11.♘d5!?.

11...♕d7

Mamedyarova also likes a sharp game. 11...0-0!? was the alternative.

12.♗xg5

12.0-0-0!?.

12...♘d4!?

Seeking counterplay in the centre.

13.♕xd7+ ♔xd7 14.♖c1 h6!?

14...♗xc4!?.

15.♗d2 ♖ae8

Attacking along the e-file. But 15...♗xc4 may have been better. Material is also important.

16.b3

16.c5!? – once again this advance.

16...♗g4 17.♔f1?!

White is afraid. 17.h3!? was possible, with the idea 17...♗xe2 18.♘xe2 ♗xg3 19.♗f1±.

17...h5

17...♔c8 18.h3 ♗d7 was preferable.

18.h3 ♗e6 19.e3 ♘c6

After a complicated fight White now wins by displaying good technique.

20.h4 ♘b4 21.♗f3 ♖h6 22.♔g2 ♖g8 23.♘e4 ♘d3 24.♖cd1 ♗g4 25.♗a5 ♗xf3+ 26.♔xf3 f5 27.♘g5 ♘c5 28.♗b4 ♘a6 29.♗a3 b6 30.♖d5 ♖f6 31.♖hd1 ♔c8 32.♔e2 ♖e8 33.♘f3 ♘b8 34.b4 ♖fe6 35.♘g5 ♖6e7 36.♖5d3 ♗f6 37.♘f3 ♘c6 38.c5 ♗e5 39.b5 ♘a5 40.cxd6 ♗xd6 41.♗xd6 cxd6 42.♖xd6 ♖c7 43.♘d4 ♖c4 44.♘xf5 ♖a4 45.♖6d2 1-0

Conclusion after Games 44-48: 6.♘f3!? is a more flexible move than the aggressive 6.♗c3. Play is not so forced either, so that both sides can always change plans..

Summary of 5.♗d2

In most of the ensuing positions White maintains a slight advantage, but I have not been able to find any quick refutation of 4...g5. Most illustrative are Games 42, 45, 46 and 48.

General Summary of 4...g5

What is Black's compensation for this risky move? In this Part he wins 5 games, draws 4 and loses 5. A 50% score, but in my database Black achieves a total of 41%, which is quite near the general 41% figure in the Budapest Gambit. This means that Black doesn't score less than in the other lines of the Gambit.

⚠ **Keep in Mind!**
Although strategically suspicious, 4...g5 creates new directions and gives you a chance to head along the road full of adventures. You will find all kinds of resources, both for the attack and the defence, allowing both sides to maintain the tension during all the stages of the game until the very end.
The 'Fianchetto' 4...g5 has great surprise value. But unfortunately, in chess pawns can only advance and not retreat to their original squares. White must try to take advantage of this rule. Having said that, if I had to meet 4...g5 today, I would choose the classical 5.♗g3.

Chapter Two

Pawns Against Pieces

1.d4 ♘f6 2.c4 e5 3.dxe5 ♘g4 4.e4

Dedicated to gentlemen playing white

World Champion Alexander Alekhine (1892-1946) was looking for a BG refutation suitable for his attacking style, and he chose 4.e4 almost exclusively.
Oddly, he was also one of the creators of the opening 1.e4 ♘f6 (the Alekhine Defence), where white pawns chase the black king's knight.

A Bit of History

After its great success in Berlin, 1918, the Budapest Gambit became known as a creative and innovative opening, and players of all levels added it to their repertoire. Among them we can find young and ambitious masters like Réti, Spielmann and Euwe.

Notably during the period 1918-1924 many games were opened with the moves 1.d4 ♘f6 2.♘f3, with the sole idea of avoiding the dangerous BG!

But the champions of the white pieces soon began to study a new idea against the Gambit. They found a method to avoid a cramped, defensive game by opening the position and fighting for the initiative with the aggressive 4.e4!.

One year after the success of the Budapest in Berlin 1918, we can find more games with the Gambit in the next tournament in Berlin, in 1919! Oddly, this was the event where the first game with the 4.e4 system was played by the two classical players Spielmann and Réti – see Game 57. The leading chess masters, Alekhine, Bogoljubow, and later Euwe and Capablanca among them, immediately picked up the idea. Alekhine began to use it almost exclusively and the line became known as the Alekhine System.

Historically, the first defender of the black pieces against 4.e4 was the Czech master Richard Réti, a talented analyst (remember the Réti Opening 1.♘f3) and also a passionate adherent of the BG. The plans conceived by Réti (even though they were made during the infancy of the variation!) are excellent examples that teach present-day students perfectly about the characteristics and the possibilities. They even contain some very original ideas that have not been further developed yet.

Strategies of 4.e4
In the first Chapter – on 4.♗f4 – we studied the material chronologically, but also along the lines of theoretical concepts: pieces fighting against pieces. In the Alekhine System Black must learn a new kind of combat: the complicated battle against central pawns.

White changes his strategy radically. Instead of defending the e5 pawn, he concentrates on domination of the centre. What does this sharp idea offer? Let's summarize the key points of the 4.e4 system.

White tries to gain space and prepares attacks in the centre and on the kingside. In some cases, positions arise that are similar to other openings, like the Maroczy Bind in the Sicilian, the Philidor Defence and the Four Pawns Attack in the Alekhine Defence as well as the King's Indian, with the same pawn structure. The difference is that in our variation the white d-pawn is gone, while his other central pawns are still weak due to his lag in development.

White
- The point of this new line is to return the extra pawn.
- While Black spends his time making knight jumps recapturing the pawn, White makes way for his pieces, taking control over the centre and preparing an outpost on d5 for his knight, the strongest white piece in this line
- White's strong centre will enable him to organize an attack.
- But his light-squared bishop is somewhat limited in mobility, as it is closed in by the pawns on c4 and e4.
- In some lines dark-square weaknesses can arise in White's camp.
- Generally in this system the exchange of dark-squared bishops is considered favourable for Black.
- The character of the opening changes radically: from the first moves onwards the game becomes very dynamic.

Black

- The key of Black's opening strategy is to invite the white pawns to attack black pieces, after which the white pawn formation is far advanced and cannot be well supported by the rest of his army.
- Black must find counterplay fast, profiting from his lead in development.
- The key pieces in the opening for Black are:
- The bishop on f8: the ...♗b4 check will be an important resource in most lines, but we must understand what is the best square for the black bishop in each line: b4 or c5? Sometimes d6 or g7 can be interesting alternatives.
- The black queen is usually placed on e7, defending the black bishop and attacking the e4 pawn. The queen exchange is generally favourable for Black, since White's pawn structure has many weaknesses.
- Black can develop the knight on b8 with ...♘c6 or use it to attack the centre with ...♘a6/d7-c5 or ...♘d7-f6.
- The bishop on c8 can move to b7, attacking along the a8-h1 diagonal and preparing to castle queenside. Sometimes it can move to g4 to pin the white knight on f3.
- Sometimes during the opening, the tactical and dynamic character can transpose into quiet, positional play.

⚠ **Keep in Mind!**

- **If we study the games in which classical-style players played White (like World Champion Alexander Alekhine or modern GMs), we find that all of them used the aggressive 4.e4 as their main weapon, in order to fight for the initiative from the very first moves.**
- **After 4.e4 it is very important for Black to counterattack quickly.**
- **This line is very dangerous if we do not have a deep knowledge of the typical plans and the available resources.**

Directions

Black can either protect the attacked knight (4...h5, the Réti Plan, Part I), continue in gambit style (4...d6, Part I), or recapture on e5 (4...♘xe5, Knight Jumps, Part II), when after 5.f4 the main possibilities are 5...♘g6 and 5...♘c6.

Part I – The Attacking Machine

1.d4 ♘f6 2.c4 e5 3.dxe5 ♘g4 4.e4 h5/d6

Introduction

The move 4.e4 against the BG officially appeared in 1919-20 and was developed by the best players of the time, among whom we find World Champions Alexander Alekhine, Max Euwe and José Raul Capablanca, and strong grandmasters like Efim Bogoljubow and Rudolf Spielmann.

Classical masters Richard Réti and Savielly Tartakower were some of the main defenders of the BG. Unfortunately, they also fell victim to the 4.e4! variation against the best attacking players.

Directions

After 4.e4 Black has two sharp replies: 4...h5 (the 'Réti Plan') and the gambit move 4...d6.

A) The Réti Plan: 4...h5

The original idea of 4...h5 (Games 49-53) is to try and maintain the knight on g4 and prepare an attack with ...♗c5!. Instead of capturing the e5 pawn, Black keeps it under fire. During 1920-1923 this was the main line against 4.e4. White must play very accurately, as the line contains some traps. To 5.♘f3? the response 5...♗c5! is good for Black, as is 5.f4?! ♗c5 6.♘h3 ♘c6 7.♗e2 0-0!.

The main disadvantage is that ...h5 is a weakening of the kingside. For example, castling kingside is temporarily prevented. In some games both sides continue playing with their kings in the centre, without castling.

Key games with 4...h5 are Weenink-Réti (Game 49) and Alekhine-Euwe (Game 50).

White's best replies in this line are 5.♗e2!? (Game 49) and 5/6. ♘h3!? (Games 50-53).

106

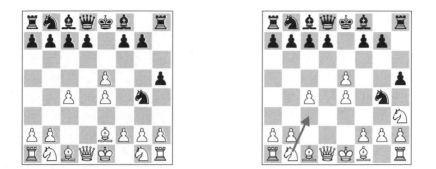

A1) 5.♗e2!?

Continuing the attack against the knight on g4. White is just threatening to take twice, as the notes to Game 49 (Weenink-Réti) show.

A2) 5/6.♘h3!? with 5/6.♘c3

White's strong centre will help him to organize an attack. Both knights are aiming for the outpost on d5, but 5.♘h3 first serves to protect f2, enabling White to develop quickly and undisturbed, and to push his f-pawn. The drawback of this line is that only one knight can occupy the d5-square. And the h3-square is in itself not a good one for the knight.

B) The Gambit Move 4...d6

The next attempt was a gambit, introduced by Janos Balogh in 1919. He tried 4...d6!?. Now, a sharp fight ensues after the acceptance of the pawn: 5.exd6! ♗xd6.

Black creates some tactical threats in the lines 6.♘f3? ♗b4+ 7.♗d2 ♗c5! or 6.h3? ♕h4! 7.♕e2, ♘f2!, but the simple 6.♗e2! (played by Capablanca) poses Black serious problems. The idea of Balogh (and maybe of Alekhine as well) was 6....h5, but after 7.♘f3! White keeps an extra pawn.

The Attacking Machine – Games

GAME 49
☐ **Henri Weenink**
■ **Richard Réti**
Amsterdam 1920 (4)

1.d4 ♘f6 2.c4 e5 3.dxe5 ♘g4 4.e4!?

An aggressive advance, attacking the ♘g4 and preparing f2-f4.

4...h5!?

In the first game with 4.e4, Spielmann-Réti, Berlin 1919, Réti replied with the more natural 4...♘xe5!? (see Game 57 in Part II of this Chapter). Another possibility is the gambit 4...d6!? – see Games 54-56.

5.♗e2!?

Other ideas are:

A) 5.h3 ♘xe5 6.♗e3 (preparing f2-f4; not immediately 6.f4?? ♕h4+!) 6...♗b4+! 7.♘c3 ♗xc3+! 8.bxc3.

analysis diagram

108

Richard Réti (1889-1929) was one of the main masters defending the colours of the BG in its early years.

This position is virtually unexplored, but it offers a very interesting game for both colours.

 8...♕f6!? – **Tricks**.

B) 5.f4?! ♗c5 6.♘h3 ♘c6 7.♗e2 (7.♘c3 0-0 8.♗e2 d6) 7...d6 (7...0-0!?) 8.exd6 cxd6 is tricky;

C) 5.♘f3? ♗c5.

The other main move is 5.♘h3!? (or 5.♘c3 ♗c5 6.♘h3), see Games 50-53.

5...♘c6!?

The (pseudo-)aggressive move 5...♗c5?! does not seem to work here: 6.♗xg4! hxg4 (6...♕h4 7.♗e2 ♕xf2+ 8.♔d2±) 7.♕xg4 d6 (7...♔f8 8.♕g3!? and Black does not have enough compensation for the two pawns) 8.♕xg7 ♕h4 9.♘f3! ♕xf2+ (9...♕xe4+ 10.♗e3 ♖f8 11.♘c3+−) 10.♔d1 ♖f8 11.♗h6 dxe5 12.♕xe5+ ♗e6 13.♗xf8+−. But the familiar check 5...♗b4+!? could be an interesting option.

For 5...d6 (by transposition), see Game 54.

6.h3

From here on, all moves are quite forced. White could have played the simple 6.♘f3!?, with a slight edge. It is interesting to notice that the g1 knight remains untouched during the next 20 moves.

6...♘gxe5 7.♗e3 ♗b4+!

A very useful check in the BG, gaining a tempo and forcing White to find a square for this 'poor' knight: ♘c3 or ♘d2 ??

8.♘d2

8.♘c3 ♗xc3+ 9.bxc3 ♕f6 △ 10...♕g6.

8...d6

8...♕f6!?; 8...♕h4!?.

9.♕c2

The position that has arisen is full of possibilities. The most important thing is not to waste any time.

9...♗e6?!

This was a good moment to complicate with 9...f5!? 10.exf5 ♕f6 or 9...♗c5!? 10.♗xc5 dxc5 or also 9...♕f6!?. In all cases Black is fighting for the initiative.

10.0-0-0

White has finished development and threatens to start an attack in the centre.

10...♕e7 11.♘b3?

A dubious move that only helps Black to gain the advantage. Better was 11.f4!.

11...a5! 12.♔b1 a4 13.♘c1

And here 13.♘d4 ♘xd4 14.♗xd4 ♘c6 with mutual chances, was preferable..

13...a3 14.b3 ♗a5!

Threatening ...♘b4.

15.♘d3 ♘xd3 16.♗xd3 0-0

16...♘b4! 17.♕e2 ♗d7.

17.g4??

Nonsense. 17.♕e2 was necessary.

17...b5!

This symmetrical reply is much more effective.

18.cxb5 ♘b4 19.♕c1

19...♗xb3!

The critical phase starts.

20.axb3 a2+

20...♘xd3!? 21.♖xd3 ♕xe4 was an easier win.

21.♔a1 ♕e5+ 22.♕b2 ♕xb2+?!

Réti is getting tired and allows his opponent to escape; 22...♘c2+ 23.♗xc2 ♗c3−+.

23.♔xb2 ♘xd3+ 24.♔c2□ ♘e1+ 25.♔b2 ♖fb8?! 26.♘e2

The knight moves at last.

26...♖xb5??

26...♘g2∓.

27.♖hxe1	**♗xe1**	**28.♖xe1**	**hxg4**
29.hxg4	**a1♕+**	**30.♖xa1**	**♖xa1**
31.♔xa1 ♖xb3 32.♔a2			**½-½**

We have analysed a typical game of the time. Both players were looking for the best continuations over the board, so it stands to reason that both made many mistakes due to their lack of knowledge of theory, concepts and tactical resources. Nowadays we all have our computer at home, full of information and with a strong analysis engine – and still we make incredible mistakes.

After 4...h5 5.♗e2 the option 5...♗b4+ might be worth a try, although the continuation in this game also offers complicated play.

The next three classical games were probably the most important ones in the developing period of the 4.e4 variation.

GAME 50
□ Alexander Alekhine
■ Max Euwe
Amsterdam free game 1921

This was a historic battle that tested the BG severely, since the two players were of the highest possible level at that time.

1.d4 ♘f6 2.c4 e5!

We're playing a 'Free Game'!

3.dxe5 ♘g4 4.e4 h5 5.♘h3!?

The main resource for White and the key move in the variation with 4...h5. The knight on the edge will have a good perspective on the d5 outpost (♘h3-♘f4-♘d5), but first it protects the weakness on f2. With ♗e2 and 0-0 White will complete his development.

5...♘c6 6.♘c3 ♗c5! 7.♘d5!?

Trying to control the centre as soon as possible, but this knight will miss the support of the undeveloped remainder of the white army. For 7.a3 see Bogoljubow-Réti, Game 51; 7.♗e2!? ♘gxe5∞; 7.e6 dxe6 8.♕xd8+ ♔xd8=.

7...♘cxe5!

Euwe follows the main idea of 4...h5 and he also increases the number of pieces in the centre. The move tried in the other test was 7...♘gxe5!?, see Euwe-Mieses, Game 4.

8.b4!?

On the eighth move we arrive at the most important moment in the opening and in the entire game. White's strategy in the 4.e4 system consists of attacking the black pieces with pawns.

8...♗e7?

The only mistake of the game, allowing White to carry out his plans. After

8...♗f8!!, Black would threaten 9...c6, attacking the white weaknesses. For example: 9.f4 ♘g6 10.f5 ♘e7!

analysis diagram

with a funny and unclear position where only pawns and knights are moving.

9.♗b2 c6?!

Now the idea does not work, which is why 9...d6!? was preferable.

10.♘xe7 ♕xe7 11.c5!± a5 12.♕d4!

We get a chance to learn from Alekhine's style. 12.a3!? was the alternative.

12...axb4 13.f3 ♕h4+ 14.♔d1 d5

14...d6 15.fxg4.

15.exd5!

Combining extraordinary calculating skills with imagination.

15...♗e6!?

16.fxg4

It looks as if the position is very complicated, but White's material advantage overcomes everything.

16...♗xg4+ 17.♗e2 0-0-0 18.d6 ♖he8 19.♗xg4+ ♘xg4 20.♔d2 ♖e5 21.♘f4 ♕g5 22.h4 ♕h6 23.♕xb4! ♖xc5 24.♕xc5 ♕xf4+ 25.♔c3 ♘f2 26.♖he1 ♖xd6

And now White takes profit of his turn.

27.♖e8+! ♔d7 28.♖ae1

Threatening 29.♖1e7.

28...♖d3+ 29.♔c2 ♕a4+ 30.♔b1 ♖d1+ 31.♗c1 **1-0**

In this dynamic game both players showed the best of their huge talent.

After the move 8.b4!?, the position was in a crisis. Unfortunately, Euwe did not find 8...♗f8! and we can but guess what would have happened if he had, but the rest of the game is impressive!

GAME 51
□ **Efim Bogoljubow**
■ **Richard Réti**
Kiel 1921 (6)

1.d4 ♘f6 2.c4 e5 3.dxe5 ♘g4 4.e4 h5 5.♘h3 ♘c6 6.♘c3 ♗c5 7.a3

With the same idea of b2-b4, like Alekhine played in Game 50. But just like in that game, Black could have obtained good counterplay quite easily.

7...♘gxe5!

This time the g4 ♘ comes into action, while the c6 ♘ controls the d4-square; 7...♘cxe5?! 8.♗e2±; 8.b4!?; 7...♗d4!?.

GM Efim Bogoljubow (1889-1952) was a player with a highly active style. Therefore, 4.e4 was the option that best suited him.

8.♗g5

White changes plans and forces weaknesses in Black's kingside pawn structure. If 8.b4 ♗d4! 9.♗b2 d6 10.b5 ♘a5 (10...♗g4!?) 11.♕xd4 ♗xh3 12.♖b1 (12.f4 ♗xg2 13.♗xg2 ♘b3⇄) 12...♕h4∞.

8...f6 9.♗d2 d6 10.♘f4

10...♘d4!?

With a very dynamic game. 10...h4!?∞; 10...♗g4!? 11.f3 ♗d7⇄.

11.h3! a5?!

Wasting an important tempo. 11...♘e6 was to be preferred.

12.♗e3 ♘ec6?

Another suspicious move. Fighting for the d4-square has no strategic sense. 12...♘e6! was much better, for example: 13.♘xe6 ♗xe6 14.♗xc5 dxc5 with a playable position.

13.♘g6

Better was 13.♘b5! ♘e6 14.♗xc5 ♘xc5 15.♗e2±.

13...♖h7 14.♗d3 ♘e5 15.♘f4 ♕e7?

The decisive error. After 15...♘e6! things would still be unclear.

16.♘fd5! ♕f7 17.♗xd4 ♗xd4 18.♘b5+– ♕g6 19.♘xd4 ♕xg2 20.♔e2! c5 21.♕g1!? ♗xh3 22.♕xg2 ♗xg2 23.♖h2 ♔f7 24.♖xg2 cxd4 25.f4 ♘d7 26.e5! 1-0

Again, master Réti did not make use of all his chances and made too many significant mistakes at key moments.

After 10.♘f4 the position is equal.

GAME 52
□ **Max Euwe**
■ **Jacques Mieses**
Hastings 1923 (3)

In this game the fifth World Champion shows an extraordinary understanding of the position, combining attacking concepts with strategic resources.

1.d4 ♘f6 2.c4 e5 3.dxe5 ♘g4 4.e4 h5 5.♘c3!? ♗c5 6.♘h3 ♘c6 7.♘d5

White's main plan in the Réti Variation 4...h5 is to neutralize Black's threats along the c5-f2 diagonal first and then prepare an attack with the f-pawn.

7...♘gxe5

Euwe preferred 7...♘cxe5! himself – see Game 50.

8.♗g5!

Creating weaknesses in Black's kingside pawn structure, an idea similar to the one used in Game 51 Bogoljubow-Réti, but with a more accurate move order.

8...f6 9.♗e3!

Taking advantage of the important role of the ♘d5.

9...d6 10.♘hf4

A critical position in this line.

10...♗g4?

Black should have chosen between 10...0-0!? and 10...f5!?, with a complicated game in both cases.

11.♗e2! ♕d7 12.f3

12.♗xg4! looks even stronger, with the idea 12...hxg4 13.♗xc5 dxc5 14.♘e6! ♔f7 15.♘xc5±.

12...♗xe3 13.♘xe3 ♗e6 14.♘xe6 ♕xe6 15.0-0

15.♕d5!?.

15...0-0

15...0-0-0!? was 'safer'.

16.♘d5

Black will have some problems with his h5 pawn.

16...♖ac8 17.♕d2!?

17.f4! ♘f7 18.♗d3↑.

17...f5?!

Trying to become active, but White is better prepared for attacking.

18.exf5 ♕xf5 19.♖ae1! ♖fe8 20.f4! ♘g6 21.♗d3 ♕f7 22.♗xg6!? ♕xg6 23.f5!

Pay attention to the role of the outpost on d5: the knight attacks c7 and helps the f-pawn to advance.

23...♕g4 24.f6 ♖xe1 25.♕xe1 ♖f8 26.f7+! ♔h7

26...♖xf7 27.♕e8+.

27.♕e8 ♕d4+ 28.♘e3 ♘e5 29.♕xf8 ♕xe3+ 30.♔h1 ♘g4

A last trap.

31.♕g8+

Not 31.♕e8?? ♘f2+ 32.♔g1 ♘h3+ 33.♔h1 ♕g1+ 34.♖xg1 ♘f2 mate.

31...♔h6 32.f8♕   **1-0**

Besides the knight on d5, White's f-pawn was the other VIP in this line.

Theoretical summary of 4...h5 5/6.♘h3: In my opinion, after 7.♘d5, the best move is Euwe's 7...♘cxe5! (Game 50), when chances are equal and the result is unpredictable.

Summarizing: Why did Black lose these three brilliant games? Simply because the white players made the best use of their resources and their attacking skills, while their opponents were not prepared for such a dynamic fight. In any case, analysis shows that during the opening phase Black was at least not worse.

Another attempt, in the spirit of the King's Indian Defence (which was not yet fashionable in the early 1920s), was tried by Rudolf Spielmann.

GAME 53
□ **Max Euwe**
■ **Rudolf Spielmann**
Bad Pistyan 1922 (2)

1.d4 ♘f6 2.c4 e5 3.dxe5 ♘g4 4.e4 h5 5.♘h3 ♘xe5!? 6.♘c3 d6

6...♗c5!?.

7.♘f4 ♘bc6

7...c6!?.

8.♗e2 g6

This fianchetto is Spielmann's new idea in this opening. It creates the possibility of organizing a counterattack on the kingside with ...♘g4, ...♗g7-e5 and ...♕h4. Black keeps the rook on h8 so that if ♗x♘g4 hxg4, it can attack along the open h-file. But this is quite a slow plan.

9.♘fd5!

White dominates the centre. One year later there was another sharp battle between two classical players: 9.0-0 ♗g7 10.♔h1?! ♘g4 11.♕e1? ♘d4! (Black is OK) 12.♗d1 ♗e5 (≥ 12...c6 13.f3 ♘e5) 13.h3 c6 14.♘d3 ♗e6 15.b3 ♗g7 16.f4 ♕a5 17.♗d2 0-0-0 18.♘b5 ♕a6 19.♘xd4 ♗xd4 20.♗c3 ♗xc3 21.♕xc3 ♕b6 22.♗f3 f5 23.c5! dxc5 24.♘xc5↑ ♗f7 25.♖ac1 ♖h7 26.e5 ♗e8 27.b4! ♔b8 28.a4 ♘h6 29.♖c2 ♘g8 30.a5 1-0 Sämisch-Spielmann, Copenhagen 1923.

9...♗e6 10.♘b5?!

Trying to gain material, but allowing Black to activate his pieces. The main attack with the central pawns was undoubtedly more effective: 10.f4! ♘d7

11.0-0 with an extremely dangerous initiative for White, who is threatening f4-f5.

10...♖c8 11.f4 ♘g4!

11...♘d7 12.0-0±.

12.♘xa7 ♘xa7 13.♕d4

13...c6!

White gains a pawn and an exchange, but loses the initiative.

14.♗xg4

14.♕xh8!?.

14...hxg4 15.♕xh8

15.♘f6+ ♔e7 is unclear.

15...cxd5 16.f5!?

The game becomes unpredictable; see also 16.exd5!? ♗xd5! 17.cxd5 ♕a5+ 18.♗d2 ♕xd5 19.0-0! ♕xd2.

16...gxf5 17.exd5 ♖xc4 18.dxe6 ♖e4+ 19.♔f2 ♕b6+ 20.♔g3 d5 21.♗f4 ♕xe6 22.♖hf1 ♘c6 23.♖ad1 d4

This position is hard to understand. However, at that time (and as in the romantic era), the attacking player used to win...

24.♖d3??

This was Euwe's decisive mistake. 24.♗g5 ♖e3+!? was still possible, or 24.h4 ♖xf4!? with a great fight.

24...♖xf4!

After this blow, the game is suddenly over.

25.♔xf4

25.♖xf4 ♕e1+ 26.♖f2 ♘e5.

25...♘e5! 26.♔g3 ♘xd3   **0-1**

A fantastic game!

Summarizing the 8...g6 plan: It looks as if Black does not have enough time to carry out the fianchetto idea in this line. For example, White could have played 10.f4! instead of 10.♘b5, with a dangerous initiative.

 **Statistics for 4...h5**

Surprisingly, after a few games the theoretical development of the line with 4.e4 h5 stopped. Black was looking for new ways to find counterplay.

Black defeats against the best players in the world may have exerted great influence on the practical use of this line, so we lack the analysis necessary to evaluate the arising positions correctly.

The statistics of 4...h5 are interesting. Only 25 games were played in total! White won 12 games, Black won 7 and 5 games were drawn, but White's rating performance was only 2033, while Black's was 2264!

Summary of the 'Réti Plan' 4...h5

- It is clear that the initial idea of keeping the knight on g4 for an attack

against f2 with ...♗c5 does not work. Still, I advise the reader to take a look at the 4...h5 line once more, as I am sure that the idea is perfectly playable.

- The secret of the positions arising after 4...h5 could lie in the search for more dynamic play. Black cannot permit himself to waste any tempi and he must use all his resources to carry on with his counterattack (see Games 49-53).

- Trying to defend first is lethal for Black in this line, and so it is for White, as is shown in Games 49-53.

- In any case, the study of the games with the 4....h5 line is helpful to apprehend the main lines of the 4.e4 variation and is useful for learning the best methods and concepts of this dangerous line.

GAME 54
□ **G. Reid**
■ **Alexander Alekhine**
Scarborough 1926

1.d4 ♘f6 2.c4 e5 3.dxe5 ♘g4 4.e4 d6!?

5.♗e2!?

White chooses to attack the g4 knight. 5.♘f3?! ♘c6!? (5...♘xe5=) 6.♘c3

(6.exd6 ♗xd6♔) 6...♘gxe5 7.♘xe5 dxe5! 8.♕xd8+ ♔xd8 9.♗e3 ♘e6! 10.g3 (10.0-0-0 c6!) 10...c6! 11.♗g2 ♘d4 12.0-0-0 (12.♗xd4 exd4 13.♘e2 ♗b4+↑; 12.0-0? ♘c2−+) 12...♗g4! 13.♖d2 0-0-0∓, Aguilera-Tartakower, Barcelona 1929. For 5.exd6! see Capablanca-Tartakower, Game 56.

5...h5!?

Old wine in a new bottle! See again the previous games with 4...h5!.

For 5...♘xe5 see Reshevsky-Denker, Game 55.

6.♘c3 ♘c6 7.h3

For 7.exd6!? see the comments to Capablanca-Tartakower, Game 56.

7...♘gxe5 8.♘f3 ♘xf3+ 9.♗xf3 g6!

The modern path introduced by Spielmann (see Euwe-Spielmann, Game 53): the idea is ...♗g7. Also, 9...♗e6!?.

10.♗e3 ♗e6 11.♘d5 ♘e5!

With a clear plan: to attack pawn c4.

12.♗d4?

Reid gets lost in a complicated position. Better was 12.♗e2!? c6.

12...c6 13.♗xe5?

This move virtually boils down to resignation. Necessary was 13.♗e2 cxd5 14.exd5 ♗f5∓.

13...dxe5 14.♘e3 ♕a5+!

Winning easily.

15.♔f1 ♗h6 16.♕e1 ♕xe1+ 17.♔xe1 ♗xe3 18.fxe3 ♗xc4 19.b3 ♗e6 20.♔f2 ♔e7 21.♖hd1 ♖hd8 22.♖xd8 ♖xd8 23.♖d1 ♖xd1 24.♗xd1 a5 25.♔e2 b5 26.a3 h4 27.♔d3 c5 28.♔c3 b4+ 29.axb4 axb4+ 30.♔d3 ♔d6 31.♗c2 ♗c8 32.♔d2 ♗a6 33.♗d3 c4   **0-1**

In this original game, in order to defend against his own favourite attacking system (4.e4), Alekhine combined three ideas: the new gambit idea 4...d6, the original 'Réti Plan' with ...h5, and Spielmann's modern fianchetto ...g6. Therefore we could name this sub-variation 'Alekhine's Hybrid'.

It is remarkable that Alexander Alekhine also played the BG as Black, showing new ideas and good results and improving its statistics. Did Alekhine win in all kinds of positions just because he was Alekhine?

GAME 55
□ Samuel Reshevsky
■ Arnold Denker
Syracuse 1934

A Wild-West game with 5.♗e2!? ♘xe5.

1.d4 ♘f6 2.c4 e5 3.dxe5 ♘g4 4.e4 d6

In this line White has a pleasant choice, since he does not have to accept the new pawn sacrifice and can just play for development, which is a plan that is more in the spirit of 4.e4:

5.♗e2!? ♘xe5

The disadvantage of this position for Black lies in the lack of targets for the f8 bishop. That might be the reason why Alekhine continued with 5...h5!?.

6.f4

6...♘g4!?

This knight is annoying. If 6...♘g6!? 7.♘f3 ♘c6?! (better is 7...♗e7 8.0-0 0-0 and ...♘d7, ...♗f6) 8.0-0 ♗e7 9.♘c3 0-0 10.♗e3± Katajisto-De Greiff, Amsterdam Olympiad 1954; Or 6...♘ec6!? 7.♘f3 ♗e7 8.♘c3 0-0 9.♘d5 ♘d7 10.0-0 ♘c5 11.e5 ♖e8?! (better was 11...dxe5 12.fxe5 ♗g4 with chances for both sides) 12.b4! ♘d7 13.b5 ♘cb8 14.♗a3!± Fomin-Miasnikov, Soviet Union 1955.

7.♘f3

7.♗xg4 ♕h4+=.

7...♘c6 8.0-0

The structure is similar to that of the Philidor Defence.

8...♗d7?

Black forgets to complete his development. Preferable was 8...♗e7 9.♘c3 0-0 10.h3 ♘f6 11.♗e3±.

9.♘c3 ♗e7 10.h3 ♘f6 11.e5 dxe5 12.fxe5 ♘g8 13.♗e3 f6

13...♗e6 14.♕e1!↑.

14.♗d3!

Looking for tactics.

14...fxe5?

14...♗e6 15.♕e2 and 16.♖ad1 wins.
And now Sam Reshevsky finished this elegant game brilliantly:

15.♘g5!

15.♘xe5!?.

15...♘f6

15...♗xg5 16.♕h5+ g6 17.♗xg6+ hxg6 18.♕xg6+ ♔e7 19.♘d5 mate.

16.♖xf6!	**♗xf6**	**17.♕h5+**	**g6**
18.♗xg6+!	**hxg6**	**19.♕xg6+**	**♔e7**
20.♕f7+	**♔d6 21.c5**		**1-0**

Mate.

A serious test of 4...d6 is 5.exd6! – the 'Technical Solution'.

GAME 56

□ **José Raul Capablanca**
■ **Savielly Tartakower**
Bad Kissingen 1928 (1)

1.d4 ♘f6 2.c4 e5 3.dxe5 ♘g4 4.e4 d6

After Alekhine's successful application of the gambit's idea, Capablanca was the first player who accepted the pawn:

5.exd6! ♗xd6

5...♕xd6!? 6.♕xd6 ♗xd6 has never been tried. Black has some compensation.

6.♗e2!

Black has some tactical points in the following lines: 6.♘f3? ♗b4+ 7.♗d2 ♗c5−+ Kinman-Koshnitsky, Perth ch-AUS 1928, or 6.h3?? ♕h4! 7.♕e2 ♘xf2 8.♘f3 ♘d3+ 9.♔d1 ♘xc1−+.

6...f5?!

The only way to sharpen up the game. The creator of the 4...d6 gambit, Janos Balogh, has suggested 6...h5, but after 7.♘f3!, point f2 is safe and White keeps his plus pawn and superiority: 7...♘c6 8.♘c3 ♗e6 9.♘b5 (9.0-0!?) 9...♗b4+ 10.♗d2± Pomar Salamanca-Myers, Lugano Olympiad 1968.

Another idea is to play the ending after 6...♗b4+!? 7.♘c3 (7.♗d2? ♗c5) 7...♕xd1+ 8.♔xd1 0-0♙ – but not against Capablanca, please!

7.exf5

🎩 **Tricks**: 7.♗xg4 fxg4 8.♕d5? ♘c6 9.a3 ♘d4! 10.c5 ♗e7 11.♔f1 ♗e6 12.♕xd8+ ♖xd8 13.♘c3 ♗c4+ 0-1 Whyte-M. Davis, Hastings 1951.

7...♕e7

8.♘f3!?

A move that fits Capablanca's style. He follows the diet of eating pawns not pieces and chooses a second-best move which yields him a very promising position.

8.c5! might be a refutation of the gambit with 4...d6 and 6...f5: 8...♗xc5 9.♕a4+! (we do not know if this was a mistake or a tricky sacrifice by Tartakower to create complications) 9...♘c6 10.♕xg4

analysis diagram

10...0-0 (10...♗xf5 11.♕xf5; 10...♘d4 11.♕h5+!? ♔f8 12.f6!+–) 11.♕c4+ ♔h8 12.♘f3 ♖xf5 13.0-0 b5!? 14.♕xb5 (14.♕c2!?) 14...♘b4 15.♘c3 ♗a6 16.♕xa6 ♘xa6 17.♗xa6 ♕f6 18.♗e2± Haider-Neubauer, Finkenstein 1992.

8...♗xf5 9.♗g5 ♘f6 10.♘c3

Later, against Tartakower, some players tried 10.0-0: 10...♘c6 11.♘c3 0-0-0 12.♕a4 ♔b8 13.♖fe1 ♗d7 14.♕c2 (14.♘b5) 14...♕f7 15.a3? ♕h5 16.♘e4?? ♘d4! 17.♕d3 ♘xe2+? (17...♘xf3+ 18.♗xf3 ♕xh2+ 19.♔f1 ♖he8–+) 18.♖xe2? (18.♕xe2) 18...♗f5? (18...♗g4!–+) 19.♘xf6 ♗xd3 20.♘xh5 ♗xe2 21.♗xd8 ♖xd8 22.♖e1 ♗xc4 23.♘xg7± Wood-Tartakower, Budapest 1948.

10...♘c6 11.♘d5 ♕f7 12.0-0 0-0-0 13.♘d4 ♘xd4 14.♕xd4 c6 15.♗xf6 gxf6

16.♕xf6?

16.♕xa7! with the idea of 16...cxd5 17.cxd5, with a promising attack.

16...♕xf6?

This is what Capablanca, the 'king of endings', had been looking for all the time. But 16...♕g6! would have been a good attempt to change the course of the game: 17.c5 (17.♕xg6? hxg6∓; 17.g4 ♗e4↑) 17...♕xf6 (17...♗xc5!?) 18.♘xf6 ♗xc5 with an initiative for Black.

17.♘xf6 ♗e5 18.♗g4 ♗xf6 19.♗xf5+ ♔c7 20.♖ad1 ♗xb2 21.♖xd8 ♖xd8 22.♗xh7 ♖d4 23.g3 ♖xc4 24.h4 b5 25.♔g2 a5 26.h5 ♗g7 27.f4 ♗h6 28.♖e1 ♖a4 29.♗g8 ♖d4 30.♖e7+ ♖d7 31.♖xd7+ ♔xd7 32.♔f3 c5 33.g4 c4 34.g5 ♗f8 35.h6 a4 36.f5 ♔c6 37.h7 ♗g7 38.f6 c3 39.♔e2 ♗h8 40.f7 **1-0**

It is possible that Capablanca chose 4.e4 against the BG knowing that in those years master Tartakower (well known for his dogmatic concepts) was one of the main defenders of the Gambit, and also of the 4.e4 d6 line.

Even though Black used the latest improvements in ultramodern theory

(6...f5?!), the third World Champion managed to steer the game into familiar paths and won the game thanks to his superior technique.

Statistics for 4...d6

In total, 36 games were played with the following results:
White wins: (15 games) = 58%
Black wins: (9 games) = 42%
Draw: (12 games)
Rating Performance White 2124, Black 2013

Summary of 4...d6
- This line is always risky.
- The possibility of continuing in gambit style with 6...f5!? has proved to have only limited resources.
- Declining the gambit with 5.♗e2 ensures White some spatial advantage.

⚠ Keep in Mind!
After 4.e4, it is advisable for Black to play 4...h5!? or immediately 4...♘xe5! (Part II of this Chapter). These variations offer Black the best prospects of satisfactory counterplay.

Part II – Knight Jumps

1.d4 ♘f6 2.c4 e5 3.dxe5 ♘g4 4.e4 ♘xe5 5.f4

Introduction

The main move 4...♘xe5! allows White to create a strong pawn centre with 5.f4. This is similar to the Four Pawns Attack in the Alekhine Defence and sometimes, after ...♗b4+ and the trade on c3, the arising positions are very similar to typical ones in the Nimzo-Indian Defence.

The black knight on g8 makes four of the first five moves, while White moves his pawns only. Remember that in the Budapest Gambit Black learns about piece play... Anyway, White weakens many squares by advancing his central pawns, like in the Four Pawns Attack in the Alekhine Defence.

In all the arising positions White's advantage lies in the control that his pawns exert over the centre, and thereby support for his pieces on the 5th rank (especially for a knight on d5).

As soon as the f-pawn advances, further weaknesses are created in Black's formation (remember f4-f5-f6-f7 from Euwe-Mieses, Game 52).

White also has some serious problems in these lines: a series of weak points behind his pawn chain that allow the black pieces to penetrate into white territory. For example, a bishop placed on c5 will prevent White's kingside castling.

If White tries to take the c5-f2 diagonal under control with ♗e3, the black bishop goes to b4 with check and after both ♘bd2 and ♘c3 ♗xc3 White can forget about his main idea to establish a knight outpost on d5.

Another good target in the white formation is the e4 pawn. Black can attack it after castling, exploiting the vis-à-vis ♕e7/♖e8 – pawn e4 – king e1.

Directions

After 5.f4 the knight can retreat either to the left (g6) or to the right (c6).

A) Jump to the Left: 5...♘g6

5...♘g6 is a dynamic retreat, exerting pressure on f4. The disadvantage is White's constant threat of f4-f5. This advance cannot be made now (and, as a rule, not in the next few moves) as Black would then gladly put his knight back on e5, the classic square of operations in the BG. White must therefore first fight to control this square.

The middlegame begins long before move 10!

Main lines are 6.♗e3 (Games 57-60) and 6.♘f3 (Games 61-63).

B) Jump to the Right: 5...♘ec6

Here the black knight is not exposed. Furthermore, 'dark' holes have appeared in White's camp, particularly on d4. The pause that this move creates allows for a more positional game. Both sides can spend a tempo to calmly prepare their plans . Time is very limited, though, as usual when White has played 4.e4.

In this line both sides often choose to castle queenside.

Just like in the event of 5...♘g6, White can continue in more than one way:

B1) 6.♗e3, the most popular move (Games 64-68);

B2) 6.a3, preventing ...♗b4+ but making his sixth pawn move in a row (Games 69-72);

B3) 6.♘f3, the most flexible move (Games 73-76).

⚠ **Keep in Mind!**
Understanding the ideas investigated earlier in this chapter will be help-ful for study of the main positions after 5...♘ec6 as well.

C) Jump Forward: 5...♘bc6

5...♘bc6!? is a highly surprising and interesting possibility. No high-level games exist with this move. But it is essential for White to decide if he is prepared for a king walk into the open for his extra piece after 6.fxe5 ♛h4+ 7.♔d2, and if 7...♛f4+ 8.♔d3! – 8.♔e1 ♛h4+ was a draw in Boyd-Hardy, Bognor Regis 1968.

Knight Jumps – Games

GAME 57
□ **Rudolf Spielmann**
■ **Richard Réti**
Berlin 1919 (1)

Oddly, it was not until the Berlin tournament one year after the introduction of the BG that the first game with the system 4.e4 occurred between two classical players.

1.d4 ♘f6 2.c4 e5 3.dxe5 ♘g4 4.e4 ♘xe5 5.f4!

This advance is the consequence of 4.e4. 5.♘c3 is also interesting, e.g. 5...♗b4 (5...♗c5!?) 6.♘f3 ♗xc3+ (6...♘bc6!?) 7.bxc3 (Tartakower-Tarrasch, Semmering 1926) 7...♘xf3+!? 8.♕xf3 0-0.

5...♘g6!?

Threatening ...♗b4+ and ...♘xf4. For 5...♘ec6 see Games 64-77.

6.♗e3

White wants to protect the c5-g1 diagonal, but defending is not the main objective of the 4.e4 system. For 6.♘f3!? see Games 61-63.

6...♗d6?!

A very interesting idea, but it does not work quite well in this move order. The best idea is 6...♗b4+!, see Games 59 and 60. 6...♘a6!? also makes sense, preparing ...♗c5 or ...♗b4+. For 6...♘c6!? see the next game.

7.♕d2!± ♕e7 8.♘c3 ♗b4

Now Réti is playing with a tempo less (6...♗d6, 8...♗b4).

9.♗d3 b6 10.♘ge2 ♗b7 11.♘g3 0-0 12.h4!?

12.♘f5!? ♕d8 13.a3±.

12...♕d8??

12...♘xh4 13.0-0-0↑; 12...♗xc3!? 13.♕xc3 f5⇄.

13.h5↑ ♘e7 14.a3 ♗c5 15.0-0-0 d6 16.♗c2 ♘d7 17.♕d3 ♗xe3+ 18.♕xe3 f6 19.e5 fxe5 20.♕d3 ♘f6 21.♘ce4

21...♗xe4??

The decisive mistake. 21...♘xe4! 22.♘xe4 ♖xf4 23.♘g5 e4! would still have offered counterchances.

22.♘xe4 ♘xe4 23.♕xe4 ♖xf4 24.♕xh7+ ♔f7 25.♖df1! ♕h8 26.♖xf4+ exf4 27.♕e4 ♖e8 28.♕xf4+ ♔g8 29.h6 g6 30.h7+ ♔g7 31.♖f1 1-0

After this important victory, the champions of the white pieces started developing the attacking system with 4.e4.

The next three games, played by the 'new generation', illustrate the search for active counterplay against White's plan with 6.♗e3.

GAME 58
□ **Igor Potiavin**
■ **Dmitry Novitsky**
St Petersburg Chigorin mem 2005 (1)

1.d4 ♘f6 2.c4 e5 3.dxe5 ♘g4 4.e4 ♘xe5 5.f4 ♘g6 6.♗e3 ♘c6!?

I analysed this game especially because of the original idea shown here by Black...

7.a3?!

To avoid the check on b4, but moving only pawns is not a good idea.

7...♗d6!?

Starting tactics! The black pieces are up against the white pawn structure. This idea is similar to the plan used in the stem game with 4.e4 by Réti (6...♗d6?! Game 57), but in this case it works perfectly thanks to the extra development tempo.

Also interesting is 7...b6! with the strategic threat of ...♗c5!, in order to dominate the dark squares first: 8.♘c3 ♗c5 9.♕d3 0-0 (9...♘a6!? and 10...♘a5) 10.♘f3 ♗a6 (10...d6!?⇄) 11.g3, with unclear play in Mikhalchishin-Lendwai, Kecskemet 1991.

8.♘h3

Other options are 8.♕f3!? 0-0 9.♘c3, or 8.e5?! ♗e7 followed by ...d6 or ...f6.
8...0-0 9.♕h5 ♕f6!

Black starts a strong attack using the queen and three minor pieces.

10.e5 ♘cxe5! 11.fxe5 ♗xe5 12.♘g5 h6 13.♘e4 ♕c6?!

There was a forced win: 13...♕e6! 14.♗d3 (14.♘bd2 f5) 14...f5! 15.♘c5 ♕e8−+.

14.♘bc3 ♖e8 15.♔d2?

Defending is always the hardest part. 15.♘d5 was the only move.

15...f5 16.♕xf5 d5 17.♘f6+ ♗xf6 18.♕xd5+ ♗e6 19.♕xc6 bxc6 20.♖e1 ♗f5 21.♔c1 ♗xc3 22.bxc3 ♖ab8   **0-1**

We have witnessed a spectacular bashing of White's plan of 6.♗e3 and 7.a3. Black demonstrated the drawbacks of White's pawn play by making good use of the available tactics.

GAME 59
□ **Alexander Jugow**
■ **René Stern**
Berlin 2006 (4)

1.d4 ♘f6 2.c4 e5 3.dxe5 ♘g4 4.e4 ♘xe5 5.f4 ♘g6!? 6.♗e3 ♗b4+!

This is the main resource for the Budapest Gambit player. In dynamic lines like 4.e4 or 4.♗f4, this tempo will be even more effective.

7.♘d2

A logical response after ♗e3. White wants to keep a healthy pawn structure and prepare his attack slowly. Black must counterattack quickly.

7...♕e7!?

Another key move in the Budapest Gambit. 7...d6!? is the alternative.

8.♗d3?

Too simple. In other variations Black also gets good counterplay: 8.f5 ♘e5! (8...♕xe4 9.♕f3∞); 8.♕c2 b6 (8...♗c5!?) 9.♘e2 ♗b7 10.♘c3 ♗xc3 11.bxc3 ♘a6 12.g3 ♘c5 13.♗g2 f5?! (13...0-0!? 14.0-0 f5) 14.♗xc5 ♕xc5 15.0-0-0 0-0-0 Munoz-Mayo Casademont, Catalunya-tt 2007; 8.♕f3 0-0 (8...d6!? and 9...♘d7) 9.♗d3 ♘c6 10.0-0-0 (a common trick is 10.♘e2?? ♘ge5!) 10...a5 11.h4 ♖e8 12.♘b3? a4 13.♘d4 a3 14.b3 ♕f6 15.e5? ♘xd4 16.♕f2 ♘xb3+! 17.axb3 a2−+ Androvitzky-Eigler, Budapest 1951.

8...♕d6!

Attacking the d3 bishop and the f4 pawn. This is one of the important tactical resources in the 'Knight Jumps' variation. It works especially well in the 'Left' line with 5...♘g6. A more risky line is 8...f5 9.♕c2!? (9.♕f3 ♘h4!?⇄ 10.♕h5+ g6 11.♕e2 fxe4 12.♗c2 c6!? 13.0-0-0 d5 14.cxd5 cxd5 15.♕b5+? ♘c6−+

Felipe-Limp, Sao Paulo 1999) 9...fxe4 10.♗xe4 d5!? 11.♗xg6+ (11.cxd5!?) 11...hxg6 12.♕xg6+ ♔f8 13.♔f2∞ Alburt-McClintock, Las Vegas 1989.

9.♕c2

9.♕b3 ♗xd2+ 10.♔xd2 ♘xf4∓.

9...♘xf4

With a technically won position.

10.♗xf4 ♕xf4 11.0-0-0 ♘c6 12.♘f3 d6 13.♔b1 ♗xd2 14.♖xd2 ♗g4 15.♖f2 ♗xf3 16.♖xf3 ♕e5 17.♖f5 ♕e7 18.c5 0-0-0 19.♕a4 dxc5 20.♖d5 ♔b8 21.a3 ♘e5 22.♗e2 c6 23.♖dd1 ♖xd1+ 24.♖xd1 ♖d8 25.♖c1 ♖d2 26.♗f1 ♕d6 **0-1**

In the next game all the tactical and strategic points are demonstrated.

GAME 60
□ **Alexey Pliasunov**
■ **Maria Zvereva**
St Petersburg 2000 (8)

1.d4 ♘f6 2.c4 e5 3.dxe5 ♘g4 4.e4 ♘xe5 5.f4 ♘g6 6.♗e3 ♗b4+ 7.♘c3

White switches to the aggressive mode.

7...♕e7

This move, combined with ...♗b4+, always serves to attack the centre directly. The other possibility is to get on with development: 7...♗xc3+!? 8.bxc3 d6!? (8...♕e7 9.♕d2 d6!? (9...♕xe4

10.♗d3 ♛e7 11.♘h3♔) 10.h4 h5
11.0-0-0 ♗g4 12.♖e1 ♘d7 13.♘f3
0-0-0! 14.♘d4 ♘c5∓

analysis diagram

15.♗d3 ♖he8 16.♗b1 ♘e5? (16...♘xe4
17.♛b2 ♛d7∓) 17.fxe5 dxe5 18.♘f5!
♛e6 19.♛b2 ♛xc4 20.♗xc5 ♛xc5♔
21.♖hf1 ♖e6 (21...a5!? 22.♘xg7? ♛c6∓
and 23...♛h6+) 22.♛b4 ♛xb4 23.cxb4
g6 24.♘e3 ♖c6+ 25.♗c2 ♗e6 26.a3 a5
27.bxa5 ♖c5 28.♖f3 ♖d4 29.♘d1 ♖dc4
30.♖f2 ♖xa5 31.♖e3 b5 32.♔b2 c6
33.♘c3 b4 34.axb4 ♖xb4+ 35.♔c1
♖a3⇄ Radulski-Moskalenko, Montcada
2007) 9.♗d3 0-0 10.♘f3 b6
(10...♘d7!?) 11.♘g5?! h6 12.h4? (a
dubious thrust) 12...♛f6 (12...♛e7!?)
13.♛d2 hxg5 14.hxg5 ♛e7 15.e5
(15.g3!?) 15...dxe5−+ Aguilera-Ribera
Arnal, Barcelona 1929.

8.♗d3 ♗xc3+ 9.bxc3

9...d6!?

Here Black has a strike which is typical
in combination with 8...♛e7: 9...f5!?.
Mostly (sometimes unnecessarily) this
move complicates the game too much:
10.♛c2 (10.♘h3!? fxe4 11.♗c2↑)
10...fxe4 11.♗xe4 ♘xf4 12.♗xf4 d5
13.cxd5 ♗f5 14.♛a4+! (14.0-0-0
♗xe4 15.♛a4+ b5! 16.♛xb5+ c6?!
17.dxc6 ♛a3+⇄ Arambel-Tovillas,
Chacabuco 1980) 14...b5 15.♛xb5+
c6 (15...♘d7!?) 16.dxc6 ♗xe4 17.c7+
♘d7 18.♘e2+− Golichenko-Malienko,
Kiev 2007.

A calmer choice is 9...♘a6!? 10.♗c2?!
b6 11.♘f3 ♗b7 12.0-0 0-0-0 13.♖e1
♘c5 14.♛d4 f6 15.a4 a5 16.f5 ♘e5
17.♘xe5 fxe5∓ Star89-Moskalenko
(CapNemo), playchess.com 2007.

10.♛c2 0-0 11.♘e2 ♘d7 12.0-0-0

White is planning a massive attack in
the centre and on the kingside. Unfortunately, in this game his plans will not
work as he expects. Black finds his way
first.

12...♖e8!

The end of the game reminds us of one
of Napoleon Bonaparte's battles.

13.♘g3 ♘f6

13...♘c5!? 14.♗xc5 dxc5⇄.

14.♗d2 ♛d7!?

The black queen moves to her own flank.

15.♞f5 ♛c6 16.♞d4 ♛c5 17.h3 ♝d7 18.g4 ♝c6 19.♜de1 ♞d7 20.h4

An attack with a legion of pawns!

20...♛a3+

20...♞gf8!?.

21.♚b1 ♞c5!

The black pieces start a counterattack on the opposite flank.

22.♝c1 ♛a6 23.h5 ♞f8 24.♜h2

24.h6!?.

24...♝a4 25.♞b3 ♞fd7 26.♝e3 ♞xd3!

In the next phase all the minor pieces are liquidated.

27.♛xd3 b5! 28.c5 ♝xb3 29.axb3 ♞xc5 30.♝xc5 dxc5 31.♛d5 ♛f6!?

31...c4!.

32.♛xc5 ♛xf4

The crop of white pawns (i.e. the legion) is ripe to be harvested.

33.♜f2 ♛xg4 34.♛xc7 ♛xh5 35.♜ef1 ♜xe4

The kingside is already wiped clean.

36.♜xf7 ♛g6 37.♚b2 ♜e2+ 38.♚a3 ♛g2 39.♛c5 ♜a2+ 40.♚b4 ♛e4+ 41.c4 a5+ 42.♚xb5 ♛e8+ 43.♚b6 ♛e6+ 44.♚c7 ♜c8+ 45.♚b7 ♛xf7+!
0-1

Summarizing 5...♞g6 6.♝e3: Generally, Black will have no trouble to obtain counterplay, thanks to his better piece development. White defends the important g1-a7 diagonal, but the black bishop on f8 has more squares available apart from c5.

GAME 61
□ Alexander Alekhine
■ Ilya Rabinovich
Baden-Baden 1925

1.d4 ♞f6 2.c4 e5 3.dxe5 ♞g4 4.e4 ♞xe5 5.f4 ♞g6 6.♞f3!

This is more natural than 6.♝e3. White continues his development and prepares f4-f5.

6...♝c5?!

This move was recommended by grandmaster Tartakower. From a positional point of view it is good: Black continues his development, taking control of the important diagonal g1-a7.

But Alekhine had found a dynamic refutation of the idea ....♗c5. Better is 6...♗b4+! (see Game 63) and Réti's classical idea is also interesting: 6...♗d6!? 7.e5 (7.f5 ♘e5) 7...♗b4+ with mutual chances.

7.f5!

True to his style, Alekhine starts fighting for the initiative immediately.

7...♘h4?!

Relatively better was 7...♘e7 8.♘c3± with a very uncomfortable, but not immediately lost position (Alekhine). 7...♘e5?? does not work in view of 8.♘xe5 ♕h4+ 9.g3! ♕xe4+ 10.♕e2 ♕xh1 11.♘g6+!+−.

8.♘g5!

A strong reply. The threat of 9.♕h5, winning the knight on h4, is already decisive. Not 8.♗g5?? ♘xf3+.

8...♕e7

If 8...h6 9.♕h5 0-0 10.♕xh4 ♗e7 11.♘c3 ♖e8 (11...hxg5 12.♕h5±) 12.♕g4!? ♗xg5 13.♗xg5 hxg5? (13...♕xg5 14.♕xg5 hxg5 15.0-0-0±) 14.0-0-0 ♘a6 15.h4+− Santos-Munoz Sanchez, Bled 2002.
9.♕g4! f6 10.♕h5+! g6 11.♕xh4 fxg5 12.♗xg5+− ♕f7 13.♗e2 0-0 14.♖f1 ♘c6 15.♘c3 ♘d4 16.fxg6 ♕xg6 17.♖xf8+ ♗xf8 18.♗h5 ♕b6

19.0-0-0!

Good enough. But not 19.♕f2? ♘c2+! 20.♕xc2 ♕g1+ with counterplay.
19...♗g7 20.♖f1 ♘e6 21.♗f7+ ♔h8 22.♗xe6 ♕xe6 23.♗f6!   **1-0**

Once more we have seen Alekhine with the white pieces executing an excellent attack, playing like an attacking machine. After this defeat, black players abandoned the idea 6...♗c5 and chose alternatives like 6...♘c6!? or 6...♗b4+!.

GAME 62
□ **Tino Laux**
■ **Normunds Miezis**
Biel 1991 (1)

1.d4 ♘f6 2.c4 e5 3.dxe5 ♘g4 4.e4 ♘xe5 5.f4 ♘g6 6.♘f3 ♘c6!?

The development of the knight to c6 allows Black to control e5, but it wastes a tempo in the fight for the initiative. White can support his central pawns and strengthen his position.

7.♗e3!?

The bishop defends the g1-a7 diagonal. 7.a3!? ♗e7 (7...♗d6!?) 8.♘c3 d6 9.♗e3 ♗g4 10.♗e2 ♗f6 11.♘d5!± Bohatirchuk-Ilyin-Zhenevsky, Leningrad ch-URS 1923; 7.♗d3 ♗b4+?! (≥ 7...♗c5!) 8.♘c3 d6 9.0-0 ♗xc3 10.bxc3 0-0 11.♘d4!?± I.Novikov-Blatny, Poznan 1987.

7...♗b4+!

This check must be executed as soon as possible.

8.♘c3 d6 9.♗d3 0-0 10.0-0 ♗xc3 11.bxc3 ♖e8

11...♘h4?! 12.♘d4! ♘xd4 13.cxd4 f5 14.e5 dxe5 15.fxe5 f4 16.♗f2± Eslon-Mejias Gonzalez, Cordoba 1995; 11...♕e7!?⇄. The black queen is well placed on this square.

12.♘d4!?

A typical position in the 4.e4 variation. The pawn structure and the game are very similar to those of the Sämisch Variation in the Nimzo-Indian Defence.

12...♘f8?!

12...♗d7!?.

13.♕f3

White does not find the right plan. With 13.♕h5!? he would have kept the initiative.

13...♗d7 14.♖ae1

14.♕g3!?.

14...♕h4!? 15.♘xc6? ♗xc6⇄

Now chances are equal.

16.♗f2 ♕e7 17.♕h5 b6 18.e5 dxe5 19.fxe5 ♖ad8 20.♖e3 ♕e6 21.♗h4 ♖xd3! 22.♖xd3 ♕xc4 23.♖e3 ♘g6 24.♗g3 ♕xa2 25.♖e2 ♕e6 26.♖ef2 ♗b5 27.♖d1 h6 28.♕f3 a5 29.h4 ♗c4 30.♕b7 ♕c8?!

30...♘xe5! 31.♕xc7 ♘g4∓.

31.♕c6 ♗e6 32.♖fd2 ♘e7 33.♕b5 ♖f8 34.h5 ♕b7 35.♖d8 ♘c6 36.♖xf8+ ♔xf8 37.♕d3 ♔g8 38.♕e4 b5 39.♗h4 a4 40.♕f3 a3 41.♗f6 ♕a7+ 42.♔h2 ♕a4

42...♕c5−+.

43.♕xc6 ♕xd1 44.♕a8+ ♔h7 45.♕e4+ g6 46.hxg6+ fxg6 47.♕a8 ♕h5+ 48.♔g1 ♗g8 49.♕xa3 g5 50.♕e7+ ♕f7 51.♕b4 h5 52.♕xb5 ♕c4 53.♕xc4 ♗xc4 54.♗xg5 ♗d5 55.♔f2 ♔g6 56.♗d8 c5 57.g3 ♔f5 58.♗e7 c4 59.♗d6 ♔e4 60.♔e2 ♗e6

½-½

6...♘c6 is a solid try, but it also allows White to develop comfortably.

In many cases the b8 knight is better placed on c5, so Black prefers continuations like ...♘d7 or ...♘a6. It is advisable for Black to insert 6...♗b4+ before moving the ♘ on b8.

GAME 63
□ **Igor Novikov**
■ **Alexander Budnikov**
Beijing 1991 (5)

This game is perfectly suited for an understanding of the best plans for both sides in the line 5...♘g6 6.♘f3.

1.d4 ♘f6 2.c4 e5 3.dxe5 ♘g4 4.e4 ♘xe5 5.f4 ♘g6 6.♘f3 ♗b4+!

129

My advice to black players is to study (in all the opening positions) Réti's old idea 6...♗d6!?, which looks quite provocative but offers a sharper game. For example: 7.e5 ♗b4+ 8.♗d2 ♕e7 9.♘c3 ♗xc3 10.♗xc3!? (10.bxc3 d6⇄) 10...♘xf4 11.♕d2 ♘e6.

7.♘c3

Virtually the only move; 7.♗d2?! ♕e7! with the threats of 8...♕xe4 and 8...♘xf4.

7...d6

The more dynamic idea is 7...♕f6 (attacking the white weaknesses with pieces; the threats are ...♘xf4 or ...♗xc3+) 8.e5! ♕b6 9.a3?! (9.f5!? ♘e7 10.♗d3 intending 11.f6) 9...♗xc3+ 10.bxc3 d6 Reshevsky-Shipman, New York 1956. Also good is 7...0-0!?.

8.♗d3

In another game (more in the spirit of Alekhine), 8.h4!? was chosen: 8...♕f6?! (8...♕e7!?⇄) 9.f5 ♘e5 10.♗g5 ♘xf3+ 11.♕xf3 ♗xc3+ 12.bxc3 ♕e5 13.0-0-0 f6 (13...♕a5!?) 14.♖d5 ♕e7 15.♗f4 ♘d7 16.c5 ♘xc5 17.♖xc5 dxc5 18.♗c4 b5? (18...♗d7□ 19.♗xc7∞) 19.♗d5 ♖b8 20.e5! ♖b6 21.♖e1 ♔d8?? 22.♖d1 ♔e8 23.♖e1 ♔d8 24.♕d1! (24.♕g3!?) 24...c4 25.exf6 ♕a3+ 26.♔b1 ♗xf5+ 27.♗e4+ ♗d7 28.fxg7 ♖e8 29.♗xh7

♖xe1 30.g8♕+ ♖e8 31.♕gd5 1-0 S. Williams-Miezis, Oslo 2004.

8...♘d7!?

Intending 9...♘c5.

9.0-0 ♗xc3!?

A thematic exchange. White will have a bad pawn structure on the queenside.

10.bxc3

This is the critical moment between the opening and the middlegame.

10...♘c5?!

The knight was well placed on d7, defending its kingside. I prefer 10...0-0.

11.♗c2 0-0

11...♗g4!?.

12.♗e3

12.f5!? ♘e7 13.♘d4! f6 14.♖f3↑ followed by ♖h3 and ♕h5.

12...b6 13.f5!

White must attack without hesitation.

13...♘e5 14.♘xe5 dxe5 15.♕h5!

15.♗xc5 bxc5 16.♕d5 ♕xd5 17.cxd5 ♗a6⇄.

15...f6 16.♗xc5

This leads to an equal position. It is important to know what happens if White continues his attack: 16.♖f3!? ♕e7 (16...♕e8!? 17.♕h4 ♕e7∞) 17.♖d1 (17.♖h3 g5!) 17...♗d7 and Black seems to be able to defend his kingside without trouble with...♖hd8.

16...bxc5 17.♖ad1 ♕e7=

The position is already blocked and it is hard to tip the balance; but 17...♕e8? was bad in view of 18.♕xe8 ♖xe8 19.♖d5.

18.♗a4 ♖b8 19.♖d2 ♖b6 20.♖fd1 ♖d6 21.♖xd6 cxd6 22.♕e2 ♗b7 23.♕d3 ½-½

 **Statistics for 5...♘g6**

Total 286 games:

White wins: 122 games = 53%
Black wins: 103 games = 47%
Draw: 61 games

Performance White: 2075, Black: 2033.

Summary of 5...♘g6

This move is perfectly playable. Black has more problems in the variation with 6.♘f3 than in the one with 6.♗e3. In both cases he should probably play 6...♗b4+!, but classical moves like 6...♗d6!? and 6...♘c6!? also deserve consideration.

In the opinion of many Budapest Gambit experts (never trust those opinions blindly!), Black has an easier task if he decides on 5...♘ec6. This will be the final subject of the Alekhine System.

Now, 6.♗e3 is the most popular move, controlling the g1-a7 diagonal.

The following two games show the possible plans in this main line with 6...♗b4+ 7.♘c3.

GAME 64
□ **Alexander Alekhine**
■ **Jakob Adolf Seitz**
Hastings 1925/26 (5)

In this classical game we will investigate the possibility of sharp counterplay for

Black with ...♕e7 and ...f5, and also some strategic alternatives.

1.c4 ♘f6 2.d4 e5 3.dxe5 ♘g4 4.e4 ♘xe5 5.f4 ♘ec6!?

The retreat 5...♘ec6 offers more positional advantages than 5...♘g6. The b8 knight will get out by way of a6-c5 or d7-f6. After 6.♘f3 ♗c5, the attack f4-f5 makes no sense (see Game 61).

Therefore Alekhine decides to prevent 6...♗c5:

6.♗e3!?

Other variations are not very promising for White: 6.♘c3 ♗c5 (6...♗b4!? also yields counterplay) 7.♕h5!? d6 8.♗d2 ♘d7 9.0-0-0 ♘f6 10.♕g5 0-0∓ Neverov-Legky, Kiev ch-UKR 1986.

6...♗b4+!

But the f8 bishop has another good square. Now, neither 7.♘d2 nor 7.♘c3 (after 7...♗xc3+ 8.bxc3) can bring White's ♘ to d5, and so the black queen will reach her post on c7. However, also possible is 6...♘a6!? and 7...♗c5 – see Game 68.

7.♘c3

For 7.♘d2!? see Games 66 and 67.

7...♕e7

A typical Budapest manoeuvre again. For 7...♕h4+!? see the next game.

8.♗d3

8...f5!?

This idea of a straight counterattack is risky, but not completely wrong, as some writers about the Budapest Gambit claim. The other, more strategic option is 8...♗xc3+ 9.bxc3 ♘a6 (9...d6) This position can also include a check on h4 by the black queen (6/7...♕h4+ g3, see Game 65). Black prefers to finish development and then to attack the structural white weaknesses by ...♘c5, ...b6, ...♗b7 and ...0-0-0.

analysis diagram

10.♘e2 (10.♕h5 b6 11.♘f3 ♘c5 12.♗xc5 ♕xc5 13.♕xc5 bxc5 14.♘d2 0-0 15.♖b1 ♖b8 16.♖xb8 ♘xb8 ½-½ Averkin-Khalikian, Yerevan 1977) 10...♘c5 11.0-0 b6 (11...♘xe4?! 12.♘d4↑; 11...0-0!? △ 12.♘g3 ♘xd3 13.♕xd3 d6⇄) 12.♘g3 g6 13.♗d4 ♖g8 14.e5 ♗b7 15.♘e4 ♘xe4

16.♗xe4 0-0-0 17.♕a4 ♔b8 18.♖ae1 ♘xd4!? 19.cxd4 ♗xe4 20.♖xe4 d5 21.♖e3 dxc4 (21...c5!) 22.♕xc4 ♕e6= Cvitan-Rogers, Vrsac 1987.

9.♕h5+

This is Alekhine's improvement. He enforces an additional dark-square weakness on Black's kingside and then exploits it. White has also tried:

A) 9.♕f3 fxe4 (9...♗xc3+!?) 10.♗xe4 ♗xc3+ 11.bxc3 0-0 12.♘e2 d6 13.0-0 ♘d7 14.♘g3 ♘f6 15.♗xc6 bxc6 16.♗d4 ♗d7 17.♖ae1 ♕f7= Asztalos-Seitz, Debrecen 1925. Obviously 9.e5?! is bad because of 9...♗xc3+ 10.bxc3 d6, winning a pawn;

B) 9.♕c2!? d6 (9...♘a6!?⇄ 10.♘e2 ♗xc3+! 11.bxc3∞; 9...♗xc3+!?) 10.♘e2 fxe4 11.♗xe4 ♗f5 12.0-0-0 (12.♗xf5!?) 12...♗xe4 13.♘xe4 0-0 14.♔b1 ♘d7 15.♗c1 ♖ae8⇄ Almond-Lochte, Dresden Ech 2007.

9...g6 10.♕f3

10...♗xc3+!

A very important exchange in the 4.e4 system! Black must do this before White plays ♘ge2, otherwise after ♘e2xc3 White's other knight will go to d5 and cause trouble. For example: 10...d6? 11.♘e2±.

11.bxc3

The critical moment in this line.

11...fxe4?

This is definitely a mistake! 11...d6! was necessary, and if 12.♘e2 (12.exf5 ♗xf5 13.♗xf5 gxf5 14.♘e2 ♘d7∞) Alekhine writes that after 12...0-0 White will have the better position. But Black has strong defensive resources: 12...fxe4! 13.♕xe4 (13.♗xe4 ♗g4! 14.♕xg4 ♕xe4 with the idea 15.♕c8+ ♘d8) 13...♗f5 14.♕xe7+ ♔xe7 15.♗xf5 ♘xf5 with a very good ending for Black.

12.♗xe4 0-0? 13.♗d5+ ♔h8 14.♘h3 d6

14...♖e8 15.♔f2+− Tartakower.

15.0-0

The struggle revolves around the possibility of ♗d4+, which will be fatal for the black king. The point of 9.♕h5+ is clear now.

15...♗xh3

Alekhine commented that all Black's moves in this position are 'equally bad': 15...♗f5 16.♖ae1 ♕f6 17.♘g5+−.

16.♕xh3 ♕d7 17.f5! gxf5

17...♖xf5 18.g4!

18.♖ab1 f4 19.♗xf4 ♕xh3 20.♗e5+!
                                    1-0

White wins after 20...♘xe5 21.♖xf8+ ♔g7 22.♖g8+ ♔f6 23.gxh3. This was the last of Alexander Alekhine's famous four victories with 4.e4.

Summarizing, in the position after 8.♗d3 two useful plans for Black apply: In the first place, the 8...f5!? break is very interesting, creating an early crisis. Black's reply 11...d6! is forced, after which chances are equal.

The second option is the strategic choice 8....♗xc3+ 9.bxc3 ♘a6!?, blocking both white bishops and attacking the pawn structure e4-f4 and c4-c3 with pieces.

With the passage of time Black found an interesting intermediate check with the queen.

GAME 65
□ **Paul Keres**
■ **Klaus Eckhardt**
cr 1933

1.d4 ♘f6 2.c4 e5 3.dxe5 ♘g4 4.e4 ♘xe5 5.f4 ♘ec6 6.♗e3 ♗b4+ 7.♘c3 ♕h4+!?

An idea inspired by Alekhine's intermediate check (♕d1-h5+-f3) in his game against Seitz (Game 64).

8.g3

From now on Black will get attacking chances along the 'Milky Way', the a8-h1 diagonal.

8...♗xc3+!

This exchange − before White has played ♘ge2 − prevents the possibility

133

of placing a ♘ on d5 and also doubles the c-pawns, which will make a good target for the black pieces.

9.bxc3 ♛e7

10.♗d3

Following Alekhine's plan. You can find other main ideas in the next illustrative games. Alternatives are:

A) 10.♔f2 b6 (or 10...d6!? and ...♘d7-f6-g4+) 11.♗d3 ♗b7 (this is the best place for the bishop in this line, especially after g3) 12.♘f3 ♘a6!.

analysis diagram

This is a typical set-up of Black's queenside pieces in this line. Now Black can choose to castle queenside, with the possibility of pawn storms on opposite flanks: 13.♖e1 ♘c5 14.♕c2 0-0 (14...♘xd3+!? 15.♕xd3 d6∓) 15.♗d4 f6 16.♖e2 ♖ae8 17.♖ae1 ♘xd3+ 18.♕xd3 ♕f7 (pressurizing the c4 pawn)

analysis diagram

19.c5 ♘b8!? (intending ...♗a6) 20.cxb6 axb6 21.♖b2 ♖e6!? (intending ...♖fe8 to target the e4 pawn) 22.♕b1 ♖fe8 23.♘d2 ♕h5 24.♔g1 f5 25.e5 ♕h3 (finally we see how Black exploits the weakness created in the opening: his idea is ...♖g6 and ...h7-h5-h4, using the control along the b7-h1 diagonal) 26.♘c4 ♖g6 27.♖e3 h5!? 28.♕f1?? ♕xf1+ 29.♔xf1 ♗a6! 0-1 Dührssen-Heidenfeld, Berlin 1930;

B) 10.♗g2!? is interesting:

analysis diagram

10...d6 (10...b6 11.♘e2 ♗b7 12.0-0 ♘a6 13.♘d4 ♘xd4 14.♗xd4 0-0 15.f5 f6 16.e5! ♗xg2 17.exf6↑ Norri-Mäki Uuro, Finland 2003; 10...0-0!?) 11.♔f2? (11.♘e2) 11...0-0 (11...♘d7!? with the idea of ...♘f6-g4+) 12.♕c2 ♘a6 13.♘f3 ♗d7

14.♖he1 ♖ae8 15.♘d2 b6 16.♔g1 ♘c5 17.h3 ♕d8 18.♖ad1 ♕c8 19.♔h2 h6 20.♗f2 ½-½ Naumkin-Koptsov, Moscow 2002.

10...d6!

Fixing White's central pawns. 10...♘a6!? 11.♗c2 (11.♘f3!? b6 12.♘d4!? ♗b7 13.0-0 0-0-0 14.♘f5 ♕f8 15.♗d4 f6 16.♘e3 ♘c5 17.♘d5 ♘a5 18.♗f2 ♗a6 19.♖e1 ♘xd3 20.♕xd3 ♗xc4∓ Ananchenko-Kahn, Budapest 2000) 11...b6 12.♘f3 ♘c5 13.0-0 ♗b7 (13...♘xe4!? 14.♗xe4 ♕xe4 15.♗xb6 0-0=) 14.e5 0-0-0 15.♘d4 f6 16.♘f5 ♕f8 17.♗d4 g6 (17...♖e8!?) 18.♘e3 fxe5 19.fxe5 ♕h6 (19...♕g7!) 20.♘d5 ♘e6 with mutual chances. Oddly, Keres repeated this a not very promising variation in a regular game several years later: Keres-Gilg, Prague 1937.

11.♔f2

The king escapes from possible dangerous pins and protects the ♗e3.

Tricks: 11.♕f3?! ♘d7! 12.♘e2? (12.♘h3= ♘de5!) 12...♘de5! 13.fxe5 ♘xe5 14.♕g2 ♘xd3+−+; Black not only has an extra pawn, but also an attack. Better is 11.♘f3!? 0-0 with the ideas ...f5 or ...♗f5, attacking along the e-file.

11...♘d7! 12.♘f3 ♘c5

12...0-0!?; 12...♘f6!?.

13.♖e1

After 13.♗xc5 dxc5 14.e5 ♗d7 Black can choose either ...0-0-0 or ...0-0.

13...♘xd3+! 14.♕xd3 ♗d7

14...0-0!? with the idea ...b6 and ...♗b7, and Black is slightly better.

15.♖ab1 b6 16.♖bd1 ♖d8 17.♗c1 0-0 18.♗a3!?

Threatening e4-e5.

18...f6! 19.♔g2 ♕f7!

Another weakness – ♘c4 – will be attacked with ...♘a5/♗e6. This idea is similar to the line with 4.♗f4 in Rubinstein-Schlechter, Berlin 1918 (Game 2).

20.♖e3 ♘a5 21.♘d2 ♗e6 22.g4 ♗xg4 23.♖g1 ♗e6!−+ 24.♔h1 ♘xc4 25.f5 ♘xe3 26.fxe6 ♕xe6 27.♕xe3 f5

27...♕xa2!?.

28.c4 fxe4 29.♗b2 ♖d7 30.♖g3 d5 31.h4 c6 32.h5 ♖f5 33.♔g2 ♖xh5 34.cxd5 ♖hxd5 35.♘xe4 ♖d2+ 0-1

Summarizing: the intermediate check 7...♕h4+ helps Black to obtain dangerous counterplay along the light squares, straight into the heart of the white position. Once development is completed, White must reinforce his centre before starting any activity, but Black has good chances of organizing a counterattack. His main weapons are the attack on White's weak pawns and breaks with his own pawns.

GAME 66
□ **Rustem Dautov**
■ **Pavel Blatny**
Bad Wörishofen 1991

1.d4 ♘f6 2.c4 e5 3.dxe5 ♘g4 4.e4 ♘xe5 5.f4 ♘ec6 6.♗e3 ♗b4+ 7.♘d2

White wants to avoid getting his pawns doubled, as would happen in case of

7.♘c3 ♝xc3+. His pieces will be slightly passive, though, while his beautiful pawn structure does not guarantee victory at the end of the battle.

7...♛e7!?

A standard attack. Black has at least three other continuations:

Maybe the safest is 7...♘a6!? 8.a3 ♝c5 9.♝xc5 ♘xc5⇄ or Panchenko's choice 7...d6!?, see Game 67. In the spirit of the line is 7...♛h4+!?. The intermediate check with the black queen always deserves attention: 8.g3 ♛e7 9.♝g2 (9.♛f3 d6⇄) 9...♘a6!? (9...a5 10.♘e2 ♘a6 with good development, Pomar-Heidenfeld, Enschede Zonal 1963. Also good is 9...0-0! 10.♘e2 ♝c5 11.♝xc5 ♛xc5= Pomar) 10.a3 (10.♘e2 ♝c5! 11.♝xc5 ♛xc5⇄) 10...♝c5 11.♝xc5 ♘xc5 (intending ...♘d3+ or ...♘xe4-f5)

analysis diagram

12.b4 (Dautov-Haas, Buhl rapid 1992) 12...♘d3+!? 13.♚e2 ♘b2 14.♛c1 ♘d4+! 15.♚f1 ♘a4 with original play.

8.a3 ♝c5!

Black can take some risks and accept the pawn: 8...♛xe4 9.♚f2 (9.♛e2!? is similar) 9...♝xd2 10.♛xd2 ♛g6!? 11.♝d3 f5. Here Black has to find a plan in order to develop his queenside.

9.♝xc5

On 9.♛f3 ♘d4!? offers counterchances.

9...♛xc5

The position is equal, but he who chooses the best moves will win.

10.♛f3 ♘d4?!

An impetuous move. The main alternative was 10...d6!?, for example: 11.0-0-0 ♘d7! 12.♘e2 ♘f6⇄.

11.♛c3 a5 12.♘df3! ♘xf3+

12...♘bc6 13.0-0-0! ♘xf3.

13.♘xf3 0-0 14.0-0-0 ♘c6 15.♖d5! ♛e7 16.e5±

Now White's pawns and pieces are dominating the board. He won the game on move 60.

Black is not forced to attack straight with the queen. It is possible to wait one more move.

GAME 67
□ **Peter Restas**
■ **Alexander Panchenko**
Budapest 1990 (7)

1.d4 ♘f6 2.c4 e5 3.dxe5 ♘g4 4.e4 ♘xe5 5.f4 ♘ec6 6.♗e3 ♗b4+ 7.♘d2 d6!

A pawn move? Sure, it is necessary to prepare the development of the queen-side pieces.
8.♗d3
8.♘f3 ♘d7!.
8...♕h4+!? 9.g3 ♕f6!
This time the attack runs along the f6-b2 diagonal. 9...♕e7!?.
10.♕c2
10.a3 ♕xb2!? 11.axb4 ♘xb4 12.♔e2 ♗g4+ 13.♘f3 ♗xf3+ 14.♔xf3 ♘xd3∞ 15.♕a4+ ♘d7!? 16.♖hb1 ♕f6 17.♖xb7? 0-0!∓.
10...♘a6! 11.♘e2 ♗c5!
The position favours Black. White has too little time to activate his pieces.

12.e5
12.♗xc5 ♘xc5 and ...♘b4 or ...♕xb2!.
12...dxe5 13.♘e4 ♕e7 14.♗xc5 ♘xc5 15.♘xc5 ♕xc5 16.♗xh7? ♗e6 17.♗e4 exf4
17...0-0-0!–+.
18.♘xf4 ♗xc4 19.♗xc6+ ♕xc6 20.0-0-0 ♗xa2 21.♖he1+ ♔f8 22.♕xc6 bxc6 23.h4 ♖e8 24.♖f1 ♖h6 25.♖f3 ♗c4 26.♖d7 ♖c8 27.♖e3 ♖d6 28.♖de7 ♗b3 29.♘d3 ♖cd8 30.♔d2 ♖xd3+! **0-1**
This dynamic game shows the disadvantages of White's plan of 6.♗e3 ♗b4+ 7.♘d2. White's pieces are passive and cannot enter the game. Meanwhile Black gets successful counterplay without hurrying, but always keeping a good pace!

We will conclude the study of 6.♗e3 with the reply 6....♘a6!?, a universal move and a classical resource for Black in the Alekhine System.

GAME 68
□ **Iosif Rudakovsky**
■ **Boris Ratner**
Moscow ch-URS 1945 (7)

1.c4 ♘f6 2.d4 e5 3.dxe5 ♘g4 4.e4 ♘xe5 5.f4 ♘ec6 6.♗e3 ♘a6!?

A universal manoeuvre with the b8 knight that has proved very effective in many lines. With solid play, Black prepares the strategic exchange ...♝c5.

7.♘c3!

Now the white pawns can't be doubled.

7...♝c5!

The line 7...♝b4 can be found in Game 77.

8.♕d2

Trying to keep the tension and preparing to castle queenside. 8.♝xc5 ♘xc5 9.♕h5!? (9.♘f3?! 0-0 10.♝d3 ♕f6!?) 9...d6 10.0-0-0 0-0 11.♘f3 f6!? 12.g4 ♕e8! 13.♕h4 a5 (13...♘b4!) 14.♖g1∞ was J. Fischer-Segal, Bucharest 1967.

8...d6 9.♘f3

9.♝d3?! ♝g4 10.♘ge2 ♕h4+! 11.♘g3 ♝xe3 (≥ 11...0-0-0!? 12.0-0 ♖he8⇄; 11...♘ab4!?) 12.♕xe3= Dautov-Köpf, Germany 1991.

9...0-0

10.♝d3

Looks natural. Some spectacular games have been played with similar ideas: 10.0-0-0!? ♖e8! (10...♝xe3 11.♕xe3 ♘c5 12.♝d3 ♘b4 13.♝b1 ♖e8 14.e5 f5 15.♕d2 ♝e6 16.♘d5 a5 17.♘xb4 axb4 18.♕xb4? ♖a4−+ Borisenko-Belova-Semenova, Riga 1955) 11.♝d3 ♝xe3 12.♕xe3 ♘c5 13.♖he1 ♘b4 14.♝b1 ♝e6 15.♘d5 (15.a3?? ♘b3 mate) 15...♝xd5 16.cxd5 c6! 17.♕c3 a5 18.a3

analysis diagram

18...cxd5! (starting a typical attack on the king) 19.axb4 axb4 (19...♘xe4!∓) 20.♕xb4 ♖a4 (20...♕c8!→) 21.♕b5 ♖a5 22.♕b4 ♕c7? (22...♕c8) 23.♔d2∞ Merriman-Anagnostopoulos, Port Erin 1994.

10...♝xe3

10...♘ab4!?.

11.♕xe3 ♘c5 12.♝c2?!

Time is too valuable for this move. On 12.0-0 Black could try 12...♖e8!?.

12...♘b4! 13.0-0-0 ♘xc2

13...♝e6!?.

14.♔xc2 ♖e8!

Undoubtedly, this position at the start of the middlegame is more promising for Black.

15.♖he1 ♝d7 16.e5 b6!?

This simple move clears a path for the black queen towards the enemy king. 16...a6!? was an alternative.

17.♔c1 dxe5 18.fxe5 ♕c8! 19.♕g5?

Preferable was 19.♕f4.

19...h6 20.♕g3 ♕a6! 21.♖d4?

21...♗f5!

Now the white king is in danger.

22.♘d2 ♖ad8 23.♖xd8

Or 23.♘d5 ♔h7!–+.

23...♖xd8 24.♖f1 ♗g6 25.♘d5 ♕xa2

0-1

So in many variations arising after the classical manoeuvre ...♘a6!? Black obtains the initiative, while the white king is still working as a goalkeeper!

Summary of 6.♗e3

The best part of almost all the lines with 6.♗e3 are the many possibilities: Black can start a counterattack immediately with 6...♗b4+ followed by 7...♕e7 or 7...♕h4+. But he can also choose the calmer 6...♘a6, developing first.

Unfortunately, nowadays the 4.e4 variation is seldom played anymore, so Black cannot put into practice all the ideas offered in Games 64-68.

A Hungarian Rhapsody

A new attempt to resurrect the 4.e4 attack was undertaken in March 1926 in Semmering, at the greatest tournament of that year. It was introduced by the famous theoretician Ernst Grünfeld. After 4.e4 ♘xe5 5.f4 ♘ec6 White can play 6.a3, avoiding ...♗b4+, even though this means making his first six moves with pawns only.

This move takes the b4-square under control and thereby supports the important knight manoeuvre to d5.

However, the first try of 6.a3 in the thematic 'Budapest Gambit' tournament revealed its main disadvantage: the waste of an important tempo.

In Semmering the struggle ended 2-1 in Black's favour: Vajda, against Tarrasch, and Réti, against Kmoch, showed the correct plan to equalize. After 6.a3 a5 7.♗e3 ♘a6 followed by ...♘c5, Black has enough counterplay (see Game 70 Kmoch-Réti).

But the real Semmering sensation was Alekhine's loss to Gilg.

GAME 69
□ **Alexander Alekhine**
■ **Karl Gilg**
Semmering 1926 (3)

This is an example where Alekhine's violent attack fails.

1.d4 ♘f6 2.c4 e5 3.dxe5 ♘g4 4.e4 ♘xe5 5.f4 ♘ec6 6.a3

Understanding whether this is a defensive or an attacking move is important here. What are White's actual threats?

6...a5

Black's customary reaction to a3. He intends to play ...♗c5. In their writings on the Budapest Gambit, some authors give the red light to the natural move 6...♗c5!? (!), claiming that it will be met by 7.b4! (?!) (if 7.♘f3 d6! and ...♗g4∓). Now, not clear is 7...♗xg1!? 8.♖xg1 0-0!, but not 8...♕h4+? 9.g3 ♕xh2 10.♖g2!±) 8.♖a2 d6!? with an unexplored position, but Black has a strong reply in 7...♗d4!. In all cases the white king will stay in the centre for the rest of the game.

7.♘c3

It looks as if Alekhine is repeating his successful idea against Euwe (see Game 50), displaying a certain obsession to bring his knight to d5 as soon as possible. A more logical option is 7.♗e3!?, see Games 70 and 71.

**7...♗c5   8.♘d5?!   0-0   9.♗d3   d6
10.♕h5**

A very optimistic attack. The only target for the white pieces is the black king. The threats of e4-e5 and ♘f3-g5 look very unpleasant. But Black is not forced to sit and wait! 10.♘f3 ♘e7⇄.

10...♘d7!?

One year later, Vajda tried to improve on this Alekhine-Gilg game, pointing his aim at White's weak centre: 10...♘d4!? (a symmetrical placement of the knights on d5-d4: Black intends to attack the ♘d5 with ...c6) 11.e5!? g6! 12.♕h6 dxe5 13.fxe5 ♖e8!.

analysis diagram

A central reaction to a flank attack! This game is a perfect illustration of that rule. 14.♕f4?! (an attempt to derive something from the placement of the ♘d5) 14...♘d7! 15.♗e3 ♘e6! 16.♕g3 c6 17.♘c3 ♘xe5! (White still has no time to castle) 18.♕xe5 ♘f4!? 19.♕xf4 ♗xe3 20.♕f1 ♗xg1+ 21.♔d2 ♗d4 22.♖d1 ♗g4 23.♖e1 ♖xe1 24.♕xe1 ♗f5 25.♕g3 ♗xd3 26.♕xd3 ♕g5+! 0-1 Gilg-Vajda, Kecskemet 1927.

11.♘f3 h6?

Exchanging the d5-knight was better: 11...♘e7!∓.

12.g4?

Played without respect for the opponent. White should have continued 12.♕h4!?, with an equal position.

12...♘f6!

12...♘d4!? 13.♘xd4 ♗xd4∓.

13.♘xf6+ ♕xf6 14.f5 ♘d4!

The knights are exchanged and White's attacking resources are vanishing.

15.g5

There is no way back.

15...♞xf3+ 16.♕xf3 hxg5 17.h4 ♖e8 18.♔d1

If 18.hxg5 ♕xf5 19.♕h5 ♖xe4+! and Black wins in all lines.

18...gxh4 19.♔c2 ♝d7! 20.♝d2

20...♖a6

Threatening 21...♖b6, but 20...♝d4 21.♖ab1 b5! 22.cxb5 ♖e5 was stronger.

21.♕h5?

A final attacking try, but this time Gilg finds the best replies.

21...♝a4+! 22.♔c1

22.b3 loses to 22...♝xb3+! 23.♔xb3 ♖b6+.

22...♖b6 23.♖a2 ♝d4 24.b4 ♝e3!

White is completely crushed.

25.♝xe3 ♕c3+ 26.♝c2 ♕xe3+ 27.♔b1 ♝xc2+

27...axb4!.

28.♖xc2 axb4

28...♖xe4−+.

29.♕xh4 bxa3+ 30.♔a2 ♕h6! 31.♕xh6 gxh6 32.♖xh6 ♔g7

With a hopeless rook ending for White...

33.♖h4 ♖b2+ 34.♖xb2 axb2 35.♔xb2 ♖h8 36.f6+ ♔g8 37.♖f4 ♔f8 38.♔c3 ♖h3+ 39.♔d2 ♔e8 40.e5 dxe5 41.♖f5 ♖h6 42.♖xe5+ ♔d8 43.♖d5+ ♔c8 44.♖f5 ♔d7 45.♖d5+ ♔e6 46.♖c5 c6 47.♖a5 ♖h8 48.♖a7 ♖b8 49.♔c3 ♔xf6 50.♔b4 ♔e5 51.♔c5 f5 52.♖a1 f4 53.♖e1+ ♔f5 54.♖e7 b5 55.♔xc6 bxc4 56.♔d5 ♖d8+ 57.♔xc4 f3 58.♔c3 ♔f4 59.♖f7+ ♔g3 60.♖g7+ ♔f2 61.♖g6 ♔f1 62.♖f6 f2 63.♖g6 ♖d5 64.♔c2 ♔e2 65.♖e6+ ♔f3 66.♖f6+ ♔e3 67.♖f8 ♖d4   0-1

After this game Tartakower exclaimed: 'The Budapest Gambit rehabilitated! (...) Alekhine's ingenious idea was refuted by strong defence!' Alekhine himself confessed he had 'underestimated the strength of his opponent' and 'had a lost position already in the opening'.

GAME 70
□ **Hans Kmoch**
■ **Richard Réti**
Semmering 1926 (10)

1.d4 ♞f6 2.c4 e5 3.dxe5 ♞g4 4.e4 ♞xe5 5.f4 ♞ec6 6.a3 a5 7.♝e3! ♞a6!

A common manoeuvre in the 4.e4 variation that virtually equalizes.

8.♘f3

In the same tournament Tarrasch tried 8.♗d3 ♗c5! 9.♕d2 ♕h4+?! (9...d6!?=) 10.g3 ♕e7 11.♘c3 ♗xe3 12.♕xe3 ♕c5 13.♕xc5 ♘xc5 14.0-0-0 d6 15.♗c2 ♗e6 16.♘d5 0-0-0 but did not obtain an advantage, Tarrasch-Vajda, Semmering 1926.

8...♗c5!

Black uses the key square c5 as an outpost for his pieces.

9.♕d2 d6! 10.♘c3 0-0

10...♗g4!?⇄.

11.♗d3 ♗xe3 12.♕xe3 ♘c5 13.0-0 ♖e8 14.♗c2 a4

14...♗e6!?.

15.♖ae1 f6

Defending against a possible e4-e5. 15...♗e6!? 16.♘d5 ♘a5! 17.♕c3 c6⇄.

16.♕f2 ♗g4 17.♘d4

17...♕d7

As usual, Réti over-complicates. Preferable was 17...♘xd4 18.♕xd4 b6=.

18.♘xc6

18.♘d5!?; 18.e5!?.

18...bxc6 19.f5?! ♗h5! 20.♕h4 ♗f7 21.♖f3 ♖e5

21...♗xc4? 22.e5!.

22.♖ee3 ♗xc4 23.♖h3 h6 24.♖eg3 ♔f8□

24...♔h8? 25.♕f4!→.

25.♖g6

25.♕f4!? would prepare for 26.♖xh6.

25...♖ae8 26.♖hg3??

Allowing a spectacular queen sacrifice. 26.♕g4!? ♖8e7 27.♖g3 was unclear.

26...♕xf5!!

With various mate threats.

27.♖xf6+

27.exf5?? ♖e1+ 28.♔f2 ♖f1 mate.

27...♕xf6

27...gxf6? 28.♕xh6+ ♔e7 29.♖g7+ ♔d8 30.exf5+−.

28.♖f3 ♖8e6! 29.♘xa4 ♘xa4 30.♗xa4 ♖xe4 31.♖xf6+ ♖xf6!

Threatening 32...♖f1.

32.g4 ♗e2   0-1

And after this victory Réti commented: 'This is a time of renaissance for the Budapest Gambit!' Geza Maroczy spoke of a 'Hungarian rhapsody'.

The following game shows how grandmasters of the late twentieth century played the Alekhine System.

GAME 71
□ **Rustem Dautov**
■ **Loek van Wely**
Germany Bundesliga B 1993/94

1.d4 ♘f6 2.c4 e5 3.dxe5 ♘g4 4.e4 ♘xe5 5.f4 ♘ec6 6.a3 a5 7.♗e3 ♘a6 8.♘c3

In another 'fresh' game White chose 8.♕d5, an interesting try to prevent ...♗c5, but the white queen will never be safe surrounded by the black army: 8...b6! (intending ...♗c5 and ...♗b7; also possible is 8...d6!?⇄) 9.♘c3 ♗c5 10.♗xc5 ♘xc5 11.♘f3 ♗b7!⇄

analysis diagram

12.0-0-0 ♕e7 (12...♕f6!) 13.♕h5 0-0-0! 14.♗d3 a4 15.♗c2 ♘a5 16.♖he1 ♘xc4 17.♘xa4? ♘xa4 18.♗xa4 ♕f6!∓ Suba-J. Gonzalez Garcia, Benasque 1996.

8...♗c5 9.♕d2 d6 10.♗d3

For 10.♘f3 see the previous game.

10...♕h4+!? 11.g3 ♕h5 12.♔f2?!

12.♗e2 ♗g4⇄.

12...0-0∓

13.♘f3

13.♘ge2? f5!∓.

13...♗g4

13...♗h3!?.

14.♗e2 ♖fe8 15.h3 ♗xf3 16.♗xf3 ♗xe3+

16...♕g6!?.

17.♕xe3 ♕c5?! 18.♕xc5 ♘xc5 19.♖ad1!±

19.♘d5 ♖ac8⇄.

19...a4!

With the idea of ...♘a5.

20.♘d5 ♘a6

20...♘xe4+? 21.♔g2±.

21.♘c3?!

21.♖he1 still offered a slight advantage.

21...♘c5 22.♘d5 ♘a6 23.♘c3   ½-½

This was a very professional game. Both gentlemen avoided bloodsheds at all stages of the game (a bit of criticism).

GAME 72
□ Vasily Ivanchuk
■ Alexander Budnikov
Moscow blitz 1993

1.d4 ♘f6 2.c4 e5 3.dxe5 ♘g4 4.e4 ♘xe5 5.f4 ♘ec6 6.♘f3 ♗c5 7.a3

The idea a2-a3 can be used at any time in the opening.

7...a5

The usual response. I like 7...d6!? more.

8.♘c3

8.♕d5?! d6! 9.f5 ♘e7?! (9...♘d7!∓) 10.♕d3∞ C. Alvarez-C. Rogers, Jakarta 1987.

8...d6

9.♕d3!?

9.h3 0-0∓ 10.♗d3 ♖e8 11.♘e2!? ♘d7 12.♕c2 f5! 13.exf5 ♘d4! 14.♘xd4 ♗xd4→ 15.♔f1 ♗b6 16.♗e4 ♘c5 17.♗d5+ ♔h8 18.♗d2 c6 19.♗f3 d5 20.cxd5 cxd5 21.g4 ♗d7 22.a4 ♖c8 23.♗c3 ♘e4 24.♖d1 ♕h4 25.♗xe4 ♕f2 mate, H. Hernandez-P. Garcia Castro, Padron 2004.

9...0-0 10.♗d2 ♗g4

10...♘d7!? 11.0-0-0 ♖e8⇄.

11.0-0-0 ♘d7 12.h3 ♗xf3 13.gxf3 ♘f6

13...♘d4!? 14.♔b1 ♘c5⇄.

14.♘d5 ♘xd5 15.cxd5 ♘e7 16.♔b1

16.f5!?.

16...c6! 17.dxc6 bxc6 18.f5 f6 19.♖h2 d5 20.♖g2 ♔h8 21.♗c1 ♖a7

21...♖b8.

22.♖c2 ♗b6 23.h4 ♖d7 24.h5 h6 25.f4 ♗c7 26.♗g2 ♕b8 27.exd5 cxd5 28.♗e3 ♗xf4 29.♗c5 ♗d6 30.♗d4 ♗e5 31.♗c5 d4!?T   0-1

31...♖b7!↑.

The legendary Austrian grandmaster Rudolf Spielmann (1883-1942) reached an extremely high level in his day. He went through all kinds of battle in chess, including some with the Budapest Gambit.

Summary of 6.a3?!

- This looks like an ambitious try to get something out of nothing.
- White does not have enough time to move with his pawns only; Black gets a good game without trouble.
- The study of the position after 6.a3 must start with the immediate attack 6...♗c5!? (see comments in Game 69, Alekhine-Gilg).

The last hope for white players might be 6.♘f3!?, the most natural, flexible and possibly most dangerous plan.

GAME 73
☐ **Frederick Yates**
■ **Rudolf Spielmann**
Karlsbad 1923 (10)

Spielmann's statistics in the Alekhine System (Chapter Two, 4.e4) are as follows. He played three games. In 1919 he won with white the original game with 4.e4 against Réti (Game 57), in 1922 he won a really tough battle against Euwe as Black (Game 53), but in 1923 he was crushed like a child by a strong English player who used a solid and natural plan with 6.♘f3!? which we might call the 'Yates Attack'.

1.d4 ♘f6 2.c4 e5 3.dxe5 ♘g4 4.e4 ♘xe5 5.f4 ♘ec6 6.♘f3!?

Obviously, developing the g1 knight is the most appropriate choice here.

6...♗c5 7.♘c3

Knights out first.

7...d6 8.♗d3 0-0!?

This could be the key position in the line with 6.♘f3. Up to now, both sides have made the most natural moves.

9.a3?!

It would be interesting to know what the real idea behind this 'discrete' move was. Later, Yates improved White's play with 9.♕e2!?, see the next game.

9...a5?!

The threat of b2-b4 is always scary, so perhaps this was a reflex. However, it is hard to believe that Black can suffer any kind of trouble in this situation. There are many more strong and creative replies: 9...♗g4!?; 9...f5!?; 9...♘d4!?.

10.♕e2 ♗g4 11.♗e3 ♘d4 12.♕f2

Another important moment in this line.

12...♗xf3?

The defensive point is to be found in the move 12...♘e6!.

13.♗xd4! ♗xd4 14.♕xd4↑

Now the white army, commanded by a talented English master, dominates.

14...♘c6 15.♕f2 ♗h5 16.0-0 f5 17.exf5 ♗g4

18.f6!

Very similar to another famous game (Game 52 Euwe-Mieses).

18...♕xf6 19.♘d5 ♕d8 20.♖ae1 ♘e5 21.♗xh7+! ♔xh7 22.♕g3 c6 23.fxe5 cxd5 24.♖xf8 ♕xf8 25.♕h4+ ♔g8 26.♕xg4 dxe5 27.♕e6+ ♕f7 28.♕xd5 ♖e8 29.♕xf7+ ♔xf7 30.♖e3 ♖c8 31.♖xe5 ♖xc4 32.♖b5 ♖c7 33.♔f2 ♔g6 34.♔f3

And old master Spielmann resigned before losing a second pawn.

I hope that this interesting classical game will help the reader understand more about the main mistakes and the moments when they are made.

In the next game we will analyse the best moves for both colours...

In the following blitz game, played on the Internet, we will analyse the line developed by master Yates more deeply.

GAME 74
□ Oleg Spirin
■ Viktor Moskalenko
Internet 2007

1.d4 ♘f6 2.c4 e5 3.dxe5 ♘g4 4.e4 ♘xe5 5.f4 ♘ec6 6.♘f3 ♗c5 7.♗d3

After 7.♘c3 d6 8.♗d3, the direct 8...♗g4 might be premature: 9.h3 ♗xf3 10.♕xf3 ♘d4?! (10...♕h4+ 11.g3 ♘d4∞) 11.♕g3 0-0 12.♗d2± I.Novikov-Moroz, Kherson 1989.

7...0-0 8.♘c3 d6

With a different order we have arrived at the main position (Yates-Spielmann, Game 73).

9.♕e2!

This seems to be the best option. White prepares ♗e3 and castling queenside. 9.♗d2?! ♘b4!? 10.♗b1 a5∓.

9...♗g4!?

A typical manoeuvre, with the threat of ...♘d4. The solid 9...♘d7!? is also interesting: 10.♗e3 ♗xe3 (10...♘b4!?; 10...♖e8) 11.♕xe3 f5 (11...♘c5!?) 12.0-0 Yates-Torres, Barcelona 1929; or 12.0-0-0!?, or 9...♘a6!?.

10.♗e3 ♘d4!?

With this new jump of the g8 knight, Black starts a counterattack with three pieces and queen. 10...♘a6!? 11.0-0-0 is unclear.

11.♕f2

11...♘e6!?

11...♗xf3!? 12.gxf3 ♘e6 (12...♘bc6 13.0-0-0!?↑) 13.f5 ♘f4 (13...♗xe3 14.♕xe3 ♕h4+ 15.♔f2 ♕xf2+ 16.♔xf2) 14.0-0 ♕g5 15.♘d5↑ Spirin-Moskalenko, playchess.com 2007; 11...♘xf3+ 12.gxf3 ♗xe3 13.♕xe3 ♕h4+ 14.♕f2 ♕xf2+ 15.♔xf2± Wood-Bakonyi, Budapest 1948.

12.g3

A position which is hard to evaluate arises after 12.f5!? ♗xe3 13.♕xe3 ♘c5 14.0-0-0 ♘bd7.

12...♘c6 13.h3

There is no danger in 13.0-0?! f5 (13...♖e8!?⇄) 14.exf5 ♗xf5 15.♗xf5 ♖xf5= Ager-Lochte, Bavaria 1999.

13...♗xf3

13...♗xe3 14.♕xe3 ♗xf3 15.♕xf3 ♘c5 (15...♘b4!?) 16.0-0-0± Spirin-Moskalenko, playchess.com 2007.

14.♕xf3

14...a6!? 15.0-0

15.0-0-0 b5!? (15...♘d4!?) 16.e5!? ♗xe3+ 17.♕xe3 ♘c5∞.

15...♘b4 16.♖ad1 ♘xd3 17.♖xd3 ♖e8 18.♔g2 ♗xe3 19.♖xe3 b5!?⇄

So far our treatment of this game. Summarizing the Yates Attack with 9.a3, Black has two options:

1) The dynamic option is a direct counterattack with three minor pieces and the queen, with 9...♗g4 and 10...♘d4;

2) Black can also follow a solid strategy, developing the rest of the army first, with 9...♘d7/a6.

In both cases the main positions of the Alekhine System (and the 6.♘f3 line) will eventually appear.

Sharper and more dangerous play for both sides occurs in the lines where White castles queenside.

Sixty years after the BG's birth in Berlin 1918, in the Chess Olympiad in Buenos Aires, we could observe an important game with the BG, this time in the Alekhine System with 6.♘f3:

GAME 75
□ **Rafael Vaganian**
■ **Tom Wedberg**
Buenos Aires ol 1978 (11)

1.d4 ♘f6 2.c4 e5 3.dxe5 ♘g4 4.e4 ♘xe5 5.f4 ♘ec6 6.♘f3

6...♗c5

This is Black's main response. Typical alternatives in the Alekhine System are:

A) 6...♘a6?! 7.a3!?±;

B) An interesting solution is 6...♗b4+!? 7.♗d2 (7.♘c3 ♗xc3+!?

8.bxc3 0-0 9.♗d3 ♘a6 10.0-0 ♘c5 11.♗e3 ♘xd3 12.♕xd3 d6 13.♘d4 ♖e8 14.♘xc6 bxc6 15.f5 f6 16.♖ae1 ♕e7 17.♗f4 ♗a6∓ Spirin-Moskalenko, playchess.com 2007) 7...♕e7!? 8.♗d3?! (8.♘c3!? ♗xc3 9.♗xc3 ♕xe4+ 10.♔f2 0-0∞) 8...♘a6?! (8...♕d6! with the possibilities of ...♕xd3 or ...♕xf4) 9.0-0 ♘c5 10.♗c2± I. Novikov-Bartsch, Neu Isenburg 1992.

7.♘c3

7.♘bd2?! d6 (7...♕e7!∓) 8.♘b3 ♗b6 (8...♘a6!?) 9.c5 (A. Kuzmin-Epishin, Tashkent 1987) 9...dxc5! 10.♕xd8+ ♘xd8=.

7...d6 8.♗d3 a5

An interesting alternative to 8...0-0. Although Black spends an important tempo, this move hampers White's play on the queenside and it will also be useful against possible queenside castling by White.

9.h3?

This is a waste of time. Better is 9.♕e2 ♗g4 (9...♘b4!?⇄) 10.♗e3 ♘d4 11.♕f2 ♘xf3+ (11...♘e6) 12.gxf3 ♗xe3 13.♕xe3 ♕h4+ 14.♔d2!? ♗e6 15.f5 ♗d7 16.♘d5 ♔d8 17.♖ag1+− S. Savchenko-A. Ivanov, Vienna 1991.

9...♘a6!

Now Black has solved all his opening problems.

10.♘d5

Once again Alekhine's optimistic move!

10...♗e6?!

10...0-0∓.

11.a3

This time this move is meant to defend the b4-square. 11.♗e3? ♗xd5 12.♗xc5 ♗xe4!∓.

11...0-0 12.f5 ♗xd5 13.cxd5 ♘e5

13...♘d4!?.

14.♘xe5

14.♗f4 ♕e7∓.

14...♕h4+!

This intermediate move delivers a heavy blow to Vaganian's position.

15.♔d2 dxe5 16.♔c2 ♗d4 17.♖f1

Better was 17.♕g4.

17...c6! 18.d6 ♘c5 19.f6 ♖fd8! 20.fxg7 ♖xd6 21.♕f3 ♖d7

21...♔xg7!? 22.♕xf7+ ♔h8∓.

22.g3 ♕e7

22...♕xh3? 23.♗c4→.

23.♗c4

23...♘xe4! 24.♗d3

24.♕xe4 ♕c5−+.

24...♘g5?!

24...♘d6? 25.♗xh7+!; 24...♘f6! 25.♕xf6 ♕xf6 26.♖xf6 e4−+.

25.♗xg5 ♕xg5 26.h4? ♕xg7−+ 27.♖ae1 ♔h8 28.♖e4 ♖g8 29.♕f5 ♖d6?!

29...f6!?.

**30.♕xf7 ♕xf7 31.♖xf7 ♖g7? **

31...♖xg3∓.

32.♖f8+ ♖g8 33.♖f7 ½-½

GAME 76

□ **Etienne Bacrot**

■ **Alexei Shirov**

Sarajevo 2000 (11)

1.d4 ♘f6 2.c4 e5 3.dxe5 ♘g4 4.e4 ♘xe5 5.f4 ♘ec6 6.♘f3 ♗c5 7.♘c3

7...0-0!?

Getting ready for tactical operations. In another well-known game, Black successfully exerted tactical and strategic pressure against the premature advance f4-f5: 7...d6! 8.f5 ♘d7! 9.♗g5 f6 10.♗f4 ♗b4!? (10...a5!?) 11.♕c2 ♘c5 12.0-0-0 ♗xc3! 13.♕xc3 a5 14.♗d3 b6 15.♗b1 ♕e7 16.♖he1 ♕f7 17.♘d4 ♘xd4 (17...♘e5!?) 18.♖xd4 ♗b7 19.b3 0-0-0!.

analysis diagram

Black is doing very well!

20.♗c2 ♘d7 21.♖ed1 ♕e7 22.a3 ♘e5 23.♔b2 ♗c6 24.b4 axb4 25.axb4 ♔b7 26.b5 ♗d7 27.♗b3 ♖a8 28.♕b4?! ♗e8 29.♕d2 ♗f7 30.♕b4 ♖a5 31.♖a1 ♖xa1 32.♔xa1 ♖a8+ 33.♔b2 ♔c8 34.h3 ♘d7 35.♗c2 ♘c5 36.♖d1 d5! 37.♔b1 dxc4 38.♖e1 ♖a1+!! 0-1 Cuartas-O'Kelly de Galway, Havana Olympiad 1966.

8.f5

The initial idea of this move is to gain time with ♗g5. In exchange, the pawn structure e4-f4 loses its dynamism.

8...d6 9.♗g5 f6

Fixing the centre.

10.♗f4 ♖e8

O'Kelly's idea is interesting here: 10...♗b4! and with the exchange ♗x♘, the e4-pawn is weakened: Black continues with ...♗xc3, ...♖e8 and ...♘a6-c5.

11.♕d5+ ♔h8 12.0-0-0 ♘d7 13.h4

With a very sharp game. Alternatives are 13.♕f7!? or 13.g4∞ (Shirov).

13...♘ce5

13...♗b4!?.

14.h5

14.♕d2!?∞.

14...h6 15.♕d2

Threatening 16.♗xh6!.

15...♘f7 16.♗d3

16...♗b4!?

The 'O'Kelly idea' is effectuated at last.

17.♗c2

17.♕c2 c6 (17...♗xc3 18.♕xc3) 18.a3 ♗a5∞.

17...♘c5 18.♕d5?!

18.♖he1 ♗d7 with mutual chances.

18...♔g8!

The king re-enters the game.

19.♘e2?

This lapsus by Bacrot allows Shirov to ignite his 'fire on board'... 19.♗d2□ ♗d7.

19...c6! 20.♕d4 ♗xf5!

20...♕a5!? 21.a3 ♗xa3! 22.bxa3 ♖xe4! 23.♗xe4 ♘b3+∓.

21.exf5 ♖xe2 22.♘g1?!

The white knights did not find good employment in this game.

22...♖xg2 23.a3

23...♕d7!

Preparing the decisive blow.

24.axb4 ♖xc2+!-+ 25.♔xc2 ♕xf5+ 26.♔c3 ♘e6 27.♕e3 ♘xf4 28.♘f3

The knight re-enters the game, in vain.

28...a5 29.♖a1 axb4+ 30.♔xb4 ♖d8 31.♖hf1 ♕c2! 32.♕c3 c5+ 0-1

33.♔b5 ♕e4 34.♔a4 b5+!-+.

A very good game by Shirov, who developed Black's attack with great energy. Summarizing the idea of 8.f5: following concepts not 'recipes', White is not ready for this kind of activity in the opening. The f4-f5 attack is premature.

Summary of 6.♘f3

● White plays solidly again, bringing his knights out first. White's aim is to complete his development and hold on to his space advantage.

● White must be very careful in lines where he chooses queenside castling.

● Black's direct counterattacks (...♕e7, ...♕h4+) are now impossible.

● Black must analyse carefully all moves and ideas in the key Game 74 (Spirin-Moskalenko). Unfortunately, we still lack the necessary practical material for a proper evaluation of the important positions of this line.

● An interesting solution is 6....♗b4+ (see comments in Game 75).

The last game in Chapter Two does not include White's hasty 5.f4, but it does contain the best plans for Black:

GAME 77
□ **Sonja Graf**
■ **Francisco Benko**
Buenos Aires 1939

1.d4 ♘f6 2.c4 e5 3.dxe5 ♘g4 4.e4 ♘xe5

5.♗e3

We know that the main move is 5.f4. However, we must also understand how to react to other moves:

A) 5.♗e2 ♗b4+ (5...♗c5!?) 6.♗d2 ♗xd2+ 7.♕xd2 d6 8.♘f3 ♗e6 9.♘c3 0-0 ⇌ Singer-G. Mohr, Graz 1994;

B) 5.♘f3 ♘bc6 6.♗e2 ♗c5 (6...♘xf3+∓) 7.0-0 d6 8.♘c3 0-0 9.♘d5 f5 10.exf5 ♗xf5 11.♗e3 ♗xe3 12.♘xe3 ♗d7 13.♕c2 ♘xf3+ 14.♗xf3 ♖xf3 15.gxf3 ♗h3 16.♕d3 ♗xf1 17.♔xf1 ♕f8 (17...♕h4! 18.♔g2 ♖f8–+) 18.♔g2 ♖e8∓ J. Gonzalez-A. Moreno, Las Palmas 1989.

5...♘a6!?

We must keep in mind that this universal manoeuvre always helps Black in the Alekhine System. Black intends ...♗c5. But in this position, the direct attack 5...♗b4+! looks stronger, for example: 6.♘c3 (6.♘d2 ♕h4!?⇄) 6...d6 and now, if 7.f4? ♘g4 and Black takes over.

6.♘c3 ♗b4

One of the key aspects in the 4.e4 system is understanding what is the best square for the f8 bishop: b4 or c5.

6...♗c5!? is an alternative here.

7.f4!

Ultimately, this advance is unavoidable. White has nothing better.

7...♘c6

We have arrived at a common position in the line with ...♘ec6.

7...♘g6!? or first 7...♗xc3+! are not bad either.

8.♘f3 ♕e7 9.♗d3 ♗xc3+! 10.bxc3 b6!?

The right plan in itself, but the best option was to activate the knight first: 10...♘c5 11.0-0 b6!?.

11.0-0 ♗b7 12.e5!? 0-0-0

Better was 12...♘c5! 13.♘d4 0-0-0.

13.♖e1

13.♗e4!? f6 14.a4∞.

13...♘c5 14.♗f1 f6

After completing his development by castling queenside, Black has the better perspectives.

15.♗f2 ♕f8 16.♖b1 ♘e6

16...fxe5!?.

17.g3?!

This allows a classical attack on the light squares.

17...g5!

17...fxe5!?.

18.f5 ♘g7 19.g4 h5!-+ 20.exf6 ♕xf6 21.♗d4 ♘xd4 22.♕xd4 ♕h6 23.♘e5 hxg4

With lots of mating threats on the kingside.

24.♕f2

24...g3! 25.♕xg3 ♘xf5 26.♕f2 ♘h4

26...g4!?.

27.♗e2 ♖df8 28.♕g3 ♘f5 29.♕f2 ♘d6 30.♘g4 ♖xf2   **0-1**

Statistics for 5...♘ec6

This is the most popular move for Black: a total of 414 games.

White wins:	200 games	= 48%
Black wins:	128 games	= 31%
Draw:	61 games	

Performance White: 2203, Black: 2092.

Summary of 5...♘ec6

- In all positions in this line both sides struggle fiercely for the initiative.
- The most tense and subtle games occur with the 'Yates Attack' with 6.♘f3.

General Conclusions on 4.e4

Thanks to Alexander Alekhine's victories, always with his incredible attacking style, the advance 4.e4 will always be a dangerous weapon against the BG.

But theory and practice follow different paths. In the thematic BG tournament in the Hungarian capital, White's main triumphs were gained with the move 4.e4!, but what was the overall result? 21,5:14,5 for Black! It would be interesting to repeat such a tournament in our day.

The strongest supporter of the 4.e4-line, Hans Kmoch, summarized: 'This variation, aimed at a quick attack, is very risky. If White is not ready to play in such sharp style, he has to choose a calmer continuation'. Our study confirms this opinion.

Next, 4.♘f3 (Chapter Three) and 4.♗f4 (Chapter One) were explored. A new generation of BG players arrived.

Chapter Three

Classical Style

1.d4 ♘f6 2.c4 e5 3.dxe5 ♘g4 4.♘f3

Dedicated to players of the new generation

Introduction

Chapter Three marks the beginning of a new era. Here we will check out modern games in a neo-classical style, emphasizing the main ideas for black players, who are already starting to attack. White discards Rubinstein's 4.♗f4 (see Chapter One) in favour of the natural knight move 4.♘f3. Development is easy here, but this line is also full of surprising moves, fascinating attacks on the enemy king and much more.

A Bit of History

In the 1930s, radical changes rule chess (as they do the world). In a brief period of time the players of the classical era almost disappear; the FIDE designs new formulas for championships; in the Eastern European countries the Soviet School is created; dogmatic chess is gone forever and a new pragmatic style appears with the systems of the patriarch Mikhail Moiseyevich Botvinnik. A new generation of strong and well-prepared chess players arrives.

Mikhail Botvinnik, the patriarch of pragmatic play: 'Chess is the art of analysis.'

'Chess is the art of analysis.' Mikhail Botvinnik, Soviet GM and World Champion.
'Chess is imagination.' David Bronstein, Soviet GM.
'Wenn Ihr's nicht fühlt, Ihr werdet's nicht erjagen.' ('If you do not feel it, you will never make it.') Johann Wolfgang Goethe; Faust.

Strategies of 4.♘f3

In the previous chapter we have studied a sharp attack by the white pawns, stopped (or softened) by adequate peregrinations or jumps by the black knights. Now, the brave Budapest Gambit player will have to deal with a new style, to discover new plans and to get to know well the abilities and manoeuvring possibilities of his pieces.

With this classic move 4.♘f3, White simultaneously protects his extra pawn on e5 and continues his development. Renouncing any attempt to refute the gambit directly, White is counting on the accumulation of small positional advantages – in particular, on the control of the d5-square.

Directions

Black now has two important continuations at his disposal:

A) 4...♘c6 and White does not play ♗f4 (Part I, Beyond Rubinstein);

B) 4...♗c5 5.e3 ♘c6, recovering the pawn (Part II, The Maroczy Attack).

> **Keep in Mind!**
> ⚠ **The bifurcation of reality: 'You must always be able to choose one of two possible alternatives.' – Talleyrand.**

Part I – Beyond Rubinstein

$$1.d4\ \text{♘}f6\ 2.c4\ e5\ 3.dxe5\ \text{♘}g4\ 4.\text{♘}f3\ \text{♘}c6$$

One possibility for Black to solve the problem posed by 4.♘f3 is the reply 4...♘c6!?, proposing to return to the Rubinstein Variation with 5.♗f4 (Chapter One). If White now desires to stick to the Knight System he must look for different continuations.

Black's main idea in Part I is developing the f8 bishop to any square but ...♗c5.

Directions
White can evade the Rubinstein Variation by 5.♗g5 (Game 78 Polugaevsky-Nunn), 5.♘c3 (see the notes to Game 78) and 5.e3 (Game 3 Khurtsidze-Gvetadze). Generally these lines follow a quieter, more classic scheme in which Black does not have much to fear theoretically.

Beyond Rubinstein – Games

GAME 78
□ **Lev Polugaevsky**
■ **John Nunn**
Biel 1986 (6)

1.d4 ♘f6 2.c4 e5 3.dxe5 ♘g4 4.♘f3 ♘c6!?

Continuing the attack on the e5 pawn.

5.♗g5!?

This manoeuvre with the Rubinstein bishop leads to simplification. Another possibility is 5.♘c3 ♘gxe5 (Black can always play 5...♗c5!) 6.♘xe5 (6.e3 ♗b4!?) 6...♘xe5 7.♕d4!? (7.e3 g6!? and ...♗g7) 7...d6 8.c5?! (8.♗f4 ♗e7!? 9.♗xe5 dxe5 10.♕xe5 0-0♛) 8...♗e7 (8...♘c6!) 9.cxd6 ♕xd6 10.♕xd6 ♗xd6= Ljubojevic-Budnikov, Moscow rapid 1993.

For 5.♕d5 see Chapter Four on rare 4th move continuations by White.

5...♗e7 6.♗xe7 ♕xe7 7.♘c3

The only chance for White in this line is to take profit of the d5 outpost with ♘d5.

7...0-0!

Giving priority to his development. A worse option is 7...♘cxe5?! 8.♘d5 (8.♕d4!?) 8...c5!? (8...♕d6 9.♕d4↑) 9.e3! (9.♘xe5?! ♕xf2+

10.♔d2 ♘xe5 11.♘xc7+ ♔d8 12.♘xa8 ♘xc4+ 13.♔c3 ♖e8→) 9...♘xf3+ 10.♕xf3 (10.gxf3!? ♘f6 11.♘xf6+ gxf6± Moskalenko-Biro, Balatonbereny 1994) 10...d6 11.♕e4+ ♗e6 12.♗e2 (12.b4!? ♕c6 13.♗e2 ♘e5 14.♕d4↑) 12...♘e5 13.f4 f5 14.♕d4 ♗xd5 15.♕xc5 dxc5 16.cxd5 ♘d7 17.g4 0-0-0 18.gxf5 ♖he8 19.♔f2 ♘f6 20.♗f3 ♘xd5 with mutual chances in Farago-Mestrovic, Bibinje 2006; or 7...♘gxe5?! 8.♘d5 ♕d8 9.♘xe5 ♘xe5 10.♕d4 with the initiative.

8.♘d5 ♕d8 9.e3 ♘gxe5 10.♘xe5 ♘xe5 11.♗e2 d6

What was Polugaevsky expecting in this balanced position? He was probably waiting for his opponent's mistakes – and they duly came.

12.0-0 c6

12...♘d7!? 13.♕d4 ♖e8 followed by ...♘c5 and ...a7-a5 is equal.

13.♘c3 ♗e6 14.b3 ♕a5?! 15.♕d2

15.♕d4!?.

15...♖ad8

16.f4

As we will soon see, this advance is an important middlegame resource for White in the Knight System.

16...♗g4

16...♘g4!?.

17.♗d1 ♗xd1 18.♖axd1 ♘g4 19.h3 ♘h6!?

19...♘f6 20.♘d5!? ♕xd2 21.♘xf6+ gxf6 22.♖xd2±.

20.e4 f5! 21.♖fe1 ♖fe8 22.♔h2 fxe4?!

22...a6!?.

23.♖xe4 ♖xe4 24.♘xe4 ♕h5

24...♕xd2 25.♖xd2 ♘f7 26.g4 ♔f8 27.♔g3±.

25.♘g5 ♘f7 26.♘f3 d5

26...♕f5 27.♖e1 d5 28.♘d4↑; 26...♖e8 27.♖e1±.

27.♕e3 ♕f5

27...dxc4 28.♖xd8+ ♘xd8 29.♕e7+−.

28.cxd5 cxd5 29.g4 ♕c2+

29...♕f6? 30.♖xd5!; 29...♕c8!?.

30.♖d2 ♕c7? 31.♖xd5!+− ♖f8 32.♔g3 ♘d8 33.♕e5 ♕c8 34.♕e7 ♕c1 35.♖f5 ♘f7 36.♕xb7 g6 37.♖f6 ♕b2 38.♕e7 ♕xa2 39.♕e6 ♕a1 40.h4 ♔g7 41.g5 a5 42.f5 gxf5 43.h5 ♕c3 44.♖xf5 ♕c7+ 45.♔h3 ♕c3 46.h6+ ♔g8 47.g6 hxg6 48.♕xg6+ ♔h8 49.♖xf7 **1-0**

A victory in neo-classical style by Polugaevsky. In the modern chess that we play nowadays, it is called a 'defensive style'. The main idea is to wait for the opportunity to punish the opponent's mistakes, increasing the positional advantage little by little. The followers of this style tend to be quite ambitious, but they prefer to safeguard their position from the very first move, no matter the colour of their pieces and no matter the position. They defend everything and they do not get tired of it until move 100! These days, this technique has grown quite popular, and it allows its followers to suffer better than other players the long duration of tournaments without wasting too much energy. It also guarantees satisfactory results, as their opponents are preparing long theoretical lines at home or intensively searching for attacks during the game, so that they get tired or bored in the end and lose due to lack of concentration.

Summary of 4...♘c6 5.♗g5: After the opening the position is balanced, but Black is slightly passive and he does not get good counterplay.

More usual after 4...♘c6 is the reply 5.e3. In the next game we will analyse typical examples of this extremely levelling line. It shows that modern analysis can find improvements in relatively old games that have not been deeply explored.

GAME 79
□ **Nino Khurtsidze**
■ **Sopio Gvetadze**
Tbilisi ch-GEO 2007 (11)

1.d4 ♘f6 2.c4 e5 3.dxe5 ♘g4 4.♘f3 ♘c6 5.e3

White rejects the transposition to the Rubinstein Variation with 5.♗f4.

5.♘c3 ♘gxe5 6.e3 ♗b4?! 7.♗d2 0-0 8.a3 ♗xc3?! 9.♗xc3± occurred in Thomas- Réti, Baden-Baden 1925.

5...♘gxe5

Or, for example, 5...♗b4+!? 6.♗d2, but not 6...♕e7? (≥ 6...♗xd2+ 7.♕xd2 0-0=) 7.♘c3! ♗xc3 8.♗xc3 ♘gxe5 9.♘xe5 ♘xe5 10.♕d4↑ Alekhine-Schenker, Zürich simul 1932.

6.♗e2

Or 6.♘xe5 ♘xe5 7.♗e2 ♗b4+!? 8.♘d2 ♕h4 (8...0-0!? 9.a3 ♗e7=) 9.0-0 0-0 10.♘b3 ♖e8 11.♘d4 ♘c6 12.♘f5 ♕f6∓ Knaak-Adamski, Sandomierz 1976.

An interesting French game continued 6.♘bd2 d5 (6...♕f6!?) 7.b3? ♕f6!? 8.♖b1 ♗f5 9.e4? dxe4 10.♘xe5 ♕xe5 11.♗b2 ♕a5 12.♖a1 0-0-0 13.♕c1 ♗b4 14.♗e2 ♗xd2+ 0-1 Le Fol (1540)-Le Pen (1330), Sautron 2006.

6...♗b4+

Another well-known idea is the fianchetto 6...g6 7.♘c3 ♘xf3+ (7...♗g7!?) 8.♗xf3 ♗g7 9.♕d2 d6 10.b3 ♘e5 11.♗b2 ♘xf3+ (11...0-0!?) 12.gxf3 0-0 13.0-0-0 (13.h4!?) 13...♗h3 14.♖hg1 ♗e6 15.♘e4 and White had an edge in Sosonko-Ree, Amsterdam 1982.

7.♗d2 ♗xd2+ 8.♕xd2 0-0

Another option was 8...♘xf3+ 9.♗xf3 ♘e5 10.♗e2 (10.♕d4!?) 10...d6 11.0-0 0-0 12.♘c3 ♗e6 13.b3 f5 14.f4± Sosonko-Hodgson, Wijk aan Zee 1986.

9.♘c3 d6 10.0-0 ♗g4!? 11.♘xe5 ♘xe5 12.♗xg4 ♘xg4 13.h3 ♘f6

13...♘e5 14.♕d4 ♖e8=.

14.♖fd1 a5 15.♘d5 ♘e4 ½-½

After natural development by both sides and due to the sparse opportunities available, the game ends before it has even begun.

It is clear that White has no advantage, although he still controls the centre. The d5-square is still available for White's knight or queen. In case of ...c6, the black pawn on d6 will be weak.

Summary of 4...♘c6

- In most continuations White has no significant advantage, but he has no problems either, due to the lack of weaknesses in his territory.
- If Black needs a draw, he can choose this variation with confidence.
- If Black is going for the win or if he simply desires a really tough game, welcome to Part II...

Part II – The Maroczy Attack

Maroczy's Bishop and Drimer's Rook
1.d4 ♘f6 2.c4 e5 3.dxe5 ♘g4 4.♘f3 ♗c5

Introduction

Black wins a tempo with this bishop development. The direct attack on f2 forces White to lock in his own Rubinstein bishop.

White loses his central domination, but square d5 is still available for his knight or queen.

Directions

The key dilemma for Black in this variation is his bishop on c5.

White has two main plans: b3-♗b2 and/or f2-f4.

After 5.e3, the black bishop's position is unsatisfactory. Meanwhile, White's bishop on c1 can be activated along the a1-h8 diagonal (b3-♗b2).

Another important resource for White is the possibility of developing a dangerous attack with the f-pawn (f2-f4-f5-f6) – the 'Smyslov/Spassky Attack'.

In order to avoid the Smyslov Attack with 8.f4, the best option is to continue with 6...0-0 instead of recapturing the pawn immediately with 6...♘xe5?!.

A counterplan for Black is the amazing 'Crazy Rook Plan', introduced by IM Dolfi Drimer in 1968. Black continues with ...a7-a5 and ...♖a6-d6-e6-g6 or h6! In many lines White must defend his fortress with great care.

The most creative player has the best chance to win, but you also need a good conceptual basis. The winner will be the player that understands best what he is doing.

⚠ **Keep in Mind!**
The best move order for Black is based on recovering the pawn only after White has played 6/7.♗e2, for example: 6.♘c3 0-0! and if 7.♗e2 ♖e8!? 8.0-0 ♘xe5!

The Maroczy Attack – Games

GAME 80
□ **Mor Adler**
■ **Geza Maroczy**
Budapest 1896

Geza Maroczy (1870-1951), the legendary Hungarian player who invented the Budapest Gambit at the end of the nineteenth century.

The stem game of the fabulous Budapest Gambit. Adler replied with the pseudo-active 6.♕d5?!.

1.d4 ♘f6 2.c4 e5 3.dxe5 ♘g4

The initial position of the Budapest Gambit. White has enough moves to defend the pawn on e5: ♘f3, ♗f4 or ♕d4/♕d5, but the move order is very important. Classic rules command us to develop the knight first, so...

4.♘f3 ♗c5!

The attack on f2 forces White to remain passive.

5.e3□

Now the Rubinstein bishop on c1 cannot reach f4 to protect the extra pawn. Not 5.♘d4?? ♘xf2!.

5...♘c6!

Black continues his attack on e5, combining it with simple development.

6.♕d5?!

In most cases, defending the e5 pawn with the queen is not successful (see Chapter Four). This idea only prevails in the Rubinstein Variation with 4.♗f4 and 6.♘c3. It does not work at a later stage either: 6.♘c3 0-0 7.a3 a5 (7...♖e8!? 8.b4 ♗f8; 7...♘gxe5!?) 8.♕d5 ♕e7 (8...d6!? 9.exd6 ♗xd6) 9.♘b5 d6 10.exd6 cxd6 11.♘c3 ♗e6 12.♕d1 ♘ce5 13.♘d5 ♗xd5 14.♕xd5 ♘xf2 15.♔xf2 ♘g4+ 16.♔e1 ♗xe3 17.♗e2 ♖fe8 18.♗xe3 (18.♕d3 ♖ac8 19.b3 ♗xc1 20.♖xc1 ♘e3 21.♔d2 ♘xg2 22.♘g1 d5–+) 18...♕xe3 19.♕d2 ♕f2+ 20.♔d1 ♖xe2?! (20...d5→)

21.♕xe2 ♘e3+ 22.♔d2 ♘xc4+ ½-½ Goldin-S. Ivanov, Leningrad 1989.

6...♕e7

7.♘c3

7.a3!? a5 8.b3?! ♘cxe5 9.♗b2 c6 (9...♘xf2!?) 10.♕e4 d6 11.♘bd2? f5 12.♕c2 ♘xf2! 13.♔xf2 ♘g4+ 14.♔g3 ♗xe3 15.♘e1 ♗f2+ 16.♔f3 (0-1 Horstmann-Saglam, Neuwied 1993) 16...♕e3 mate.

7...♘gxe5 8.♗e2 d6 9.♘e4?

White keeps pursuing a bad plan and now the game will soon be over.

9...♗e6

9...♘b4!? 10.♕d2 ♗f5↑.

10.♕d1 ♗b4+ 11.♗d2 0-0-0 12.♗xb4 ♘xb4 13.♕b3 ♘xf3+ 14.♗xf3 d5! 15.♘d2 dxc4 16.♘xc4 ♖d3 17.♕a4 ♗xc4 18.♕xa7 ♘c2+   0-1

It's mate next move.

Games 81-85: Drimer's Rook

The next subject is the natural white development plan with b3-♗b2 or a3, countered by an idea that IM Dolfi Drimer introduced in 1968/69.

Drimer's Rook comes into play after 6.♘c3! 0-0! 7.♗e2 ♖e8! 8.0-0 ♘xe5 9.♘xe5 ♘xe5 10.b3 a5!? 11.♗b2 ♖a6!.

With great chances of a successful attack!

The next five games are good examples of sharp and strategic lines with 12.♘e4/♘a4/♕d5, attacking the

Maroczy bishop, and Black's alternatives ...♗a7/♗f8, as well as the 'neutral' move 12.♘d5.

GAME 81
□ Lembit Oll
■ Alfonso Romero Holmes
Groningen Ech-jr 1984 (4)

This important black victory made the plan ...a5 and ...♖a8-a6 very popular.

1.d4 ♘f6 2.c4 e5 3.dxe5 ♘g4 4.♘f3 ♗c5 5.e3 ♘c6 6.♘c3 ♘gxe5

Important notes:

1) The best move order for Black is first 6...0-0! in order to avoid the immediate f2-f4, as in 6...♘gxe5?! 7.♘xe5 ♘xe5 8.f4!, which transposes to the Smyslov Attack, where White wins a tempo continuing with 9.♗d3! – see Game 89.

2) An even more suspicious line is taking the e5 pawn with the c-knight 6...♘cxe5?! on account of 7.h3! ♘xf3+ 8.♕xf3 with the idea 8...♘e5 9.♕g3!.

7.♘xe5 ♘xe5 8.♗e2 0-0 9.0-0 ♖e8

This is the main tabiya of the Maroczy Variation.

10.b3

With the idea to complete his development and to activate the Rubinstein bishop on the a1-h8 diagonal.

10...a5!?

Preparing an ambitious counterplan. The most natural response would be 10...d6!?, a move we will investigate in Games 94 and 95.

11.♗b2

This seems like a natural move. Alternatives are 11.♘e4 (Game 86) and 11.♘a4 (Game 87).

11...♖a6!?

12.♘e4

One of the key moments in this line. When the c5 bishop is under attack, Black can choose between two paths.

12...♗a7!

This is the most aggressive retreat. Black avoids f2-f4 and threatens to start a straight attack with ...♖h6 and ...♕h4. The other option 12...♗f8 may be safer because the bishop protects g7. But after leaving the a7-g1 diagonal the bishop cannot take part in the attack: 13.♘g3 (13.f4!? ♘g4 (Antoshin-Drimer, Havana 1968) 14.♗xg4 ♖xe4 15.♗e5!?∞) 13...♖ae6 14.♕d5 b6! 15.♖ad1 (15.f4? ♖d6! 16.♕b5 c6 17.♕a4 ♘d3 18.♗a3 ♘b4∓) 15...d6 16.♖fe1 ♗d7 17.♕d2 ♖h6! 18.f4?! ♘g4 19.♘f1 ♘f6 20.♗f3 ♘e4 21.♕d5 ♕e7?! (21...c6! 22.♕d4 f5∓) 22.♘g3 ♘xg3 23.hxg3 ½-½ Bischoff-Hort, Dortmund 1989.

13.♕d5!?

There is no time for typical advances like 13.c5?! ♖h6! 14.♕d4 ♕h4 15.f4? (15.h3 d6→) 15...♕xh2+ 16.♔f2 ♖g6 17.♘g5 ♕h4+ 18.♔g1 d6!−+ Klinger-Lendwai, Vienna 1991; or 13.f4? ♗xe3+ 14.♔h1 ♖h6, threatening ...♖xh2+! ♔xh2 ♕h4+.

13...♖ae6

The modern idea is 13...♖h6!, see the next game.

14.♕xa5!?

At least White gets a new extra pawn in the BG. If 14.c5 c6 (14...♕h4! and ...c6-♗b8-♖h6→; 14...♕e7?! 15.♖ac1 ♗b8 16.♖fd1 ♖h6 17.g3 c6 18.♕d4 ♕e6 19.h4± Remlinger-Svidler, Gausdal 1991) 15.♕d2 d5 16.cxd6?! (16.♘d6!?) 16...♕h4?! (16...♖h6!⇄) 17.♗xe5 ♖xe5 18.d7 ♗xd7 19.♕xd7 ♖5e7 20.♕d2 ♖xe4 21.♕xa5 ♗b8 22.g3 ♕h3 23.♕h5± M. Gurevich-Kortchnoi, Madrid 1988.

14...♗b6 15.♕c3 ♕h4 16.f4 ♖h6!

Drimer's Rook has become a Crazy Rook. 16...d5!?.

17.h3 d5!?

17...♖g6 18.c5 d5 19.♘g5 ♗a7.

18.cxd5??

This is the losing move. The only chance was 18.c5! with complex tactical play. For example: 18...dxe4!? (or 18...♖g6 19.♘g5 ♗a7 20.♖ad1 c6⇄; 18...♗xh3 19.♕e1) 19.fxe5 ♖g6 20.♖f2 ♗a7 and the situation is highly unclear.

18...♗xh3!

Blasting open the kingside.

19.gxh3 ♕xh3 20.♔f2 ♕h4+ 21.♘g3 ♕h2+

Even stronger was 21...♖g6! 22.♖g1 ♕xf4+! 23.♔e1 ♗xe3−+.

22.♔e1 ♕xg3+ 23.♔d1 ♘d7 24.♖f3 ♕g2 25.♖f2 ♕xd5+ 26.♔c2 ♖c6 27.♗c4 ♕e4+ 28.♔d1 ♘f6 29.♖e2 ♖d6+ 30.♖d2 ♖ed8 **0-1**

A good example of the great potential of the plan with ...a7-a5 and ...♖a8-a6, with the Drimer Rook marching along the sixth rank.

Now for the improvement 13...♖h6!?.

GAME 82

□ **Tomi Nybäck**

■ **Shakhriyar Mamedyarov**

Antalya Ech 2004 (12)

1.d4 ♘f6 2.c4 e5 3.dxe5 ♘g4 4.♘f3 ♗c5 5.e3 ♘c6 6.♗e2 0-0 7.0-0 ♘gxe5 8.♘xe5 ♘xe5 9.♘c3 a5 10.b3 ♖e8 11.♗b2 ♖a6 12.♘e4 ♗a7 13.♕d5 ♖h6!?

Black temporarily sacrifices his knight. This is an improvement on 13...♖e6, implemented by master Gusev in 1989.

14.♗xe5

Seems forced. Otherwise, Black develops his initiative easily:

A) 14.g3? c6 15.♕d1 ♘xc4! 16.♘f6+ gxf6 17.bxc4 d5 18.cxd5 ♕d7! 19.h4 ♕h3! 20.♗d4 ♖xe3! 21.♗xe3 ♗xe3 22.h5 ♕xg3+ 23.♔h1 ♕h3+ 24.♔g1 ♗f4 0-1 Lembak-Kantorik, Slovakia 1995;

B) 14.c5? c6 (14...d6!?) 15.♕d4 d5 16.♘g3 b6 17.cxb6 ♗xb6 18.♕c3 ♕h4−+ 19.h3 ♗xh3 20.gxh3 ♕xh3 21.♖fc1 ♕h2+ 22.♔f1 ♖f6 0-1 Eslon-Porper, Benasque 1992;

C) 14.♕xa5? ♗b6 15.♕b5 c6 16.♕b4 ♗a5 (16...d5!?) 17.♕a4 ♕h4 18.h3 ♕xe4 19.♕xa5 ♖g6→.

14...c6 15.♗f6

Again the only move. Worse is 15.♕d3? ♖xe5 16.♘d2 d5! 17.♘f3 ♖eh5 18.♖fd1 ♗f5 19.♕c3 ♗b8 20.g3 ♗e4 21.cxd5 ♖xh2! 22.♘xh2 ♖xh2 23.f4 ♖xe2? (Black wins with 23...♖g2+! 24.♔f1 ♖xg3 25.♕d4 ♗g2+ 26.♔e1 c5 27.♕xc5 ♗d6−+) 24.dxc6⇄ Polovodin-Chigvintsev, Moscow 1999.

15...gxf6 16.♕d3

If 16.♕f5 ♗b8!? 17.♘g3 ♗e5 18.♖ad1 d6 19.♕f3 f5↑.

16...d5

With this move Shakhriyar Mamedyarov opts for play in the centre, manipulating his d- and f- pawns. However, I prefer the straight attack with the other pawn by 16...f5!, as happened in the stem game of this original line: 17.♘d2? (17.♘g3 f4! 18.♘f5 ♖f6 19.♘d6 fxe3! 20.♘xe8 exf2+ 21.♔h1 ♕xe8↑; 17.♘d6?? ♕c7!–+) 17...f4! 18.exf4 ♕h4 19.♘f3 ♕xf4∓ and Black has the initiative, Legky-Gusev, Leningrad 1989.

Another interesting option could be 16...♗b8!?, planning to meet 17.♘d6 with 17...f5! 18.♘xf5 ♗xh2+ 19.♔h1 ♖ee6 with chances of developing a successful attack.

17.♘g3 ♖e5

With very dynamic play.

18.♖ad1

18.♖fd1 f5! 19.♘f1?! ♕f6 with an edge for Black, Ambartsumian-Kretchetov, Costa Mesa 2003.

18...f5 19.cxd5 cxd5 20.♕c3 ♖e8 21.h3 d4! 22.♕d3 ♕g5

22...♕e7!?.

23.♕b5 ♕e7 24.♘xf5 ♗xf5 25.♕xf5 dxe3 26.♔h1?! exf2 27.♗c4 ♕f6 28.♕xf6 ♖xf6∓

And the game ended in a draw on move 82.

Summary of 13...♖h6: This rook manoeuvre is certainly stronger than Romero's less aggressive 13...♖e6. After 15.♗f6 gxf6 the black pawn structure is not perfect, but it is very dynamic. A more interesting option is 16...f5! with the idea ...f5-f4, but 16...d5!? and ...d5-d4 is not bad either. Black keeps the initiative during the complex middlegame thanks to his very active pieces: both bishops, the queen, the rook on e8, but especially the powerful Drimer Rook on h6!

GAME 83

□ Zsuzsa Polgar
■ Jesus Maria De la Villa Garcia
New York Open 1989 (7)

1.d4 ♘f6 2.c4 e5 3.dxe5 ♘g4 4.♘f3 ♗c5 5.e3 ♘c6 6.♘c3 0-0 7.♗e2 ♘cxe5 8.b3 ♖e8 9.0-0 a5 10.♘xe5 ♘xe5 11.♗b2 ♖a6 12.♘a4 ♗f8!?

The gin returns to the bottle. Since the bishop is a fast-moving piece, it decides to remain behind its army for now. Undoubtedly, a more aggressive option is 12...♗a7!? with the idea 13.c5 ♖g6!? (13...♖h6 14.♕d4!?) 14.f4 ♘c6 15.♗d3 (15.f5!? ♖h6 16.f6 gxf6⇄) 15...♖h6 16.♕d2 ♕h4 17.g3 ♕h5 18.♖f2 d6 Neyhort-Mukabi, Thessaloniki Olympiad 1988. Another interesting possibility is the rook dance 12...♖d6!? 13.♕c2 ♗a7 14.♖ad1 ♖h6!.

13.f4?!

White wants to punish Black for playing 12...♗f8, but his own 12.♘a4 should also be considered. In case of 13.♕d5 there are attacking tricks like 13...♖h6!, and if 14.♗xe5? ♖xe5! 15.♕xe5 ♗d6 16.♕d4 ♗xh2+

17.♔h1 ♗f4+! 18.♔g1 ♖h1+!
19.♔xh1 ♕h4+ 20.♔g1 ♕h2 mate.

13...♖d6!

A logical and strong intermediate move,
activating the Drimer Rook before playing ...♘c6. Worse is 13...♘c6?! 14.c5
♖a8 15.♖f3 (15.♗c4!?) 15...d6
16.♖g3 (16.cxd6 ♕xd6 17.♕xd6
♗xd6 18.♖g3 ♗f8 19.♘c3 ½-½
Shaked-Lalic, London 1997) 16...dxc5
17.♕c2 (17.♗d3 g6 18.♕f1 ♗g7
19.♗xg7 ♔xg7 20.♗b5 ♕f6 21.♘xc5
b6 22.f5 ♗xf5 23.e4∓ ½-½ Kjeldsen-
Jaksland, DEN-chB 1989) 17...♕e7
18.♗d3 ♘b4 19.♗xh7+ ♔h8 20.♕b1
♖a6 21.f5 ♖h6 22.f6 ♖xf6 23.♗xf6
♕xf6 24.♖f3 ♕h6 25.♗e4??−+ ½-½
Smyslov-Drimer, Hastings 1969/70.
14.♕c2 ♘c6 15.♖f3 ♖h6!

The black rook dominates.

16.♖d1 d6 17.♘c3 ♕h4

With attacking ideas akin to all other
lines with the Drimer Rook.
18.h3 ♖g6 19.♔f1 ♖g3 20.♗c1 ♗xh3
20...♘b4!? 21.♕d2 ♗f5 with the
initiative; 20...♗e7!?.
**21.♖xg3 ♕xg3 22.gxh3 ♕xh3+
23.♔e1??**
This square looks safer, but Black will
bring on new resources. 23.♔f2 was
the only move.
23...♘b4! 24.♕b2

24...♗e7!

The Maroczy bishop shoots! (while
Rubinstein's remains on its original
square).
25.♔d2 ♗f6! 26.e4 ♗d4

Black would also have won easily with
26...♘xa2!.
**27.♖f1 ♕e3+ 28.♔d1 ♗xc3 29.♗xe3
♗xb2 30.♔d2 ♖xe4 31.♗f3 ♗c3+
32.♔xc3 ♖xe3+ 33.♔d2 ♖d3+
34.♔e2 ♖c3 35.♗xb7 ♖c2+ 36.♔f3
♖xa2 37.♔g4 ♔f8 38.f5 ♘d3 39.f6
gxf6 40.♖xf6 ♘e5+ 41.♔g5 ♖b2
42.c5 ♖xb3 43.♗d5 ♖b5   0-1**

Here are some more examples of the
Drimer Rook effect during the
1980s-1990s.

GAME 84
□ **Spyridon Skembris**
■ **Nikolay Legky**
Vrnjacka Banja 1989 (7)

1.d4 ♘f6 2.c4 e5 3.dxe5 ♘g4 4.♘f3 ♗c5

Another nice miniature was 4...♘c6 5.♘c3 ♗c5! 6.e3 ♘gxe5 7.♗e2 0-0 8.0-0 a5 9.b3 ♘xf3+ 10.♗xf3 ♘e5 11.♗e4 ♖a6!? 12.g3 ♖h6 13.♘a4 ♗a7 14.♗g2 d6∓ 15.♕e2 ♖e8 16.f3 ♕g5 17.♘c3 ♕h5 18.♔h1 ♘xc4 (threatening 19...♖xe3!) 0-1 Karolyi-Hector, Copenhagen 1985.

5.e3 ♘c6 6.♗e2 ♘gxe5 7.♘xe5 ♘xe5 8.0-0 0-0 9.♘c3 ♖e8 10.b3 a5 11.♗b2 ♖a6 12.♕d5

Attacking the Maroczy bishop with the queen.

12...♗a7! 13.♖ad1

White is playing classical chess in the centre, placing his pieces as 'correctly' as possible. 13.♘e4 transposes to Games 81 and 82. After 13.c5, 13...♖h6! looks good, for instance: 14.♘e4 c6 15.♕d4 d5! 16.♘g3 b6! 17.cxb6 ♗xb6 18.♕c3 ♕h4–+ 19.h3 ♗xh3 20.gxh3 ♕xh3 21.♖fd1 ♕h2+ 22.♔f1 ♖f6 0-1 Polovodin-Miezis, Moscow 1992.

13...♖g6!

But Black, does not waste any time and starts a direct attack against the white king's fortress. Also interesting is 13...♖h6!?.

14.♔h1?!

Fear. 14.♕xa5 ♕g5! 15.♕d5□ d6→; 14.♘e4 c6!? 15.♕d2 ♕h4→.

14...c6 15.♕d2 ♕h4! 16.f4 ♖h6 17.h3

17...♕g3!!

Preparing 18...♖xh3.

18.♕e1

Or, for example: 18.♗c1 ♖xh3+ 19.gxh3 ♕xh3+ 20.♔g1 ♘xc4 21.♗xc4 ♗xe3+ 22.♕xe3 ♖xe3 23.♗xe3 ♕xe3+ 24.♔g2 ♕xc3–+.

18...♖xh3+! 19.gxh3 ♕xh3+ 20.♔g1 ♖e6 21.♗h5 ♕xh5 22.fxe5 ♖g6+ 23.♔f2 ♕h2+ 24.♔f3 ♕g2+

Followed by 25...♕g4 mate.

0-1

GAME 85
□ **Yury Drozdovsky**
■ **Igor Smolkov**
Alushta ch-UKR 2002 (2)

1.d4 ♘f6 2.c4 e5 3.dxe5 ♘g4 4.♘f3 ♗c5 5.e3 ♘c6 6.♗e2 0-0 7.0-0 ♖e8 8.♘c3 ♘gxe5 9.b3 a5 10.♗b2 ♘xf3+ 11.♗xf3 ♘e5 12.♗e2 ♖a6 13.♘d5

White prepares f2-f4, but does not attack the Maroczy bishop. So...

13...♖h6! 14.g3

To defend against the threat of ...♕h4. In case of 14.f4, the c3 pawn is weakened and Black gets counterplay easily with 14...♘g6 (14...♘c6!? 15.♖f3 ♘b4!? with chances for both sides) 15.♗d4 ♗xd4 16.♕xd4 d6 17.f5 ♘e7 18.♗d3 ♘xd5 19.cxd5 c5 20.♕f4 ♕f6∓ 21.g4 ½-½ Kantsler-Gusev, Belgorod 1990.

14...d6

The rook on h6 is real. Black must push on with his attack.

15.♗d4

In another game Black missed a good chance to score a resounding victory: 15.♘f4 ♕d7!? 16.h4 ♘g6! 17.♘g2 ♕h3! 18.♗f3 ♗d7?! (the winning move was 18...♘xh4!! 19.gxh4 (if 19.♘xh4 ♖xe3!) 19...♖g6−+) 19.♗d4 ½-½ Panchenko-Kiselev, Cheliabinsk 1993.

15...♘g6

Black was also close to victory after 15...♕d7!? 16.h4 ♘g6!? 17.♗f3 ♘xh4! 18.gxh4 ♖g6+ 19.♗g2 ♖xg2+ (19...♖e4 20.f3 ♗xd4 21.fxe4 ♖xg2+ 22.♔xg2 ♕h3+=) 20.♔xg2 ♕h3+ 21.♔g1 ♖e4 22.♘f4 ♖xf4 23.exf4 ♗xd4 24.♕xd4 ♕g4+ 25.♔h2 ♕xh4+ 26.♔g1 ½-½ Vyzhmanavin-Lendwai, Gelsenkirchen 1991.

16.♕d2 c6!

Building the 'Boleslavsky Wall'. As in the Indian Defences, the pawn on c6 controls the d5-square.

17.♘c3 ♕d7!

A logical attack over the light squares.

18.f4

18...♖xh2!?

The positional method was also still available: 18...♕e7!? followed by ...♘f8-♖e6 with pressure along the e-file.

19.f5!

The only defence. If 19.♔xh2? ♕h3+ 20.♔g1 ♕xg3+ 21.♔h1 ♕h3+ 22.♔g1 ♘h4!? 23.♗f2 ♗xd4 24.exd4 ♗g4 with a winning attack.

19...♗xd4 20.exd4 ♖h3! 21.♔g2

Or 21.fxg6 ♖xg3+ 22.♔f2 ♖xg6→.

21...♖h6 22.♗d3

The key moment of the game. Time-trouble is approaching and both

players miss their chances in an extremely sharp struggle.

22...c5?

22...♘f8!?∓.

**23.♘e4 cxd4? 24.♕xh6! ♖xe4
25.♕h5 ♖e5 26.♕g4 b6?! 27.♕xd4
♗b7+ 28.♔h2 ♕e7 29.♕xb6? ♖e2+
30.♖f2 ♖xf2+ 31.♕xf2 ♕g5 32.♗f1
♕h6+ 33.♗h3 ♘e5 34.♖e1 g5
35.♖xe5 dxe5 36.♕d2 ♕c6 37.♕d8+
♔g7 38.♕xg5+ ♔h8 39.♕d8+ ♔g7
40.♕g5+ ♔h8 41.♕d8+   ½-½**

In almost all the games with 13.♘d5
that we have analysed, the white players
were about 200 Elo points above their
opponents. Maybe that difference is the
reason why White escaped from several
totally lost positions.

Some Anti-Drimer Rook variations are
based on earlier deviations like 11.♘e4
(Game 86), 11.♘a4 (Game 87) or
6-10.a3 (Game 88).

GAME 86
□ Robert Bator
■ Peter Svidler
Copenhagen 1991 (10)

Many players, like, for example, Illescas
(see Game 90) and Svidler, have played
the BG when they were young. Playing a
gambit seems like a good idea for a
growing player since it helps him to
learn about the value of the pieces.
When these players grow up, they
choose a safer repertoire.

**1.d4 ♘f6 2.c4 e5 3.dxe5 ♘g4 4.♘f3
♗c5 5.e3 ♘c6 6.♗e2 0-0 7.0-0 ♖e8
8.♘c3 ♘cxe5 9.♘xe5 ♘xe5 10.b3 a5
11.♘e4**

11...♗f8

Another good option is 11...♗a7 when,
although the Drimer Rook does not
leave the a8-square, Black's position is
satisfactory: 12.♗b2 d6 13.♘d2 ♗f5
14.♘f3 ♗e4 (14...♕f6!? 15.♕d2
♗e4∓) 15.♘xe5 dxe5 ½-½
Giorgadze-Epishin, Tbilisi 1989.

12.c5

The idea is to avoid Black's plan with
...♖a6. Other possibilities are:

A) 12.f4 ♘g4 (12...♘c6!?) 13.♗xg4
♖xe4 14.♕d3 ♖e8 15.♗b2 ♕e7
(15...♖a6!? and 16...♖h6) 16.♗f3 d5!
17.♗xc8 dxc4 18.♕xc4 ♖axc8 19.♖g3

In his early chess-playing days, Peter Svidler
played the Budapest Gambit – a good way to
learn about the value of the pieces.

♕b4= Salov-Illescas Cordoba, Barcelona 1989;

B) 12.♘g3 ♖a6 13.e4?! ♗c5!↑ 14.♔h1 ♕h4! 15.f4 ♖d6!∓ Naumkin-Zakharov, Moscow 1994;

C) 12.♗b2 ♕h4 (12...d6=) 13.♘d2 d6 14.♘f3 ♕h6 (14...♕f6!?) 15.♕c2 ♕g6 16.♕xg6 hxg6 ½-½ Cruz-Moskalenko, Sabadell 2007.

12...♕h4!

Attack! 12...♘c6!?∓.

13.f4

13.♕d5!? d6 14.cxd6 ♗d7!? with chances for both sides.

13...♘c6

There were two other interesting alternatives: 13...d5!?, with many tactical possibilities, and 13...♘g4!? 14.♗xg4 ♖xe4.

14.♘g5 ♘d8 15.♖f3?

15.♕c2 ♘e6!?∞.

15...♗xc5

Black is better after the ensuing tactical operations.

16.♗d3

16.♖h3? ♕xf4!.

16...d6! 17.♗xh7+ ♔f8 18.♕f1 ♗g4

18...g6!.

19.♖g3 g6 20.♗d2??

There is no time. The lesser evil was 20.♕c4 ♗f5! 21.♕c3 ♘e6!?∓.

20...♘e6

20...♗f5!.

21.♘xf7 ♕xh7 22.♘xd6 cxd6 23.♖xg4 ♘g7 24.♕d3 ♘f5 25.♖e1 ♖e6 26.♔h1 ♖ae8 27.e4 ♕e7 28.♖f1 ♖xe4 29.♖xg6 ♕f7 30.♖g5 ♘e3 31.♖f3 ♖d4! 32.♕c3 ♕h7 33.♖xc5 ♕b1+ 34.♗e1 ♘d5! 0-1

GAME 87

□ Francisco Vallejo Pons
■ Alfonso Romero Holmes
Ayamonte tt 2002 (1)

1.d4 ♘f6 2.c4 e5 3.dxe5 ♘g4 4.♘f3 ♗c5 5.e3 ♘c6 6.♘c3 ♘gxe5 7.♘xe5 ♘xe5 8.♗e2 0-0 9.0-0 ♖e8 10.b3 a5 11.♘a4 ♗f8!?

Now 11...♗a7 would block the rook on a8 and could be cut off with c4-c5, as White's knight is more stable on a4 than on e4. After 12.♗b2 White has a small advantage.

12.f4!?

The best resource for White.

12...♘g6!?

Black went to the Right (see Chapter Two, Part II) with 12...♘c6!? 13.♗f3 d6 (13...♖a6!?) 14.♕d2 ♗f5 15.♘c3 ♕b8 16.a3 ♕a7⇄ in Agdestein-Haik, Marseille 1987.

13.♕d2 b6!?

13...c6?! 14.♗b2 (14.f5!? ♘e5 15.f6↑) 14...d5 15.cxd5 ♗f5 16.♗d4 b5 Cu.Hansen-Miezis, Copenhagen 2004; 13...♘h4!? 14.♗d3 b6⇄.

14.♗b2 ♗b7= 15.♗f3 ♕b8?!

A suspicious manoeuvre; 15...♗c6!? 16.♖ad1 ♕e7 offered more chances.

16.♖ad1 ♘h4 17.♗d5 ♘f5?

Allowing a thematic bishop sacrifice.

18.♗xf7+! ♔xf7 19.♕xd7+ ♔g6 20.g4! ♘xe3 21.f5+ ♔g5 22.f6!

Another winning option was 22.♕f7!? ♘xg4 23.f6+−.

22...♕c8 23.fxg7 ♗d6 24.g8♕+! ♖xg8 25.h4+!

Forcing mate.

25...♔xh4

25...♔h6 loses after 26.♖f6+ ♖g6 27.♖xg6+ hxg6 28.♕g7 mate.

26.♕xh7+ ♔g3

26...♔xg4 27.♖d4+ ♔g5 28.♕h4+ ♔g6 29.♖f6+ ♔g7 30.♕h6 mate.

27.♕h2+ ♔xg4 28.♖d4+   1-0

It's mate in five.

Black was OK after the opening and he had some options to balance the game.

The idea of 6-10.a3 is to threaten the Maroczy bishop on c5.

GAME 88
□ **Laszlo Zsinka**
■ **Boris Galanov**
Budapest 1991 (8)

1.d4 ♘f6 2.c4 e5 3.dxe5 ♘g4 4.♘f3 ♗c5 5.e3 ♘c6 6.♗e2

6.a3 is usually met by 6...a5 (6...♘gxe5!? is also good; 7.♘xe5 ♘xe5 8.b4 ♗e7⇄) 7.b3 (7.♘c3 0-0! 8.♗d3 ♖e8) 7...0-0 8.♗b2 ♖e8 9.♗d3 d6!? 10.exd6 ♘xf2! (10...♕xd6!?♔) 11.♔xf2 ♖xe3 12.♔f1 ♗g4! 13.♗e2 ♗xf3! 14.♗xf3 ♕h4 15.♖a2 ♖ae8! 16.♗c3 cxd6 17.g3 ♕h3+ 18.♗g2 ♕f5+ 19.♖f2 ♕xf2+! 20.♔xf2 ♖d3+ 0-1 Yrjölä-Liew, Dubai Olympiad 1986.

6...0-0 7.0-0 ♖e8 8.♘c3 ♘gxe5 9.♘xe5 ♘xe5 10.a3

Trying to gain space and to vacate square b2 for the bishop with tempo. But now this idea doesn't make sense. Black brings out the Crazy Rook with an extra tempo.

10...a5!

10...d6 11.b4 ♗b6 12.♘d5±.

11.b3

11.♖b1 d6!? (11...b6 12.f4!?∞) 12.b4 ♗a7!.

analysis diagram

13.♘b5 ♗b8 (13...♗f5 14.♖a1 ♗b6) 14.♗b2 (14.f4 ♘d7∞) 14...c6 15.♘d4 ♕h4! 16.f4 ♘g4 17.♗xg4 ♗xg4 18.♕d3 axb4 19.axb4 ♕e7 20.♖be1 ♕e4 21.♕c3 f6 22.h3 ♗d7 23.♘b3 ♗f5 (23...♕g6!? 24.♔h2 ♗f5) 24.g4 ♗g6 25.f5 ♗f7 26.♘d2 ♕e5 (26...♕e7!? 27.g5 d5 28.gxf6 gxf6⇄) 27.♕xe5 dxe5 28.♖a1= ♗c7 29.♔f2 ♖ad8 30.♔e2 ♖d7 31.♖fc1 ♖ed8 32.♗c3 ♔f8 33.c5 ♖b8 ½-½ Grigore-Moskalenko, Sitges 2007.

11...♖a6

12.♘d5

If 12.♗b2?! ♖h6! 13.g3 (13.♘d5 d6 14.♘f4 c6∓) 13...d6∓ 14.♘e4 ♕d7! (14...♗a7∓) 15.♘g5 f6 16.♕d5+ ♔f8! 17.f4 c6 18.♕d2 ♘xc4! 19.♘xh7+ ♖xh7 20.♕c2 ♗xe3+ 21.♔h1 ♖xh2+! 22.♔xh2 ♕h3 mate, Jug-Petek, Slovenia 1992; or 12.♕d5 ♗a7! and ...♖g6-♕g5 or ...♖h6-♕h4.

12...♖d6

12...♖h6!? 13.e4 (13.b4!? ♗a7 14.c5 d6 15.e4!?∞) 13...♖h4 14.♕c2 ♘c6 15.♗d3 ♘d4 (15...d6!?) 16.♕d1 d6 17.♘e3 ♕f6 18.b4 ♗a7 19.♖e1 ♕e5 20.g3 ♖xe4!? 21.♗d2 ♗h3 22.♗c3 ♕e6 23.♗xe4 ♕xe4 24.♗xd4 ♗xd4 25.♕c2 ♗xa1∓ Grdinic-G. Mohr, Pula 1993.

13.♕c2 c6 14.b4 ♗a7 15.♘f4

15.c5!?.

15...♖h6! 16.c5 d5 17.cxd6 ♕xd6 18.g3

18...g5!

With a winning attack.

19.♘g2

19.♘h5 ♕e6−+.

19...♕e6!

Threatening ...♕h3.

20.f4 ♕h3 21.fxe5 ♕xh2+ 22.♔f2

The white king starts to run...

22...♖h3 23.♖g1

... but he can't hide!

Romanian IM Dolfi Drimer (born 1934) was the inventor of the dangerous L-shaped attacking manoeuvre with the Drimer Rook.

23.♖d1 ♕xg3+ 24.♔g1 ♕xe5 25.♗d2 ♕h2+ 26.♔f2 ♖exe3–+.

23...♖xe5! 24.♗d3 ♖e6 25.♗f5 ♕xg3+ 26.♔e2 ♖f6 27.♗xc8 ♖f2+ 28.♔d3 ♕d6+ 29.♔c3 ♗d4+ 30.♔b3 ♕d5+ 31.♔a4

31...b5+   **0-1**

32.♔xa5 ♕d8+ 33.♔a6 ♕b6 mate.

Summary of the Drimer Rook plan

In many games Black wins by a direct attack on the king, thanks to the activity of the a8 rook. The safest solution for White might be to study the anti-Drimer lines or to abandon the defensive plan

b3-♗b2 and try to find some attacking plan, as did Vassily Smyslov and Boris Spassky, the best representatives of the new generation – see the next two games.

An important resource for White is the idea of these two champions to attack aggressively with f2-f4 on move 8-14. White loses no time fianchettoing his queen's bishop; he immediately starts operations on the kingside. This is slightly similar to the Alekhine System with 4.e4 (Chapter Two).

GAME 89
□ **Vasily Smyslov**
■ **Ralph Blasek**
Gelsenkirchen 1991

1.d4 ♘f6 2.c4 e5 3.dxe5 ♘g4 4.♘f3 ♗c5 5.e3 ♘c6 6.♘c3 ♘cxe5?

A serious mistake in this system. Necessary is 6...0-0! and if 7.♗d3 ♖e8!, but not 7...♘gxe5? 8.♘xe5 ♘xe5 9.♗xh7+!.

7.♘xe5

After 7.h3!? ♘xf3+ 8.♕xf3 ♘e5 9.♕g3! ♘g6 10.♗d2 ♗d6 11.f4 ♗e7 12.0-0-0 ♗f6 13.♕f3 d6 14.♘d5 White also has the upper hand, P. Nikolic-Barbero, Skien Wch-jr 1979.

7...♘xe5 8.f4!

Generally, this advance is White's main resource in the Knight System.

8...♘c6 9.♗d3!

White wins a neat tempo in comparison with other positions of the Knight System.

9...h5?

This move does not solve Black's problems. In case of 9...d6 10.0-0 0-0 White is still a tempo up – see Games 90 and 91; 9...♕h4+ 10.g3 ♕h3 11.♘d5↑.

🎩 **Tricks**: 9...0-0? 10.♕h5! f5 11.♗xf5+– Razuvaev-Bardel, Geneva 1995.

10.0-0 d6 11.a3 a5 12.♗d2 ♗g4 13.♕c2 h4 14.h3 ♗d7 15.♘e4 ♔f8 16.♘xc5 dxc5 17.♗c3+ ♕e7 18.♖ae1 ♖d8 19.♗e4 ♖h6 20.f5 b6

21.♗xc6! ♗xc6 22.♖f4 ♕d6 23.♕f2 ♕d3 24.♖xh4+– ♔e8 25.♖g4 ♖h5 26.e4 ♔d7 27.♕e2 ♕xe2 28.♖xe2 ♖e8 29.♗xg7 ♖xf5 30.♖d2+ **1-0**

After the error 6...♘cxe5?! Smyslov found the main weapon for White, 8.f4!, and then played on with great vigour to gain the victory.

However, the Budapest Gambit has a lot of resources.

Black can avoid the direct Smyslov Attack by first playing 6...0-0!? 7.♘c3 ♖e8 8.0-0 ♘xe5 9.♘xe5 ♘xe5. Only

now can White play his attacking move 10/11.f4. This is the method that World Champion Boris Spassky has introduced.

A dangerous resource for White is taking his own rook to the third rank. But like the Nautilus, the Budapest Gambit remains alive!

GAME 90
☐ **Boris Spassky**
■ **Miguel Illescas Cordoba**
Linares 1990 (7)

1.d4 ♘f6 2.c4 e5 3.dxe5 ♘g4 4.♘f3 ♗c5 5.e3 ♘c6 6.♗e2

Remember 6.♘c3 0-0!.

6...♘gxe5!?

Now the f1 bishop has moved to e2, this is possible.

7.♘xe5 ♘xe5 8.♘c3 0-0 9.0-0 ♖e8 10.♔h1!?

Preparation for f2-f4. For the immediate 10.f4!? see the next game.

10...a5!?

This move keeps all Black's counterchances alive: ...♖a6, ...♗a7 and ...♗f8. Another possibility is 10...d6!?. Now White can trade off the c5 bishop with 11.♘a4, but this does not seem dangerous as Epishin shows: 11...♕h4!? (11...♗b6 12.♘xb6 axb6=;

Former World Champion Boris Spassky refined the Smyslov Attack by postponing f2-f4, turning it into one of the most dangerous weapons for White against the Budapest Gambit.

♕c6 22.a3 f6 23.♗e3 b6 24.♗f2 a5 25.♖d1 ♖ed8 26.♖de1 a4 27.♗e3 ♗f7 28.♖d1 ♕e6 29.♗d3 ♕e5 30.f4 ♕h5 31.♖d2 ♕g4 32.f5 ♘c6 33.h3 ♕h4 34.♗c2 ♖xd2 35.♗xd2 ♘e5 36.♖f4 ♕h5 37.♗xa4 ♕e2 38.♗e1 ♘d3 39.♗g3 ♘xf4 40.♗xf4 ♕f1+ 0-1 Vaisser-Epishin, Sevastopol 1986.

11.f4!

White sticks to his plan. An interesting tactical fight would ensue after 11.a3 ♖a6 (11...d6⇄) 12.f4 ♖d6! 13.♕c2 ♘c6 14.♘e4 ♖h6

analysis diagram

15.♗f3 (15.♘xc5 ♕h4 16.h3 d6 △ 17.♘e4?? ♗xh3-+) 15...♗a7 16.c5 d5!? 17.cxd6 cxd6 18.♘g5 d5 19.♕d3 ♘e7! 20.e4 dxe4 21.♕xd8 ♖xd8 22.♗xe4 ♘f5∓ (threatening 23...♘g3 mate)

analysis diagram

11...♗f5!?⇄; 11...b6?! 12.♗d2 a5 13.♘xc5 bxc5 14.f4 ♘d7 15.♗f3 ♖b8 16.♕c2 a4 17.♖ae1 ♘f6 18.♗c3 ♘g4 19.e4± Beliavsky-G. Mohr, Portoroz 1997) 12.♘xc5 dxc5 13.f3 (13.♕d5 ♗e6!? 14.♕xb7 ♗xc4⇄) 13...♗f5∓

analysis diagram

with a long-term initiative for Black: 14.♕e1 ♕e7 (14...♕xe1!? 15.♖xe1 ♗d3 16.b3 ♖ad8∓) 15.♕c3 ♖ad8 16.e4 ♘c6 17.♗f4 ♗g6 18.♗d3 ♘d4 19.♖ae1 ♖d7 20.♗b1 ♕f6 21.♗c1

23.♗xf5 ♗xf5 24.h3 ♖c6 25.♘f3 ♖c2
26.♗d2 ♖cxd2 27.♘xd2 ♖xd2
28.♖ad1 ♖xd1 29.♖xd1 ♗b6 30.♖d5
♗e4 31.♖b5 ♗c7 32.♖c5 ♗c6 0-1
Fries Nielsen-Svidler, Gausdal 1992.
11...♘c6
11...♘g6?! 12.f5 ♘e5 13.f6↑.
12.♗d3

12...d6!
The critical moment: 12...♗xe3?
13.♗xe3 ♖xe3 14.♗e4±.
13.♕h5!?
Spassky prefers to attack with his pieces.
13.f5 f6⇄; 13.♘e4?! ♕h4!.
13...h6?
On move 13 Black makes an important
mistake. The right defence was the
blockade idea 13...g6! 14.♕h6 f5 and
White has difficulties to develop his initiative on the kingside. See also the analysis of the next game.

14.♖f3!
This rook manoeuvre is White's ulti-
mate attacking resource – similar to the
black rook manoeuvres in other games
in this chapter.
**14...♘b4 15.♗e4 c6 16.♖g3 ♕f6
17.♗d2 ♘a6 18.a3! ♔f8 19.♗d3 ♗a7
20.♘e2+− ♘c5 21.♗c3 ♕xc3
22.♘xc3 ♘xd3 23.♖f1 ♗xe3 24.♕e2
♘xf4 25.♕d1 1-0**
Black will lose even more material.
Summary of this important game:
Spassky conducted the attack in exem-
plary fashion. But after the correct
13...g6! the position is totally unclear.
Another interesting alternative for Black
is 10...d6, with a balanced game.
We can observe an important tendency
in the Knight System: in many games,
the first player that places his rook on
the third rank wins!

GAME 91
□ **Antonio Gual Pascual**
■ **Javier Avila Jimenez**
Spain 2006 (7)

In this game my student (Black) shows
his knowledge of the Budapest Gambit.
**1.d4 ♘f6 2.c4 e5 3.dxe5 ♘g4 4.♘f3
♗c5 5.e3 ♘c6 6.♗e2 0-0! 7.♘c3
♖e8!? 8.0-0 ♘gxe5 9.♘xe5 ♘xe5
10.f4!?**

White's trump card in this aggressive variation (as Spassky showed in the previous game) is his mobile f-pawn, in combination with his control of the vital d5-square and attacking moves like ♗d3, ♕h5 and ♖f3.

10...♘c6 11.♗d3 d6

Accepting the pawn is very dangerous: 11...♗xe3+? 12.♗xe3 ♖xe3 13.♘d5! (13.♕d2?! ♖e8∞) 13...♖e8 14.♕h5 g6 15.♕h6 f5 16.♗xf5! with a decisive advantage for White, Lombart-Marlier, Charleroi 2004.

12.♕h5

The idea of GM Comas was 12.♘e4!? ♗b6 (Black also has the strong defensive resource 12...♕h4! with the idea 13.♘xc5 dxc5 with counterplay; or first 12...♘b4!?) 13.♕h5 g6! 14.♕h6 f5! 15.♘g5

analysis diagram

15...♕e7?? (after 15...♖e7□ 16.♖f3 ♕f8!? Black would be OK) 16.c5! (now this gives White a winning attack) 16...♗xc5 17.♗c4+ ♔h8 18.b4 ♗xe3+ 19.♗xe3 ♕xe3+ 20.♔h1 ♕e7 21.♖ae1 1-0 Comas Fabrego-Altisen Palmada, Spain 1995. If 12.♘d5!? f5!? (12...♘b4!?; 12...♘e7!?) 13.♕h5 ♘e7!⇄.

12...g6! 13.♕h6

13...f5!

The best defence is this blockade. The white 'screwdriver' cannot proceed now, while his bishops are temporarily out of the game. 13...♘e7? 14.b4!? ♗xb4 15.♗b2+−.

14.♘d5?!

Looking for new attacking resources, but now Black controls the board. 14.♖f3!? ♘b4! 15.♗b1 (15.♖h3 ♖e7 16.♗b1 d5!) 15...d5! 16.a3 d4! 17.axb4 ♗f8, with chances for both sides, may have been a better bet.

14...♘b4! 15.♖f3 ♘xd5

✏ **Tricks**: 15...♘xd3? 16.♖h3 ♖e7 17.♕g5!±.

16.cxd5 ♕f6 17.h4 ♕g7 18.♕g5 h6 19.♕g3

White has lost his initiative and now has an uncomfortable game.

19...h5?!

19...♔h7! gives Black an edge.

**20.♗d2 ♔h7 21.♗c3 ♕f7 22.♔h2?
♗d7**

22...♕xd5!∓.

23.♖e1 ♖g8?!

23...c6!?⇄.

**24.♕g5 ♖ae8 25.♖g3 ♕f8 26.♖e2
♕h6 27.e4 ♕xg5 28.♖xg5 fxe4
29.♗xe4 ♔h6 30.♗d3 ♖xe2 31.♗xe2
♗e3 32.g3 ♖f8 33.♔g2 ♖f5 34.♗d3
♖xg5 35.hxg5+ ♔h7= 36.♔f3 ♗c5
37.b4 ♗g4+ 38.♔g2 ♗e3 39.b5 ♗d7
40.a4 ♗f5 41.♗xf5 gxf5 42.a5**

42.♗a5 ♗b6=.

**42...a6 43.bxa6 bxa6 44.♔f3 ♗c5
45.♗e1 ♔g6 46.♔e2 ♔f7 47.♗d3
♔g6 48.♔c2**   ½-½

Teacher's summary: In the opening my student showed a very good understanding of the position. White's attack was successfully slowed down with the key moves 6...0-0!, 12...g6!, 13...f5!, and 15...♘b4!. Unfortunately, in the middlegame he was not in best shape and made some mistakes. But we will do more hard work!

Summary Smyslov/Spassky Attack:

In order to avoid Smyslov's Attack with 8.f4, the best option is to play 6...0-0! instead of the immediate 6...♘xe5. The best defence against White's attack with f2-f4, ♗d3 and ♕h5 is the blockade with ...g6 and ...f5 — see the analysis in Games 90 and 91.

GAME 92
□ **José Raul Capablanca**
■ **J.H. White**
London casual 1919

Without a doubt, World Champion José Raul Capablanca was a hero of the classical style and also one of the main founders of the new generation and the modern chess style, developed by players in the 20th and 21st centuries.

**1.d4 ♘f6 2.c4 e5 3.dxe5 ♘g4 4.♘f3
♗c5 5.e3 ♘c6 6.♗d2**

This move cannot yield White an advantage, but it produced one more interesting game for your collection.

6...0-0

6...a5?! 7.♗c3 ♕e7 8.♗d4 (8.♕d5!?) 8...♘gxe5 9.♘xe5 ♘xe5 10.♘c3 ♗b4 11.♗e2 d6 12.0-0 ♗xc3 13.♗xc3± Moskalenko-Budnikov, Beijing 1991; 6...♘gxe5=.

World Champion José Raul Capablanca (1888-1942), hero of the classical style, nearly tripped in a foggy casual game with the Budapest Gambit in London.

7.♗c3 ♖e8 8.♗e2 d6

An aggressive idea. Simpler is 8...♘gxe5!?=.

9.exd6 ♗xe3 10.fxe3 ♘xe3 11.♕d2 ♘xc4 12.♕g5 f6 13.♕d5+ ♗e6⇆ 14.♕d3 ♘xd6

15.0-0??

The London fog may perhaps be blamed for this mistake. 15.♘bd2±.

15...♗c4 16.♕xc4+□ ♘xc4 17.♗xc4+ ♔h8∓

Now Capablanca starts to play more seriously. And he creates some chances.

18.♘bd2 ♕d6 19.♔h1 ♖ad8 20.♖ae1 ♕c5 21.♖xe8+ ♖xe8 22.a3 b5 23.♗a2 a5 24.♘b3 ♕c4 25.♘fd2 ♕e2 26.♘c1 ♕e3 27.♘f3 ♖d8 28.♖e1 ♕c5 29.♘b3 ♕b6 30.♘bd4 ♘xd4 31.♗xd4 c5 32.♗g1 ♕c6 33.h4 h5?!

33...c4 would have been winning.

34.♗f7! f5? 35.♘g5 ♕c7 36.♗xh5 ♕g3?

37.♘f3?!

37.♖e3! ♕xh4+ 38.♖h3 ♕xg5 39.♗f7+ ♕h6 40.♖xh6+ gxh6 41.♗xc5±.

37...♕d6 38.♘e5 ♕f6 39.g3 ♖d2? 40.♗xc5 ♖c2 41.♗d4 ♕a6 42.♘f7+ ♔h7 43.♘g5+ ♔h6 44.♗f3! ♕c8 45.♖e6+ g6 46.♖e7 ♖c1+ 47.♔h2 ♖c2+ 48.♔h3 f4+ 49.g4 ♕g8 50.♘f7+ ♔h7 51.♘e5+ 1-0

GAME 93
□ **Ashot Anastasian**
■ **Alex Yermolinsky**
Soviet Union 1987

1.d4 ♘f6 2.c4 e5 3.dxe5 ♘g4 4.♘f3 ♗c5 5.e3 ♘c6 6.b3?!

White's kingside is too undeveloped to successfully complete his fianchetto with ♗b2.

6...♘gxe5!

A good possibility to equalize was 6...0-0 7.♗b2 ♖e8 8.♘d3 ♕e7 (the gambit idea is 8...d6!? 9.exd6 ♗xe3 10.0-0 ♘xf2 11.♖xf2 ♕xd6∞) 9.0-0 ♘gxe5 10.♘xe5 ♘xe5 11.♘c3 ♘xd3 12.♕xd3= (Lputian-Panchenko, Sochi 1987) 12...c6!?. Black can also play in gambit style rightaway with 6...d6!? 7.exd6 ♕f6! 8.♗a3 ♘b4!?.

7.♘xe5 ♘xe5 8.♗b2 d6∓

9.♗e2

There is no other way to castle. If 9.♗xe5?! dxe5 10.♕xd8+ ♚xd8 11.♘c3 c6∓.

9...♕g5!

But now Black attacks first, this time with his entire army.

10.0-0 ♗h3 11.♘f3 0-0-0! 12.♘c3 h5! 13.♔h1 ♗g4 14.♗e2 ♕h4 15.♕e1?

15.♘d5 was the only move.

15...♗xe2 16.♕xe2 ♖de8! 17.♘a4?

A somewhat optimistic manoeuvre.

17...♘g4!

Now Black finishes the game immediately.

18.h3

Black to play and win!

18...♖xe3!!　　　　　　　　**0-1**

This is much worse than just a Crazy Rook: 19.fxe3 ♕g3 20.hxg4 hxg4+ 21.♔g1 ♗xe3+ 22.♖f2 ♕h2+ 23.♔f1 ♕h1 mate.

GAME 94
□ Enrique Ibanez
■ Alexander Alekhine
Buenos Aires exh 1926

1.d4 ♘f6 2.c4 e5 3.dxe5 ♘g4 4.♘f3 ♝c5 5.e3 ♘c6 6.♘c3 ♘gxe5 7.♘xe5 ♘xe5 8.♗e2 d6!?

With this classical move Black is looking for a more natural development for his pieces. This is a good alternative to the aggressive plan with ...a5-♖a6, even though it is a pity that the Drimer Rook was not known at the time.

9.0-0 0-0

9...♗e6!? 10.b3 ♕h4!? (10...h5 11.♘a4!?) 11.♘a4 0-0-0∞.

10.b3

White can exchange the Maroczy bishop by 10.♘a4 ♗b6 (10...♗f5!?) 11.b3 ♗d7 12.♘xb6 axb6 13.♗b2 ♕e7 14.♕d4 f5 15.a4 (15.f4 ♘g6 16.♖f3 ♗c6 17.♖g3 ♖f7 18.♗h5 ♖e8 19.♖e1 ♕h4 20.♕d1 ♖e6= Rivas Pastor-West, La Valetta Olympiad 1980) 15...♖ae8 16.♖ae1 ♗c6 17.♗d1 ♖f6! (here the ♖f8 makes an L-shaped move to h6) 18.f3 ♖h6 19.♗c2 ♖f8 20.♕f4 ♘g6 21.♕g3 ♘h4 22.♕f4?? ♖g6 (22...♘xg2! 23.♔xg2 ♖h4-+) 23.♖e2 ♖f7 24.♔h1? ♘xf3! 25.♗xf5 (25.gxf3 ♖g4-+) 25...♘h4 26.♗xg6 ♖xf4 27.♗xh7+ ♔xh7

28.♖xf4 ♘xg2 29.♖xg2 ♕xe3 30.♖f1
♕e2 31.♖g1 ♕xb2 0-1 Radulescu-
Bakonyi, Budapest 1948.

10...♕h4

This manoeuvre of the black queen is
very popular in the Knight System. But I
think it is better to begin with 10...a5!?,
providing more squares for the bishop
on c5, for instance: 11.♗b2 ♖e8
12.♘d5?! c6! (the Boleslavsky Wall)
13.♘f4 ♕g5! 14.♗d4 ♗f5↑ C. Flear-
Gurieli, Biel 1991. Also good is
10...♗d7!?, controlling the a4-square.

11.♘a4!?

11.♘d5!? c6 12.b4 cxd5 13.bxc5 ♘xc4
14.♕xd5 ♗e6⇄.

11...♖d8

11...♗b6!? 12.♘xb6 axb6=.

12.♗b2 ♗f5

The game is balanced. An alternative here
is 12...♘g4!? with the idea 13.h3 ♘xf2!.

13.♕e1!? ♘c6?!

Maybe due to the Buenos Aires heat,
Alekhine does not make his usual fas-
cinatingly strong moves, but in the end
he wins in Capablanca style.

Preferable was 13...♘g4!? 14.h3 ♘f6
15.♘xc5 dxc5 16.♖d1 ♕g5.

14.♕c3 ♕g5 15.♘xc5 dxc5 16.h4?!

Better was 16.♖ad1±.

**16...♕h6 17.g4 ♗xg4 18.♗xg4 ♕g6
19.♕xg7+ ♕xg7 20.♗xg7 ♔xg7**

21.♖fd1 ♘e5 22.♖xd8 ♖xd8 23.♖d1
♖d6 24.♗e2 ♔f6 25.f4 ♘c6 26.♔f2
♘b4 27.♖xd6+ cxd6 28.a3 ♘c6
29.♔f3 ♘a5 30.♗d1 a6 31.♗c2 h6
32.♔e2 b5 33.cxb5 axb5 34.a4?! b4
35.e4 ♔e6 36.♔f3 f6 37.♔e3 d5
38.exd5+ ♔xd5 39.♗e4+ ♔d6
40.♗c2 c4 41.bxc4 ♘c5 42.♔e4
♘xc4 43.a5 ♘d6+ 44.♔e3 ♔b5
45.♔d4 ♔xa5 46.♔c5 ♘b5 47.♗b3
♘c3 48.♔d4 ♔b5 49.♗c2 ♔c6
50.♗b3 ♔d6 51.♗c4 ♘b1 52.♔d3
♔c5 53.♗b3 ♘c3 54.♔e3 ♘b5
55.♔e4 ♘d6+ 56.♔d3 ♘f5 57.h5
♘d4 58.♗a2 b3 59.♗b1 ♘b5 60.♔e3
♘c3 61.♗d3 b2 62.♔f3 ♔d4   0-1

Our study of the Knight System ends
with an attack by the friendly GM
Vasilios Kotronias, who plays 10...d6
two moves later and uses his other rook
to perform the same Drimer trick.

GAME 95
□ **Alexey Vyzhmanavin**
■ **Vasilios Kotronias**
Moscow B 1987

1.d4 ♘f6 2.c4 e5 3.dxe5 ♘g4 4.♘f3
♗c5 5.e3 ♘c6 6.♗e2 ♘gxe5 7.♘xe5
♘xe5 8.0-0 0-0 9.♘c3 ♖e8 10.b3
d6!?

This move is easier to understand than the mysterious 10...a5! and 11...♖a6!.

11.♗b2

The problem with playing ...d6 before ...a5 is that White can try to exchange the Maroczy bishop with 11.♘a4!? b6 (11...♗f5!? 12.♘xc5 dxc5) 12.a3!? (12.♘xc5 bxc5 13.f4 ♘d7 14.♗f3 ♖b8⇄ W. Schneider-Roscher, Germany 1989) 12...a5 13.♗d2 ♗d7⇄ Sieglen-Schnepp, Württemberg 1996.

11...♖e6!?

Another rook, but with the same objective: ...♖g6 or ...♖h6! Some interesting alternatives are:

A) Not so clear is 11...a5 12.♘a4!? b6 13.♘xc5 bxc5 14.f4 ♘d7 15.♗f3 ♖b8 16.♕d2 (16.♕e1!?) 16...a4⇄ Osnos-Yermolinsky, Leningrad-ch 1977;

B) Black is also doing well after the development of his c8 bishop: 11...♗d7! (or 11...♗f5!?) 12.♔h1 ♖e6!? 13.f4 ♖h6! M. Larsen-P. Nielsen, Vanlose 1991; if now 14.fxe5?? ♖xh2+! with mate in 4.

🎩 **Tricks**: 11...♕h4?! 12.♘d5 ♖e6 13.b4?? (13.♘xc7? ♖h6 14.h3 ♗xh3 15.g3 ♕g5−+; the best move is 13.g3!±) 13...♖h6 14.f4 ♕xh2+ 15.♔f2 ♕h4+ 16.♔g1 ♕g3! 17.fxe5 ♖h2 18.♗f3 ♕h4 0-1 Roth-Rauch, Germany 1991/92.

12.g3?

Weakening the light squares on the kingside. 12.♘a4!? b6 13.♘xc5 bxc5 14.f4 ♘d7! (14...♘c6?! 15.♗f3 ♗b7 16.f5±) 15.♗f3 ♖b8 would be unclear.

12...a5!∓

Giving the bishop on c5 more space.

13.♔h1?! b6

More effective was 13...♗d7!, controlling a4 and threatening 14...♗c6.

14.e4 ♖g6?!

Defending the g4-square, but White is well prepared for the attack with his pawns.

15.f4!? ♘g4 16.f5!

Now incredible complications start.

16...♘e3 17.♕d3

17.fxg6? ♘xd1 18.gxf7+ ♔f8 19.♖axd1 ♗h3 20.♖f3 c6 21.♘a4 ♕e7∓.

17...♖h6 18.♖f4 ♕g5

18...g5!?.

19.♖g1! ♗b7 20.♗f3 ♖h3

20...♖e8 21.♗c1 ♘xf5 22.♖xf5 ♖xh2+ 23.♔xh2 ♗xg1+ 24.♔xg1 ♕xc1+ 25.♗d1±.

21.♘a4

21.♗c1!? ♕h6 22.♖h4.

21...♕h6 22.♖h4! ♖xh4 23.gxh4 ♕f4! 24.♖g3?

24.♖xg7+ ♔f8 25.♖g3 ♖e8 26.♘xc5 bxc5 27.♗c1 would have won.

24...♖e8 25.♘xc5 bxc5 26.♗xg7?

26...♘g4!!
The star move, forcing the win.
27.♕f1
27.♖xg4 ♕xg4 28.♗xg4 ♗xe4+ 29.♕xe4 ♖xe4—+; 27.♗h6 ♕xg3!—+; 27.♕e2 ♗xe4 28.♗c3 ♔f8 29.♗xa5 ♗b7 30.♕g2 ♖e4!—+.
27...♗xe4 28.♗c3 h5 29.♔g1 ♕e3+
Even stronger was 29...♗xf3 30.♕xf3 ♕c1+ 31.♕f1 ♕c2 32.♕g2 ♕b1+ 33.♕f1 ♕xa2—+.
30.♔h1 ♕xc3
30...♔f8!?.
31.♗xe4 ♕d4 32.♗f3 ♔h8
32...♕d2!? 33.♖g2 ♖e1 34.♖xd2 ♖xf1+ 35.♔g2 ♘e3+ 36.♔g3 ♘xf5+∓.
33.h3?
33.♗xg4 hxg4∓.
33...♕c3 34.♖g1 ♖e3 35.hxg4   0-1
(time) 35...♖xf3 would have won anyway.
Summarizing this beautiful (though not classical) game strategically: it seems that White must play ♘a4 and ♘x♗ as quickly as possible, since the bishop on c5 will be very powerful when Black starts his attack on the kingside.
To avoid the exchange of the Maroczy bishop on c5 it was sufficient to play 13...♗d7!, controlling the a4-square.

Statistics for 4...♗c5 5.e3 ♘c6

In total 2412 games.
White wins:	950 games	= 53%
Black wins:	793 games	= 47%
Draw:	667 games	

With an approximately equal rating performance.

Summary of the Maroczy Attack
- Thanks to the developing tempo with 4...♗c5, Black gets good chances to fight for the initiative, especially in the lines with Drimer's Crazy Rook.
- White, as usual, tries to stabilize the position and to derive a classical advantage from his space surplus and better pawn structure.
- But after 4...♗c5! White cannot play defensively, since Black is threatening to gain the initiative and be the first to attack.
- Generally speaking, if both sides play as actively as possible, fighting to win, many tense and quite attractive ideas can be found.

Chapter Four

War and Peace

Rare Systems and Declining the Gambit

War (Part I)

Peace (Part II)

Introduction

In this chapter we complete the study of the Budapest Gambit with the exception of 3...♘e4, which is the subject of the final Chapter Five: Knight Fiction.

Here we will analyse some key positions that occur after unusual and irregular possibilities against the Budapest Gambit.

Some of these lines are not so popular in tournament practice, but are very often used in Internet games.

A Bit of History/Directions

After 3.dxe5 ♘g4 4.e3 e5 (Part I – War), the strange-looking manoeuvre 5.♘h3!? was very fashionable in the 1980s/1990s when the Budapest Gambit had its second heyday.

Garry Kasparov introduced the subtle alternative 5.♘c3!? in two simultaneous games in the 1990s, which had a strikingly similar course.

Declining the gambit is also possible (Part II - Peace), but so far this has mainly been tried in Internet games in the past few years. Usually, play transposes to other well-known openings, but to lines that are not very dangerous for Black.

Part I – War

Irregular Systems – 1.d4 ♞f6 2.c4 e5 3.dxe5 ♞g4

Dedicated to victims of the Budapest Gambit

Introduction

For those who want to avoid the main variations presented in the previous Chapters, there are some minor lines after 3.dxe5 ♞g4.

Directions

Usually these rare systems are divided into two groups:

White protects the pawn on e5 by various moves other than 4.♞f3 and 4.♝f4, fighting for his extra pawn. These systems have taken many white victims, so we may call these alternatives grave errors.

We will show the following lines:

1. 4.♕d4 (Game 96 Beliavsky-Epishin, 4.♕d5 is similar)
2. 4.f4 (Game 97 Max-Reinhardt).

As the games show, we cannot recommend these lines. Black can quickly grab the initiative and gain the advantage with the natural ...d7-d6.

Other moves (after 4.e3 ♞xe5):

1. 5.♞h3!? (Game 98 Gurevich-Tisdall): the knight heads for the d5-square via the passage h3-f4-d5, as the other knight does via c3-d5.

2. Kasparov's waiting move 5.♞c3!? (Game 99 Kasparov-Europ Chess) has the idea to carry through the f2-f4 push quickly. This leads to positions similar to the Smyslov/Spassky Attack. Anyway, the classical advance f2-f4 will always be White's most dangerous weapon against the BG.

Irregular Systems – Games

GAME 96
□ **Alexander Beliavsky**
■ **Vladimir Epishin**
Reggio Emilia II 1991 (7)

Another famous example, similar to Berlin 1918. Perhaps GM Beliavsky did not know the games of the classic masters, nor the main ideas of the Gambit.
1.d4 ♘f6 2.c4 e5 3.dxe5 ♘g4 4.♕d4

Vladimir Epishin was the greatest advocate of the Budapest Gambit in the 1980s-1990s. Unfortunately, in this millennium he prefers to play it with the white pieces.

5.exd6 ♗xd6

This early queen sortie seems justified, as it both defends the pawn and attacks the knight on g4. Black has no time for the immediate 4...♗c5 or 4...♘c6, but soon the queen in the centre will become a target, giving Black a lead in development. Another possibility is 4.♕d5 ♗b4+ (4...d6! 5.exd6 ♗xd6⩱) 5.♘c3 ♕e7 6.♘f3 ♗c5? (6...♗xc3+ 7.bxc3 ♘c6 8.♗f4 f6 see Chapter One, Part I) 7.e3± Siviotti-Le Masson, Rio de Janeiro 2000.

4...d6!

Black obtains more than enough compensation for the pawn. Not so clear is 4...h5 5.♘f3 (5.h3 ♘c6 6.♕e4 ♘gxe5 and if 7.f4?! ♕h4+↑) 5...♘c6 6.♕d5 ♗b4+? (6...d6!? 7.♗g5 ♕d7∞) 7.♘c3 ♕e7 8.♗f4± Esser-Breyer, Budapest 1916.

6.♕e4+

It is not possible to play with the queen all the time. If 6.♘f3 0-0 7.♗g5 ♕e8 8.♘c3 ♘c6 9.♕d2 ♗e6 (9...f6!?) 10.e3 f6 11.♗h4 ♖d8 12.0-0-0?? g5!–+ and White loses material, Stephan-Pohle, Bavaria 2002.

Tricks: 6.♕xg7?? loses immediately to 6...♗e5.

6...♗e6 7.♘c3

7.♕xb7 ♘d7 8.♘f3 0-0↑.

7...0-0

Even better is 7...♘c6! 8.♘f3 ♕d7 with the idea ...0-0-0 and ...♖he8.

8.♘f3 ♕d7 9.♘d4 ♗xc4

Now White has neither the material nor the position.

10.♘f5 ♗e6 11.♘xd6 cxd6 12.g3 d5 13.♕f4 d4 14.♘e4 ♗d5 15.f3 f5! 16.♘c5 ♕e7 17.♘d3

17.♕xd4 ♗xf3→.

17...♘c6

Zugzwang! There is no good move for White.

18.h3 ♘ge5 19.♘xe5 ♘xe5 20.♔f2 d3!? 21.♗d2 dxe2 22.♗xe2 ♗xf3! 23.♗b4 ♕e6 24.♖he1 ♗xe2 25.♕e3 f4! **0-1**

Conclusion: After 4.♕d4+?! (or 4.♕d5) d6! it is much easier to play with the black pieces.

GAME 97
□ **B. Max**
■ **Bernd Reinhardt**
Zell 1977

1.d4 ♘f6 2.c4 e5 3.dxe5 ♘g4 4.f4?

This way of defending the extra pawn is totally erroneous.

4...♗c5! 5.♘h3

Defending f2. But now it will be difficult for the white king to castle

kingside. If 5.e3 d6! 6.exd6? (6.♘f3 0-0↑) 6...0-0! 7.♘c3 ♗xe3 8.♗d3? ♗xg1 (8...♖e8!–+) 9.♖xg1 ♕h4+ 10.♔d2 ♕f2+ 11.♘e2 ♘c6→ Akhundov-Simonenko, Ashkhabad 1990.

5...d6!

Opening the centre works in favour of the black army.

6.♘c3 ♘h6?!

This retreat is not necessary. The correct move is 6...0-0! 7.exd6 cxd6 and Black has an attacking position.

7.♘f2 ♘f5 8.♕d3 0-0

8...♘c6!?.

9.exd6? ♘xd6 10.♘fe4?

10.e4 ♘c6⌘ was better.

10...♗f5 11.♕f3 ♘xe4 12.♘xe4 ♗xe4! 13.♕xe4 ♘c6

There is no escape for the white king.

14.♗d2 ♖e8 15.♕d5 ♕e7 16.♗c3
♗b4 17.♕g5 ♗xc3+ 18.bxc3 ♕e3
19.♕g3 ♕c5 20.♕d3 ♖ad8 21.♕c2
♕xc4 22.♕b3 ♕xf4 23.g3 ♕e4
24.♖g1 ♘e5 25.♖g2 ♘f3+ 　　0-1
26.♔f2 ♕e3 is mate.

Summarizing the lines where White
defends the e5 pawn by 4.♕d4/♕d5
or 4.f4: White's position is immediately
worse, due to his difficulties to complete his development satisfactorily.
Black takes the initiative with the key
move ...d7-d6!.

GAME 98
□ **Mikhail Gurevich**
■ **Jonathan Tisdall**
Akureyri 1988 (2)

**1.d4 ♘f6 2.c4 e5 3.dxe5 ♘g4 4.e3
♘xe5 5.♘h3**

This manoeuvre against the BG was
very fashionable in the 1980s-1990s.
The knight on g1 heads for the d5-
square via the passage h3-f4-d5, as the
other knight does via b1 to c3-d5. The
question is: what are so many knights
doing on one single square?
5...g6!?
Here we will study some examples
with this original fianchetto idea,

which leads to positions similar to the
King's Indian. Black has several other
options:

A) Of course 5...♗c5!? is also a normal move, for example: 6.♘f4 0-0
7.♘c3 a6 (7...d6!?) 8.b3 ♖e8 9.♗b2
♘bc6 10.♗e2 d6 11.♘cd5 ♘g6
(11...♘b4!?) 12.♘h5 ♘ce5 13.0-0 c6
14.♘c3 ♕h4!

analysis diagram

with a nice mating combination:
15.h3? ♗xh3! 16.gxh3 ♕xh3 17.f4
♘h4 18.♖f2 ♗xe3 19.♕f1 ♘ef3+
20.♗xf3 ♘xf3 mate, Ivanisevic-Tovizi,
blitz game ICC 2003;

B) 5...d6!? 6.♘f4 ♘bd7!? (6...g6!?
7.♗d2 ♗g7 8.♗c3 0-0 9.♗e2 ♘bd7
10.♘d2 ♘c5 11.0-0 a5 12.♕c2 ♖e8
13.♖ad1 c6 14.♗d4 ♕c7 15.♘b3 ♗f5
and the game ended in a draw,
Krasenkow-Del Prado, Ponferrada 1991)
7.♗e2 ♘f6 8.♘c3 c6 9.0-0 ♗e7 10.b3
0-0 11.♕d2 ♕c7 12.♗b2 ♗f5 13.f3
♖ad8 14.e4 ♗c8 15.♔h1 ♖fe8= V.
Milov-Gonzalez Arroyo, Merida 2006;

C) Sometimes Black plays 5...♘g6!?,
preventing ♘f4.
**6.♘f4 ♗g7 7.♗e2 0-0 8.0-0 d6 9.♘c3
♘bd7 10.♕c2**
10.e4 ♘c5 11.♗e3 c6 (11...f5!?⇄)
12.♕d2 ♘e6 13.♖ac1 ♘xf4 14.♗xf4

♗e6= Malaniuk-S.B.Hansen, Lyngby 1991.

10...a5 11.♗d2

11.b3 ♘c5 12.♗b2 c6 13.♖ad1 ♕c7 (13...♕e7!?) 14.♕d2 ♖d8 15.e4 ♕b6⇄ Agrest-Budnikov, Katowice 1992.

11...♘c5 12.♖ad1=

12...f5

Simpler is 12...c6!? with a balanced game.

13.♘a4 b6 14.♘c3 ♗b7 15.♘cd5

White's great dilemma in the line with 5.♘h3 is which knight to put on d5.

15...♖f7 16.♗c1 ♕h4!?

A typical queen manoeuvre in these lines. Black is looking for attacking chances on the kingside.

17.b3 ♖e8 18.♗b2 ♗c8 19.f3 g5 20.♘d3 ♘cxd3 21.♗xd3 f4

21...g4!?↑.

22.♗e4 ♗e6 23.♕f2 ♕h5 24.♗c1 ♖ef8 25.♖fe1 fxe3 26.♘xe3?

Surprisingly, the following game phase contains many lapses.

26...h6?

26...g4!−+.

27.♕e2 ♔h8 28.♖f1 ♘g6?!

28...g4!→.

29.♗b2 ♗xb2 30.♕xb2+ ♘e5 31.♗d3 g4!

Finally this move.

32.fxg4 ♗xg4 33.♖xf7 ♖xf7 34.♖f1 ♕g5!

And now for a dramatic finish.

35.♕d2?

Or 35.♖xf7 ♕xe3+ 36.♔h1 ♕xd3−+.

35...♗f3

Even stronger was 35...♘f3+!.

36.♗c2? ♗xg2! 37.♖xf7 ♗c6+ 38.♔f1 ♘xf7   **0-1**

This was a catastrophe for the white player. On the other hand, with a suspicious, even if fashionable manoeuvre like 5.♘h3?! you do not win games! It seems better for White to return to the more natural Knight System (4.♘f3), which we have studied in Chapter Three.

GAME 99
□ **Garry Kasparov**
■ **Europ Chess**
Madrid simul 1997

1.d4 ♘f6 2.c4 e5 3.dxe5 ♘g4 4.e3 ♘xe5 5.♘c3!?

A waiting move. Kasparov's idea is to advance f2-f4 immediately. This is similar to the classical Smyslov/Spassky Attack in Chapter Three – The Knight System.

Garry Kasparov tried 4.e3 ♘xe5 5.♘c3 against the Budapest and avoided falling victim to the Gambit in two simul games.

5...♘bc6

This move is possible but not necessary. It is better to first develop the bishop with 5...♗b4!? or 5...♗c5!?. In this position, 5...g6 is not so clear; after 6.f4!? ♘ec6 7.♘f3 ♗g7 8.♗d3 0-0 9.e4 d6 10.0-0 White can gain an initiative, as in one of the lines of the King's Indian Four Pawns Attack.

6.a3!?

Another delay. 6.f4 ♘g6 is unclear.

6...♗e7

An improvement. During a simultaneous exhibition at Simpson-in-the-Strand Kasparov had encountered 6...a6 7.f4 ♘g6 8.g3?! ♗c5! 9.b4 ♗a7 10.♘f3 d6 11.♗g2

analysis diagram

11...♗e6 (11...0-0 12.0-0 ♖e8⇄) 12.♕d3 ♕d7 13.0-0 ♘ge7? 14.♔h1 ♗g4 15.♘d5 ♖b8? 16.♗b2 0-0 17.♘g5! f5 18.♕c3 ♘xd5 19.♗xd5+ (19.cxd5!?) 19...♔h8 20.♖ae1 ♖be8 21.e4?! ♗d4?? (a blunder; 21...fxe4 is unclear) 22.♗xc6!+− ♗xc3 23.♗xd7 ♗xb2 24.♗xe8 ♖xe8 25.h3 ♗c3 26.hxg4 ♗xe1 27.♖xe1 h6 28.♘f3 ♖xe4 29.♖xe4 fxe4 30.♘d4 c6 31.♔g2 d5 32.cxd5 cxd5 33.♘e6 ♔g8 34.♔f2 b6 35.♔e3 ♔f7 36.♘c7 a5 37.♘xd5 1-0 Kasparov-Mercury Asset Management, London simul 1993.

7.f4!? ♘g6

But now the position is very similar to those in 'Knight Jumps', Part II of Chapter Three.

8.g3?!

The same move as in the London simul. More natural is 8.♘f3 ♘h4!? or 8.♗d3!?.

8...d6 9.♗g2 ♗e6 10.♘d5 ♕d7 11.b4 ♗g4 12.♕d3 0-0 13.♘f3 a5 14.b5 ♘d8 15.♗b2 ♘e6 16.0-0 ♘c5 17.♕d4 f6 18.♖ad1 ♘b3 19.♕c3 ♘c5 20.♗a1 ♗d8!? 21.♕c2 ♖e8

21...c6! 22.♘c3 ♗b6 was a better try.

22.♖fe1 ♘e4?! 23.♖d4! ♘c5 24.e4 c6 25.♘e3 ♗xf3 26.♗xf3 ♗b6 27.bxc6 bxc6 28.♖dd1 ♕c7 29.♔h1 ♖ad8 30.♘f5 ♘e7 31.♘d4 a4 32.♗g4 ♘g6 33.h4 ♗a5 34.♖e2 ♖b8 35.h5 ♘f8 36.♖e3 d5 37.cxd5 cxd5   ½-½

There is still a lot of tension on the board.

Summarizing the move 5.♘c3 with the idea of f2-f4: These were two interesting simultaneous games by Kasparov. Mysteriously, they were very similar. So maybe both games were against the same opponent...?

Anyway, with 5.♘c3!? the 13th World Champion managed to avoid becoming a victim of the Budapest Gambit.

Part II – Peace

Declining the Gambit: 1.d4 ♘f6 2.c4 e5

Introduction
Declining the Budapest Gambit is very rare in tournament practice, although not in Internet Chess.

Directions
Games 100-102 contain some interesting ideas.

They illustrate three main ways to decline the Budapest Gambit:

A) 3.d5 b5!? – from the Budapest to the Volga-Benko;

B) 3.♘f3 – proposing to transpose to the Maroczy scheme;

C) 3.e3 – often transposing to the Exchange Variation of the French Defence.

Neither of these lines poses Black great difficulties.

Declining the Gambit – Games

GAME 100
□ **Jan Malec**
■ **Olaf Heinzel**
Plzen 2004 (1)

1.d4 ♘f6 2.c4 e5 3.d5

This is also a common move at the level of Internet games. The positions that arise are similar to the Indian Defences. Here, I would like to offer the lovers of the Gambit style an original and quite creative idea, which turns one gambit into another:

3...b5!?

From the Budapest to the Volga-Benko. Black also has an excellent game after the natural 3...♗b4+!? 4.♗d2 ♗xd2+ (the exchange of dark-squared bishops strategically favours Black) 5.♕xd2 d6 6.♘c3 0-0 7.e4 ♘bd7 8.♗d3 ♘c5⇄ Marmol Villalba-Figueiredo, Guaymallen 2001; or 3...♗c5 4.♘c3 e4!? 5.e3 d6 6.♕c2 ♕e7 7.♘ge2 ♗f5 8.♘g3 ♗g6 9.♗d2 ♘bd7 10.♘b5?! ♖c8 (10...♘e5 was preferable) 11.♗c3 0-0 with mutual chances in Hook-Yabra, Havana 1970.

Tricks: 3...♗c5 4.♗g5? ♘e4 or 4...♗xf2+.

4.♕c2

There are only few games with this line and there is still much ground to explore. We will briefly analyse the practiced alternatives:

A) 4.♘f3?! bxc4 (4...e4! 5.♘d4 bxc4∓) 5.♘c3 d6?! ½-½ Gonzalez Zamora-Villegas Corona, Hermosillo ch-MEX 2003; 5...♗b4!?⇄;

B) After the acceptance of the gambit with 4.cxb5!? Black can fight for the initiative with 4...a6! (less good is 4...♗b7 5.♘c3 ♗b4 6.♗g5± Peschardt-Abrahamsson, Copenhagen 2005) 5.bxa6 ♗xa6 (or 5...♘xa6!?) 6.♘c3 ♗b4 7.a3 ♗xc3+ 8.bxc3 ♗c4 (8...♕e7!?) 9.♗g5 ♕e7⇄ Fuchs-Fohler, Endingen 1987;

C) 4.e3 ♗b7 (4...bxc4!? 5.♗xc4 ♗a6⇄) 5.♘c3 b4! (5...♗b4 6.♗d2 (Fajman-Doring, Czechia 2001) 6...c6!?) 6.♘ce2 c6 7.d6 c5 8.b3 (8.♘g3 ♕b6∓) 8...♕b6 9.♘g3

9...♕xd6 (9...♗xd6∓) 10.♕c2 ♕e6 11.♗b2 d6 12.♘f3 h6 13.0-0-0 ♘bd7 14.♘d2 e4!? 15.f3 ♗e7 16.♘dxe4 ♘xe4 17.fxe4 0-0 18.♗e2 g6 19.h4 ♘e5 20.h5 ♗g5 21.♔b1 a5 22.♖d5 a4 23.♖hd1 axb3 24.axb3 ♗xd5 25.exd5 ♕e7 26.♘e4 ♗xe3 27.♖f1 f5 28.♘g3 ♕g5 29.♘h1 ♗d4 30.♘f2 ♗xb2 31.♕xb2 ♖a3 32.♘h3 ♕e3 0-1

Shengelia-Moskalenko, Banyoles rapid 2007;

D) 4.♗g5 bxc4 5.♘c3 h6!? 6.♗h4 ♗b4 (6...♘a6!?) 7.e3 (Berciano-Martin Estupinan, Gran Canaria 1989) 7...♗a6 8.♕a4 ♕e7 with chances for both sides.

4...bxc4

Interesting is 4...♘a6!?, a typical Benko Gambit manoeuvre that maintains the dynamic tension.

5.e4 c6!?

This position is just the ticket if you enjoy creative play.

6.♗xc4 cxd5 7.exd5 ♗b4+

7...♕c7!?.

8.♗d2 ♗xd2+ 9.♕xd2 0-0 10.♘c3 d6 11.♘ge2 ♘bd7 12.0-0 ♕c7 13.♗b5 ♗b7 14.♖fc1 ♕b6 15.b4 a6 16.♗d3 g6 17.♖ab1 ♘g4 18.♘g3 f5 19.h3 ♘gf6 20.♕g5 ♔h8 21.♗c4? ♖ac8∓ 22.♘a4 ♕d4 23.♘e2

Your move (check yourself):

23...♕xf2+! 24.♔xf2 ♘e4+ 25.♔g1 ♘xg5 26.b5 a5 27.b6 ♘e4 28.♖b5 ♗a6 29.b7 ♖xc4 30.♖xc4 ♗xb5 31.♖c8 ♔g8 32.♘b6 ♘b8 33.♘c3 ♗a6   0-1

It seems that this Budapest-Benko Hybrid is very interesting and playable. It can be a disagreeable surprise for the white player, who is trying to avoid gambit play.

GAME 101

□ **Julio Granda Zuniga**
■ **Viktor Moskalenko**
Tamarite 2007 (8)

1.d4 ♘f6 2.c4 e5 3.♘f3

White attempts to enter a scheme similar to the Maroczy, but here Black has the possibility of advancing the e-pawn:

3...e4!?

Or 3...exd4!? 4.♘xd4 ♗c5 or 4...♗b4+!?.

4.♘fd2 c6!?

More aggressive is the pawn sacrifice 4...e3!? 5.fxe3 d5!? (5...♗b4!? 6.♘c3 ♕e7≌ Hünnekes-Heinzel, Kleve 2001) 6.g3 (6.cxd5?! ♘xd5 7.♕b3 ♘b6!?≌) 6...h5 (6...♘g4!?) 7.♘f3 h4!→ Broekman-Thevenot, Sautron 2005.

5.e3 d5 6.♘c3

We find ourselves in a typical position of the Reversed French.

6...♗d6

Surely better is 6...♗e7!? with a balanced (French) game.

7.♕b3 ♗e7 8.♗e2 0-0 9.0-0 b6 10.a4 ♘a6 11.♖d1 ♘b4 12.♘f1 h5

Better was 12...dxc4!? 13.♗xc4 ♗g4∓.

13.♗d2 a5 14.cxd5 cxd5 15.♘b5 ♗a6 16.♖ac1 ♗xb5 17.♗xb5 ♖c8 18.♖xc8 ♕xc8 19.♖c1 ♕b8 20.♗xb4 ♗xb4 21.♖c6!↑ ♕d8

21...♖c8? 22.♖xf6!.

Wolfgang Uhlmann is a great expert of the French Defence. Budapest Gambit players can learn from his games if they are faced with the line 4.e3 exd4 4.exd4 d5 5.♘c3.

22.h3 g6 23.♘g3 h4 24.♘f1 ♔g7 25.♘h2 ♕b8 26.♗e2 ♖c8 27.♕c2 ♖xc6 28.♕xc6 ♕d8 29.♗d1 ♗d6 30.♘g4 ♘xg4 31.♗xg4 ♕c7 32.♗d7

32.♕xd5?? ♕c1+ 33.♗d1 ♕xd1 mate.

32...♔f6 33.♔f1 ♕xc6 34.♗xc6 ♔e6

½-½

After 3.♘f3 e4!? 4.♘fd2 Black has a pleasant choice between the solid plan with 4...c6 and 5...d5 (playing a French Defence Reversed), or the gambit with 4...e3!?, in both cases with a satisfactory game.

The line 3.e3 exd4 4.exd4 d5 5.♘c3 is a way to enter the Exchange Variation of the French Defence, which can also arise via other move orders. For example 1.c4 e5 2.e3 ♘f6 3.d4, or 1.e4 e6 2.d4 d5 3.exd5 exd5 4.c4 ♘f6 5.♘c3. We can learn from the specialists of this system.

GAME 102
□ **Dragoljub Velimirovic**
■ **Wolfgang Uhlmann**
Skopje 1976 (1)

1.e4 e6 2.c4 d5 3.exd5 exd5 4.d4 ♘f6

White will have an isolated pawn on d4.

Here we learn how to play in such situations.

5.♘c3

5.♘f3 ♗b4+!? 6.♗d2 ♗xd2+ 7.♘bxd2 0-0 8.♗e2 dxc4 9.♘xc4 ♘c6 10.0-0 ♗g4 11.♘ce5 ♗xf3 12.♘xf3 ♕d6⇄ Khachian-Akobian, Los Angeles 2001.

5...♗e7!?

This is a solid continuation. The alternatives are:

A) 5...♗b4!? 6.♘f3 0-0 (6...♘e4?! 7.♕b3 ♕e7 8.♗e3± Alekhine-Schwartz, Montreal 1923) 7.♗e3 (7.♗e2 dxc4 8.♗xc4 ♕e7+!? 9.♗e3 ♗e6 10.♗xe6 ♕xe6= Farina-Naumkin, Montecatini Terme 2000) 7...♖e8 8.h3?! ♘e4 9.♕b3 ♕e7 10.0-0-0 ♗xc3 11.bxc3 c6⇄ Rabinovich-Mieses, Prague 1908;

B) 5...c6 6.♘f3 ♗d6 7.cxd5 ♘xd5 8.♘xd5 cxd5 9.♗b5+?! ♘c6 10.0-0 0-0 11.♖e1 ♗g4 12.♗xc6 bxc6∓ Teske-Knaak, Zittau ch-DDR 1989.

6.♘f3

6.cxd5 ♘xd5 7.♗c4 ♘b6 8.♗b3 ♘c6 9.♗e3 0-0 10.♘ge2 ♗f5 was equal in Tartakower-Balogh, Bardejov 1926.

6...0-0 7.♗e3

A) 7.♗e2 ♗e6!? (7...♘c6 8.0-0 ♗e6 9.cxd5 ♘xd5 10.♗b5 ♘cb4 11.♖e1 a6 12.♗f1 ♖e8 13.♗d2 ♘c6 14.h3 ♗f6 15.♖e4 ♕d7∓ Miezis-Short, Leon 2001) 8.c5?! b6 9.cxb6 axb6∓ Buturin-Malaniuk, Kiev 1986;

B) 7.♗d3 dxc4!? 8.♗xc4 ♗g4 9.♗e3 ♘c6 (9...♘bd7!?∓) 10.0-0-0= S. Hansen-Spraggett, Ubeda 1996.

7...c6 8.♗d3 dxc4 9.♗xc4 ♘bd7 10.0-0

10.h3?! ♘b6 11.♗b3 ♘bd5 12.0-0 ♗e6= Kharlov-Voldin, Dos Hermanas 2004.

10...♘b6 11.♗b3 ♘bd5 12.♘e5 ♗e6 13.♗g5 ♖e8 14.♖e1 ♕a5 15.♕f3 ♖ad8

Black is more comfortable here. Soon after, he gained the initiative and the full point.

16.♖ad1 ♗b4

16...♘c7!?.

17.♘xd5 ♗xd5 18.♗xd5 ♕xd5 19.♗xf6??

More resistance would have been offered by 19.♖e3 ♕xf3 20.♘xf3 ♗e7!?∓.

19...gxf6 20.♕xf6 ♖d6! 21.♘d7 ♗xe1

0-1

German GM Wolfgang Uhlmann is a great specialist of the French Defence. In this game he showed clearly that White is unable to obtain something in this line. In other well-known examples Black did not have any opening problems either.

Summary

Normally, Black does not have problems in the secondary lines of the BG. Sometimes they transpose to positions of other openings. But in this Chapter (like in the others) I have looked for the most creative and original ideas for both players – **they are the ones who must choose between War and Peace!**

Chapter Five

Black Knight Fiction

Fajarowicz-Richter System 1.d4 ♘f6 2.c4 e5 3.dxe5 ♘e4

Dedicated to Sammi Fajarowicz and Kurt Richter

Introduction

Sammi Fajarowicz and Kurt Richter were the two German players who drew attention to the possibility of the ingenious move 3...♘e4.

According to theoretical sources, the variation 3...♘e4 is known as the Fajarowicz Gambit (A51), whereas the previously analysed 3...♘g4 is known as the Budapest Gambit (A52). This denomination creates a certain confusion.

The gambit is introduced by Black's move 2...e5, so if on the third move White does not accept the gambit, it should be called a declined gambit. If White accepts the pawn by playing 3.dxe5, Black's various replies should be variations of the same gambit, not two different gambits!

However, the theoretical confusion started with 3...♘g4, and 3...♘e4 appeared later, so to avoid any confusion, from now on we will treat A52 and A51 as two different variations.

Sammi Fajarowicz was one of the inventors of the 'spiritual' Fajarowicz-Richter System 3...♘e4.

197

The other interpretation, though, is 'spiritual' and is called the Fajarowicz Gambit ('FG' in this book) because instead of trying to get the pawn back immediately by playing 3...♞g4 as in the 'normal' Budapest Gambit, Black declines the possibility of recapturing the pawn.

It is in the spirit of the FG not to try and win the pawn back for the moment, but to develop and create complications!

A Bit of History

The stem game was played by Fajarowicz against Herman Steiner in Wiesbaden 1928 (see the note to 8.g3 in Game 103, Van Doesburgh-Richter).

During the initial period of this system Black achieved several quick and pretty tactical wins. A cruel result for white players, but actually this is quite common statistically and historically, whenever a sharp line is introduced.

Strategies of 3...♞e4

The two main motifs in the Fajarowicz-Richter System are the idea of the 'Trojan Horse' (the knight on e4) and the 'Milky Way', diagonal a8-h1.

Black

The super-aggressive 3...♞e4!? puts the knight, like the Trojan Horse, on the hottest spot on the board, in the centre of White's fortress.

Black makes use of classic tactical BG resources and plans like ...♝b4+, ...♛h4 (attacking f2 and defending the Trojan Horse on e4), ...d7-d6 (attacking the e5pawn), or ...d7-d5 (defending the knight). Sometimes ...f7-f5 is played to protect the knight. Another important opening resource is ...b7-b6/...♝b7, playing along the Milky Way.

The knight on e4 can always escape via c5.

The great popularity of this variation is due to the following reasons:
- The main ideas of 3...♞e4 are easy to study;
- Action starts at an early stage;
- There are many tactical tricks in the opening, like 4.a3 d6 5.exd6 ♝xd6 6.g3?? ♞xf2! 7.♚xf2 ♝xg3+.

- The plans in the middlegame are easy to understand. For example, in positions with an extra pawn for White on e3, Black prepares queenside castling and then attacks with ...g7-g5-g4 and ...♗xh2+!.

Game 111 Mayo-Herms
after 13...♗xh2+!

- ...b7-b6 on move 4 or at any other time during the opening is an important resource that opens up new routes along the Milky Way that are full of surprises. See the following positions:

Game 108 Ciszek-Pielaet: 5...♗b7!

Comments Game 115 Kelecevic-Gümsberg: 5...♘c5!

- If White tries to play it safe by simplifying, Black will recover the e5 pawn and the resulting endings are balanced.

White

Generally speaking, the white player is not as well prepared as Black and he tends to have little knowledge of theory and tactics, so he must trust his own judgment. But you can play the Fajarowicz and the Budapest Gambit with both colours!
Therefore:
- During the opening, White should aim for simplifications, defending the strategic key point e5 (where the extra pawn is located) and preparing quick development of his kingside.

- Fighting for the initiative and attacking is advisable after kingside castling (in certain situations, White can also choose to castle queenside).
- White should carefully consider any decision to accept more material. For example, taking a pawn by exd6 is virtually forbidden, since in many lines Black will obtain a long-term initiative, see Games 111 and 115. Sometimes the best option is to return the extra pawn in order to gain tempi for more important actions.
- Immediately attacking the Trojan Horse on e4 can be a waste of time (see Part I). But after 4.a3!? White is already threatening 5.♕c2! (see Part III).
- One of the opening possibilities is the fianchetto g3-♗g2, with counterplay along the Milky Way, like in the Catalan Opening.

⚠ Keep in Mind!
- **Before playing the FG (3...♘e4), it is advisable to study the typical ideas and concepts of the classical BG (3...♘g4) first.**
- **After 3...♘e4, during the opening Black should avoid the exchange of his Trojan Horse!**

Last warning!
If you are still interested and ready for pure action with the FG, all that remains is:

Directions
After 3...♘e4, there are three main lines that we shall analyse in detail:
1. Attacking the e4 knight with queen moves (Part I, The Trojan Horse);
2. Classical development of the white knights: 4.♘f3, 4/5.♘d2 or 4.♘c3?! (Part II, Knight Poker);
3. Avoiding the ...♗b4 check by playing 4/5.a3!? is the modern idea (Part III, The Milky Way).

Part I – The Trojan Horse

Introduction

To begin with, it is important to check the most logical idea for White: attacking the Trojan Horse with the queen. But as the given material shows, rather than having to defend his knight, Black can often use it to carry out his own aggressive plans.

Directions

There are two different ways for White to attack the knight with the queen: via c2 or via the d-file.

A) 4.♕c2 - Here Black has two main replies:

A1) 4...d5 (Game 103 Van Doesburgh-Richter) - This typical FG move defends the knight and prepares the development of the c8 bishop - preferably to f5 to threaten the white queen.

A2) 4...♗b4+ (Game 104 Stohl-Trapl) is a typical Budapest check which is also useful in the FG. Only here it is mostly followed up by the FG thrust ..d7-d5, developing quickly and immediately creating dangerous threats in the centre.

B) 4.♕d5/d4/d3 - queen on the d-file (Game 105 Karpov-Hajenius)

After 4.♕d5/d4, the 4...♗b4 check promises Black already a lead in development. Moreover, it turns out that 4.♕d5 does not prevent the opening of the Milky Way with ...b6, as in many cases the queen can be caught after taking the rook on a8. On 4.♕d3, 4...♘c5 is more accurate.

The Trojan Horse – Games

GAME 103
□ **Gerrit van Doesburgh**
■ **Kurt Richter**
Munich ol 1936 (1)

1.d4 ♘f6 2.c4 e5 3.dxe5 ♘e4!?

Here we go! Instead of the classical BG move 3...♘g4, attacking the pawn on e5, Black suddenly changes his strategy, aiming for direct complications and entering a kind of Pulp Fiction game!

4.♕c2

Attacking the Trojan Horse with the queen is the first possibility both players must consider. For other moves with the white queen (to d5-d4-d3) see Game 105. In any case, the most absurd idea for White would be trying to attack the knight with the f2 pawn; 4.f3? ♕h4+ 5.g3 ♘xg3 6.hxg3 ♕xh1–+.

4...d5!?

A common resource in the FG. It defends the Trojan Horse and prepares the move ...♗f5. For the BG check 4...♗b4+!? see Game 104. A complicated line is 4...♘c5 5.b4?! (better is 5.♘c3 or 5.♘f3) 5...♘e6 with counterplay: 6.a3 a5 (6...d6!?) 7.b5 d6 8.♘f3 (8.exd6!? ♗xd6 9.♗b2 0-0∞)

8...dxe5 9.♘xe5 ♘d4! 10.♕d3 ♗f5 (10...♗d6!) 11.e4 ♗d6⇄ Roesner-Richter, Berlin 1951.

The critical position in this line.

5.exd6!?

Other moves are worse, for example: 5.e3?! ♘c6 (5...♗f5!?) 6.♘f3 ♗f5 7.♕d1 (7.♗d3?? ♘b4) 7...dxc4 8.♕xd8+ ♖xd8 9.♗xc4 ♗b4+! 10.♔e2 ♘a5 11.♗b5+ (11.♗d3 ♖xd3!; 11.b3 ♘xc4 12.bxc4 ♗c3!; 11.♗b3 ♘xb3 12.axb3 ♘c5∓; 11.a3!? ♗e7 with initiative) 11...c6 12.♗a4 ♘c5–+ S. Rubinstein-A. Becker, Vienna 1932.

5...♗f5

The main idea of the FG is quick piece development. Pawns are of later concern. Another interesting option is 5...♘xd6!? 6.♘c3 ♘c6 7.♘f3 ♗f5 (7...♗e6!?) 8.e4 ♘xe4 9.♘xe4 ♗b4+ 10.♗d2 ♕e7 11.0-0-0? (≥ 11.♗d3∞) 11...♗xe4 12.♗d3 ♗xd2+ 13.♖xd2?! ♘b4 14.♕a4+ b5!? 15.cxb5?? ♕c5+? (15...0-0-0! 16.♗xe4 ♕xe4 would have won) 16.♔b1 ♗xd3+ 17.♖xd3 0-0∞ Mandel-Richter, Berlin 1951.

6.♕a4+?

White wastes a lot of tempi moving only his queen and pawns.

🎩 **Tricks**: 6.f3?? ♕h4+!.

If 6.♕b3?! ♗xd6 7.♞d2 (7.♕xb7
♞d7⊜) 7...0-0 (7...♞c6! is better)
8.♕xb7 ♗c5 (≥ 8...♖a6! 9.♕xa6 ♗b4
10.♞f3 ♞c5 11.♕c6 ♖e8 12.e3
♗e4−+) 9.e3 ♕e7

analysis diagram

10.♞df3?? (10.♕xa8 ♞xd2!? followed
by ...♗e4! winning the ♕a8)
10...♗b4+! 11.♗d2 ♞xd2 12.♞xd2
♗e4 13.♕b5 ♖d8 14.0-0-0 ♕d6−+
Gilfer-Richter, Munich Olympiad 1936.
A better option for White seems to be
6.♞c3!? ♞xd6 7.e4!? ♞xe4!

analysis diagram

8.♞xe4 ♗b4+ 9.♗d2 ♗xd2+
10.♕xd2 ♗xe4 11.♕xd8+ ♔xd8
12.0-0-0 ♞d7 13.♞h3!?± h6 14.♞f4
c6 15.f3 ♗h7 16.♗d3 ♗xd3 17.♖xd3
♔c7 18.♖e1 ♖he8 19.♖de3 ♖xe3
20.♖xe3 ♔d6 21.♞h5 g6 22.♞g3 ♞f6

23.♔d2 a5 24.♔c3 b5= Strunsky-
Heinzel, Ditzingen 2006.
6...♞c6 7.♞f3 ♗xd6

After only seven moves, the black pieces
dominate the board.
8.g3
The stem game continued 8.a3 ♕f6!?
9.g3 0-0-0 (9...♗c5! 10.e3 ♗g4−+)
10.♞bd2 ♞c5 11.♕d1 ♖he8 and Black
was totally winning, H. Steiner-
Fajarowicz, Wiesbaden 1928.
8...♗c5!
8...♗b4+!?.
9.♗e3 ♕f6?!
Unnecessarily complicating the game.
A stronger option was 9...♕e7!
10.♗g2 ♗xe3 11.fxe3 ♞c5−+.
10.♗xc5 ♞xc5?!
10...♕xb2! 11.♗d4 ♕c1+ 12.♕d1
♕xd1+ 13.♔xd1 0-0-0∓.
11.♕a3 ♕e7 12.e3??

Just a blunder.

12...♗xb1 13.♖xb1 ♕e4 14.♘d2 ♕xh1 15.♕xc5 ♕xh2 16.♘f3 ♕h6 17.♖d1 ♕f6 18.♗h3 ♖d8 19.♖xd8+ ♕xd8 20.♘g5 h6 21.♘e4 ♕e7 22.♕d5 0-0 23.♘c5 ♘b4   0-1

24...♕xc5 25.♕xc5 ♘d3+ is next.

Summary of 4.♕c2 d5: from the 4th move on Black obtains the easier game. But after 5.exd5 ♗f5, White can play 6.♘c3, forcing an ending with a slight edge.

GAME 104
□ **Igor Stohl**
■ **Jindrich Trapl**
Namestovo 1987 (5)

This is one of the most tense and beautiful games ever played with the FG. Both players went through unforgettable moments from the beginning to the end.

1.d4 ♘f6 2.c4 e5 3.dxe5 ♘e4 4.♕c2 ♗b4+!?

A typical BG move and a much-appreciated friend of black players! Gaining a tempo is always useful.

5.♘d2

There is nothing after 5.♗d2 ♘xd2 6.♘xd2 ♘c6 7.♘f3 ♕e7 8.a3?! ♗xd2+ 9.♕xd2 ♘xe5 10.♘xe5 ♕xe5

11.e3 d6= Meins-Gutman, Höckendorf ch-GER 2004.

Nor is there after 5.♘c3 d5!? (5...♘xc3 6.bxc3∞) 6.cxd5 (6.exd6 ♗f5 7.♗d2!? ♗xc3!? (better is 7...♘xd6 8.e4 ♗xc3 9.♕xc3 ♘xe4 10.♕e5+±) 8.♗xc3 0-0⇄) 6...♕xd5!? 7.♗d2 (if 7.♕a4+?! ♘c6 8.♕xb4 ♘xb4 9.♘xd5 ♘c2+ 10.♔d1 ♘xa1 looks better for Black) 7...♕xd2+! 8.♕xd2 ♘xd2 9.♔xd2 ♘c6 10.♘f3 ♗g4 (10...♗f5!?) 11.e3 0-0-0↑ Cruz Lopez Claret-Bellon Lopez, Spanish Championship, Lleida 1991.

5...d5!

The same strike.

6.♘f3!?

Development is important, but with this move White accepts that his attack 4.♕c2 was not so effective. The alternatives are:

A) 6.a3?! (intending to simplify) 6...♗xd2+ 7.♗xd2 ♗f5!

analysis diagram

8.♘f3 (8.♕c1?! dxc4∓; 8.♕d3 d4!?⇄) 8...♘g3?! (too hurried; 8...♘c6 or 8...0-0!? are better) 9.e4! ♗xe4 (9...♘xe4 10.cxd5 ♕xd5 11.♗c4 ♕d7 12.♗d3±) 10.♕a4+ b5 11.cxb5?? (11.♕xb5+ c6 12.♕b7 ♘xh1 13.♕xa8∓) 11...♘xh1 12.b6+ (Kallio-Kahn, Budapest 2002) 12...♘d7∓;

B) 6.exd6?! ♗f5! 7.♘f3?! (7.dxc7?! ♕xc7 8.♕a4+ ♘c6 9.♘f3 0-0-0! 10.e3 ♘c5→ Benitah-Aubert, Orange 1993) 7...♘c6 (7...♕xd6!?↑) 8.♕a4 ♕xd6 9.a3 ♘c5! 10.♕d1 0-0-0!→

analysis diagram

11.e3 ♖he8 12.♗e2 ♘d3+ 13.♗xd3 ♗xd3 14.axb4 ♘xb4 15.♕a4 ♘c2+ 16.♔d1 ♕g6 17.♕xa7 ♕xg2−+ Galarza Bilbao-Basto Auzmendi, Erandio 2005;

C) 6.cxd5?! ♕xd5 7.♘f3 ♗f5!

analysis diagram

with several threats that are hard to deal with: 8.a3 ♘xd2 9.♕a4+ b5 (9...♘c6!) 10.♕xb4 ♘b3∓ 11.♗g5 ♘c6 12.♕f4 ♘xa1 13.♕xf5 f6 14.♗d2 ♖d8 15.♕b1 ♘xe5 16.♗e3 ♘b3 (16...♘a2!!) 17.g3 ♘xf3+ 18.exf3 ♘d2 19.♗g2 ♘xb1 0-1

Fahnenschmidt-Kratochwil, Germany 2000.

6...♘c6!

At this point things are not so clear: after 6...♗f5 7.♕b3!? ♘a6 8.cxd5 0-0 (8...c6!?) 9.e3?! (9.a3 ♗xd2+ 10.♗xd2 ♘ac5 11.♕c4 b5 12.♕a2∞) 9...♕e7? (9...♘ec5 10.♕c4 ♗e4♔) 10.♗e2 ♖ad8 11.0-0± Matamoros Franco-Quadrio, Loures 1998. But an interesting try is 6...0-0!?.

7.e3 ♗g4!?

Fighting for the initiative. 7...♗f5!? 8.♗d3 0-0 9.0-0 ♘xd2 10.♗xd2 ♗xd3 11.♕xd3 ♗xd2 is equal.

8.cxd5!?

8...♗xf3

8...♕xd5?? 9.♗c4.

9.dxc6?!

This move complicates things too much. After 9.gxf3 ♘xd2 10.♗xd2 ♕xd5 11.♗xb4 ♘xb4 12.♕a4+ ♘c6 both sides have chances.

9...♕h4!

Another common shot in the BG.

10.g3 ♘xg3?!

The game gets out of hand. Easier was 10...♘xd2!? 11.♗xd2 ♕e7 12.cxb7 ♗xd2+ 13.♕xd2 ♖d8 14.b8♕ ♖xb8 15.♖g1 ♕xe5.

11.fxg3

The critical response was 11.cxb7!?, creating incredible complications, for example: 11...♘xh1 12.bxa8♕+ ♗xa8 13.♗b5+ ♔f8 14.♕f5! ♗b7 and the position remains unclear.

11...♕h6!

Now the white king is not very happy.

12.♗b5!?

Strange as it may seem, the same position occurred in a later game: 12.♕b3 (a very suspicious attempt at an improvement) 12...0-0! 13.♖g1

analysis diagram

13...♗xd2+? (what if 13...♗d5! or 13...♕xh2?! 14.♕xb4 ♗xc6 15.♘f3! ♗xf3 16.♕f4±) 14.♗xd2 ♕xh2 15.e4! ♕xg1 16.♕xf3+– Finegold-Vokler, Groningen 1990.
If 12.♔f2? ♗xh1–+.

12...♕xe3+ 13.♔f1 0-0!

It is not clear who is better in this position, but we know that defending is always harder than attacking.

14.♘xf3? ♕xf3+ 15.♔g1 ♗a5?

The right move was 15...♕d5! setting up the dual possibilities of 16...♗c5+ and 16...♕xb5.

16.h3

16.h4!? was more aggressive.

16...♕xg3+ 17.♕g2 ♕e1+? 18.♕f1?

After 18.♗f1 ♕xe5 19.♖h2! White is better.

18...♕g3+ 19.♕g2 ♕xe5

Better was 19...♗b6+!→.

20.♕e2 ♗b6+ 21.♔g2 ♕d5+ 22.♔h2 ♖ae8!

23.♕c4??

This move loses immediately. Necessary was 23.♕d3 ♕e5+ 24.♔g2 ♖d8↑.

23...♕e5+ 24.♔g2 ♖e6

24...a6!?.

25.♖d1 ♖g6+ 26.♔h1 ♕h5 27.♕d3 ♖d6   **0-1**

This game deserves an applause. Summarizing: the move 4.♕c2 does not look too useful. In the typical examples with 4...♗b4+! or 4...d5!?, Black develops quickly, creating dangerous threats (like ...♗f5 or ...♗g4) in the centre.

GAME 105
□ **Anatoly Karpov**
■ **Willem Hajenius**
Antwerp 1997

1.d4 ♘f6 2.c4 e5 3.dxe5 ♘e4 4.♕d5

Against 4.♕d3 the best continuation would probably be 4...♘c5!?, threatening the queen (if 4...♗b4+ White now has 5.♘c3!?±; less good is 5.♘d2 ♘c5 6.♕c2 ♘c6 7.♘f3 d6! 8.exd6 ♕f6!? and 9...♗f5) 5.♕c2 (5.♕g3 ♘e4!?) 5...♘c6 6.♘f3 d6!?⇄.

analysis diagram

A typical break in the FG. 7.♗g5 ♕d7 8.exd6 ♗xd6 9.a3 0-0 10.b4?! ♘e6 11.c5 ♘cd4! 12.♘xd4 ♘xd4 13.♕d3 ♗e5∓ 14.♖a2? (14.♘c3 ♕g4↑) 14...♕g4 15.f4 ♗xf4 16.♗xf4 ♕xf4−+ Jakab-Kahn, Budapest 2002. But after 4.♕d4, 4...♗b4+! (or also

4...♘c5!? 5.♘c3 ♘c6♕) is possible: 5.♘c3 (5.♘d2 ♕h4! 6.♘f3 (6.g3 ♘xd2! 7.♕xh4 ♘f3+ 8.♔d1 ♘xh4 9.gxh4 d6!?⇄) 6...♘c6! 7.♕e3 ♘xd2! 8.♗xd2 ♕xc4↑ Svela-Gundersen, Norway 1992) 5...♘xc3 6.bxc3 ♘c6↑ 7.♕e3 ♗a5 8.♗a3 ♕h4∓ Mohd-Halim, Kuala Lumpur 1996.

4...♗b4+!

The typical BG check.

The situation is unclear after 4...f5 5.exf6 (5.♘c3!? ♗b4 6.♗d2) 5...♘xf6 6.♕d1 ♗c5 7.♘f3 ♘c6 8.♘c3 d6 9.e3 (9.♗g5!?) 9...0-0 10.♗e2 ♗g4 (10...♕e8!?) 11.h3 ♗d7 with some compensation for the pawn; 12.a3 a5 13.b3 ♕e8 14.♗b2 ♕g6 15.♘d5 ♘e4 16.g4 ♖ae8 17.♖h2 ♕h6 18.♕c2 ♖f7 19.♘xc7 ♘xf2 20.♘xe8 ♕xe3 21.♕c3 ♕xe8 22.♖xf2+− Alterman-Kogan, Tel Aviv 1996.

A worse option is 4...♘c5?! 5.♘f3±.

5.♘d2 ♘c5!?

A way to balance the game could be 5...♘xd2 6.♗xd2 ♕e7, recovering the pawn on e5 sooner or later (with ...♘c6, ...0-0-0, ...♖e8), but if then 7.f4, Black can continue 7...♘c6 8.♘f3 0-0 9.0-0-0 a5!?⇄ or 9...d6!?; 9...♖d8!?.

6.a3

Obviously, Karpov wants to defend his pawn and gain the bishop pair, but White cannot play calmly anymore. To 6.♘f3 a strong reply could be 6...b6!? (6...♘c6!?⯗ is also good)

analysis diagram

Tricks: 7.♕xa8?? ♗b7∓.

7.e3? ♗b7 8.♕d4 ♗e4! and the white queen has some problems; 9.e6 0-0 10.exf7+ ♖xf7 11.♘e5 ♘c6 12.♘xc6 dxc6! 13.♕xd8+ ♖xd8 14.f3 ♗g6 15.♔e2 ♗d3+ 16.♔d1 ♖fd7 17.♗xd3 ♖xd3 0-1 Ledfuss-E. Fischer, Bavaria 1996.

6...♗xd2+

6...♘b3!? is unclear.

7.♗xd2

7...b6!

An important resource in the FG that we can find in all main lines. Black

transfers the action to the new Milky Way, the diagonal a8-h1. The line starting with 7...♘b3 turns out to be better for White: 8.♖d1 ♘xd2 9.♖xd2 0-0 10.♘f3 ♘c6 11.e3 ♕e7 12.♗d3!? ♖e8 13.♗f5±.

8.♖d1

Quite a humble response. Let us look at some other possibilities:

A) 8.♕f3 0-0!?⯗;

B) **Tricks**: 8.♕xa8? ♗b7 9.♗g5 (9.♕xa7 ♘c6∓) 9...♕c8 10.♕xa7 ♘c6 11.♕xb7 ♕xb7∓ N. Müller-Piotraschke, Germany 2000;

C) 8.e6!?

analysis diagram

8...dxe6 (8...fxe6? 9.♕h5+ g6 10.♕e5↑; maybe the best idea is 8...0-0!?∞) 9.♕xd8+ ♔xd8 10.♖d1 ½-½ Beikert-Bräuning, Bad Wildbad 1993;

D) 8.♗g5 ♕xg5 9.♕xa8 ♕xe5 10.0-0-0 0-0 with an unclear position.

8...♗b7

Now Black must be OK.

9.♕d4 ♕e7!?

9...0-0!.

10.♕g4 f6

Better was 10...0-0!? 11.♘f3 f5! with the idea 12.exf6 ♘d3 mate.

11.b4

🎩 **Tricks:** 11.exf6?? ♘d3 mate.
11...♘e4 12.exf6 ♕xf6
12...♘xf6!?.
13.♘f3 0-0
Black has won the opening battle.
14.e3 ♘xd2 15.♖xd2 ♕a1+ 16.♔e2?!
A powerful king move; 16.♖d1 ♕xa3↑.
16...♕xa3 17.h4 ♕xb4−+

18.♖h3
White lacks forces on the queenside, but the old idea of the Crazy Rook allows him to save the game: He intends to continue with ♖g3, threatening ♕g7 mate.
18...♗a6?!

18...♘c6!?.
19.♔e1 ♕b1+ 20.♖d1 ♕b4+ 21.♖d2
♕b1+   ½-½
The black player was happy to repeat moves against his strong opponent.

Summarizing the lines with 4.♕d5/d3/d4: it seems that Black has enough resources to defend successfully. In certain variations he can even aim to play more aggressively by using typical 'Trojan Horse' plans.

Summary of 'The Trojan Horse'
After queen moves on move 4, White does not have enough resources to play actively. The Trojan Horse on e4 helps the black pieces to attack and slows down White's development.
The disadvantage of attacking the Trojan Horse immediately with the queen is that White loses an important tempo, allowing Black to obtain counterplay and in certain lines even to fight successfully for the initiative.

Part II – Knight Poker

Introduction

White usually chooses these continuations when he is not theoretically prepared and prefers a solid and natural game.

4/5.♘f3 defends the extra pawn on e5, while the natural move 4/5.♘d2 attacks the dangerous knight on e4.

Directions

A) **4.♘f3** may again be met by the BG check:

A1. 4...♗b4+, and now there are the following possibilities:

A11. 5.♗d2 (Game 106 Smyslov-Steiner) gives up the bishop pair, but gets rid of the Trojan Horse. after the exchange on d2 and 6...♘c6, 7.a3! is crucial, as it allows White to defend his extra pawn on e5.

A12. 5.♘bd2 (Game 107 Topalov-Romero) is more flexible and less forcing, offering both players more options, such as (again) a3 or simple development with e3 or g3. It is like playing poker with the knights.

A2. The second black option is 4...b6 (Game 108 Ciszek-Pielaet), seemingly inviting 5.♕d5, with a myriad of complications. White can also react with the calmer 5.♘bd2 here.

B) **4.♘d2** was Alekhine's favourite move against the FG. Now the lines branch as follows:

B1. 4...♘c5 (another possible order is 4.♘f3 ♘c6 5.♘d2 ♘c5), Game 109 Alekhine-Tartakower;

B2. 4...♗b4 5.g3 – the old Catalan Way, Game 110 Epishin-Bellon Lopez.

Knight Poker – Games

GAME 106
□ **Vasily Smyslov**
■ **Herman Steiner**
Groningen 1946 (2)

In this game, played during the Staunton Memorial, grandmaster Smyslov found a creative manoeuvre: 11.♖d5!. I will baptize this rook the Staunton Rook.

1.d4 ♘f6 2.c4 e5 3.dxe5 ♘e4 4.♘f3!?

World Champion Vasily Smyslov used to surprise his opponents with fascinating opening ideas, even when facing the Budapest Gambit.

A natural response, played by White in half of the games with the FG.

4...♗b4+

The BG check is also the most popular move in this position, although it is less effective now. Another plan is 4...♘c6!? 5.♘bd2 (5.a3!? see Game 113) 5...♘c5!?, see Game 109.

5.♗d2

The move 5.♘bd2!? offers more options for both players: 5...d5!? (or for example 5...♘c6 6.a3! ♘xd2!? (like playing poker with the knights) 7.♘xd2!? trying to keep both bishops on the board; or 5...d6 6.a3 ♗xd2+ 7.♘xd2!? ♘xd2 8.♕xd2±) 6.exd6 (an option deserving closer analysis is 6.♕b3!?) 6...♕xd6 7.e3 ♘c6 8.♗e2 ♗f5 9.0-0 ♕h6 10.♘xe4 ♗xe4

11.♕a4 0-0-0 12.a3 ♗d6♔ (intending ...g5-g4)

analysis diagram

13.h3 f5 14.♘d2 ♖he8? (a clear oversight. 14...♗xg2! 15.♔xg2 ♕g5+ 16.♔h1 ♕h4 17.♔g2=) 15.♘xe4± Ivkov-Persitz, Copenhagen Wch-jr 1953.

5...♘xd2

In the variation 5...♗c5 6.e3 ♘c6 7.♘c3 ♘xd2 8.♕xd2 0-0 9.♘d5!? White keeps some advantage.

6.♘bxd2 ♘c6

211

7.a3!

The only way to try and keep the material advantage. 7.e3?! allows Black to recover the e5-pawn – see also Game 107 (6.e3/g3) 7...♕e7 8.♗e2 ♘xe5 9.a3 ♘xf3+ 10.♗xf3 ♗d6!? 11.♕c2= Züger-Romero Holmes, Manila Olympiad 1992.

7...♗xd2+?!

I think that this exchange is not necessary, although in practice it is played automatically. An alternative more in the spirit of the variation is the absurd-looking retreat 7...♗f8!? (the gin goes back into the bottle!), for example: 8.♘e4 (8.♕c2!?) 8...♕e7 9.♕d5 b6 10.g3 ♗b7 11.♗h3 0-0-0 12.0-0-0 ♘xe5! 13.♕xe5 ♗xe4 14.♖he1 f5 15.♕xe7 ♗xe7 16.♘e5?! ♖hf8∓ Benitah-Toulzac, Mulhouse 2000.

8.♕xd2 ♕e7 9.♕c3

This is the first critical position of the line with 4.♘f3 ♗b4+.

After simplifications, even if the Trojan Horse is exchanged, Black has (albeit not too great) attacking resources. The only plan is to finish development and try to get the e5 pawn back.

9...0-0

Another important possibility is 9...b6!?, preparing queenside castling, and now: 10.e3 (an interesting idea is 10.g3!? ♗b7 11.0-0-0! and now:

🎩 **Tricks:** A) 11...♘xe5? 12.♕xe5 ♕xe5 13.♘xe5 ♗xh1 14.f3±;

B) 11...0-0-0 12.♗h3 ♖he8 13.♖d5! ♘b8 14.♖d3 (14.♖hd1!?) 14...♘a6?! (14...h5!?) 15.b4 c5? (15...♘b8) 16.♖hd1 cxb4 17.axb4 (17.♖xd7!) 17...♘b8 18.c5 bxc5 19.bxc5 ♗xf3 20.exf3 ♕xe5 21.c6+− E. Toth-Kahn, Budapest 2007) 10...♗b7 11.♗e2.

analysis diagram

Waiting to see Black's reaction. 11...0-0-0!? is the most aggressive option; now castling kingside would lead to a position similar to the main game. 12.0-0-0 g5!? (a kind of 'Black Jet' attacking idea that I consider very interesting in this position. If 12...♖he8 13.♖d5! ♘b8 14.♖d4 (Smyslov's patent idea would be the rook sacrifice 14.♖hd1!?) 14...♘c6 15.♖g4 White is slightly better, as in Solo-zhenkin-Weemaes, Bethune 1992) 13.h3 h5 14.♗d3 (14.♖d5 g4∞) 14...♖he8!=.

analysis diagram

Black has equalized, for instance: 15.♗e4 ♘xe5 16.♗xb7+ ♔xb7 17.♘xe5 ♕xe5 18.♕xe5 ♖xe5 19.♖d4 d6 20.♖hd1 ♖f5 21.♖1d2 ♖e8 22.♖d5 ♖ee5 23.♖xe5 ♖xe5 24.♖d5 ½-½ Summermatter-Bellon Lopez, Bern 1995.

The Spanish GM Juan Bellon Lopez, an FG expert, is a fan of the move ...b7-b6 and of playing along the Milky Way (see also Game 110).

10.♖d1!

Preparing a surprise.

A more risky line is 10.0-0-0 ♖e8 11.♖d5 (also played by Zviagintsev) 11...b6 (11...d6!? 12.exd6 cxd6 13.e3 ♗e6⇄) 12.e3 ♗b7 13.♗e2 a5 (13...♘d8∞) 14.♖hd1 ♘b4 15.axb4 ♗xd5 16.♖xd5 axb4 17.♕d4+− Rogozenko-Kahn, Budapest 1995.
10...♖e8 11.♖d5!

Here is the 'Staunton Rook', dedicated to the memory of master Staunton.
11...b6!?
Black opens a new path along which to continue the battle.
12.e3 ♗b7 13.♗e2
Another important moment in the opening.
13...♖ad8
Defending the pawn on d7 first seems logical, but this way White gains a tempo to complete his development.
A worse move is 13...♘a5?! 14.b4!? (14.♖d2!?) 14...♗xd5 15.cxd5 ♘b7 16.♕xc7 (16.0-0!?) 16...d6 17.♕xe7 ♖xe7 18.exd6 ♘xd6 19.♘d4± Haba-Heinzel, playchess.com 2005, but a plausible alternative is 13...♘d8 14.♖d2 ♘e6, and if 15.0-0 ♘g5!? 16.♘xg5 ♕xg5 17.g3 ♖ad8 18.f4 ♕e7 Black has certain compensation for the pawn.
14.0-0 ♘b8!?

213

15.♖c1!?

This is the point of White's plan: he sacrifices the Staunton Rook in order to dominate with his central pawns. This brilliant idea is still an important resource in this line. If 15.♖d2 ♗xf3 16.♗xf3 ♕xe5 (= Smyslov) 17.♖c1 ♕xc3 18.♖xc3 d6 19.♔f1 ½-½ Gilman-A. Gulko, Quebec 2001.

15...♗xd5 16.cxd5

Black is slightly passive and it is hard for him to improve his position.

16...d6

Maybe better is 16...c5!? 17.♗b5 f6!? with the idea 18.d6 ♕f8 19.b4 ♔h8 20.bxc5 ♖c8 with mutual chances.

17.♗b5! ♖f8 18.e4! a6 19.♗d3 dxe5?

Black may have more chances in the variation 19...♖fe8!?, for example: 20.♕xc7 ♕xc7 21.♖xc7 dxe5 22.a4 ♖d7!? 23.♖xd7 ♘xd7 24.♗xa6 ♘c5

25.♗b5 ♖a8 and there are still certain possibilities of counterplay.

20.♘xe5 ♖d6?!

20...♖fe8 21.f4±.

21.♘c4 ♖h6

A very modest attack.

22.♘e3 ♕h4 23.♕xc7

Black's position is completely hopeless.

23...♖f6 24.g3 ♕h5 25.e5 ♖h6 26.h4 ♕f3 27.♖c4 b5 28.♖f4 ♕h5 29.♘g4 ♖g6 30.♗xg6 ♕xg6 31.e6 ♕b1+ 32.♔h2 f5 33.e7 ♖e8 34.♕d8   1-0

Summary of 4.♘f3 ♗b4+: White develops and simplifies, trying to defend the e5 pawn. In main lines Black must fight hard for equality, but there are still some lines, like 7... ♗f8!? instead of 7...♗xd2, that leave room for creativity.

GAME 107
□ Veselin Topalov
■ Alfonso Romero Holmes
Las Palmas 1992

1.d4 ♘f6 2.c4 e5 3.dxe5 ♘e4 4.♘f3

Against 4.♘c3 the most creative response would be 4...♕h4!? (4...♘xc3 5.bxc3∞) 5.♘xe4 ♕xe4 (attacking two pawns) 6.♘f3 ♕xc4⇄.

4...♗b4+

4...♘c6!? 5.♘bd2 (for 5.a3 see Game 113) 5...♘c5!? see Game 109.

5.②bd2 ②c6

A) 5...♕e7 6.a3 ♗xd2+ 7.②xd2!?
(7.♗xd2 ②c6 8.♗e3!?) 7...♕xe5
8.g3?! (8.②xe4 ♕xe4 9.♕d5±)
8...②c5 (8...②xd2!?) 9.②f3 ♕h5
10.b4 ②e6 11.♗g2± Herraiz Lopez-
Torres Dominguez, Torrelavega 2002;

B) 5...d6 6.a3 ♗xd2+ 7.♗xd2
(7.②xd2!?) 7...②c6 8.exd6 ♕xd6
9.♗e3 ♕e7 10.g3 0-0 11.♗g2 ♗e6
12.♕c2 ②d6 13.♗c5! b6 14.♗xd6
cxd6 15.0-0 ♖ac8 16.♕d3 ♖fd8
17.b3?! d5!⇄ Dautov-Gutman,
playchess.com ch-GER blitz 2003.

6.e3

White opts for the completion of his
development, but allows Black to regain
the pawn on e5. A quite similar option
is 6.g3 ♕e7 7.♗g2 ②xd2 8.♗xd2
♗xd2+ 9.♕xd2 ②xe5 10.②xe5 ♕xe5
11.0-0 0-0 12.b4 ♖b8 (12...d6) 13.f4
♕e7 14.f5 ♖e8 15.f6 ♕e3+ 16.♕xe3
♖xe3 17.♖ad1 d6 18.c5 ♗e6
(18...♖xe2=) 19.cxd6 cxd6 20.♖xd6
♖xe2 21.a4 b6 22.fxg7 ♖c8 23.♗c6
½-½ Kasparov-Arts, Rotterdam simul
1987.

The most ambitious move is 6.a3!? similar to the ideas shown in the previous
game.

6...♕e7 7.♗e2

Slightly better is 7.a3!?.

7...②xe5=

8.0-0 ②xf3+

8...②xd2 9.♗xd2 ②xf3+ 10.♗xf3
♗xd2 11.♕xd2 d6 12.b4 0-0 13.♖ac1
♖b8 14.c5 dxc5 15.bxc5 b6 16.♕c3
♗e6⇄ Volkov-A. Gulko, playchess.com
blitz 2004.

9.②xf3 0-0

9...a5 was better.

**10.②d4 ♗c5 11.♕c2 c6 12.b3 d5
13.♗b2 ♗d7 14.♗d3 ♖fe8 15.f3 ②f6
16.♖ae1 dxc4 17.bxc4 ♖ad8 18.♗f5
♗xd4 19.♗xd4 ♗xf5 20.♕xf5 ②d7
21.♕a5 c5 22.♗a1 ②b6 23.e4 ♖d3
24.♖c1 ②c8 25.♗c3 ♕d6 26.♗e1 b6
27.♕a6 ♕d7 28.a4 ♖a3**

28...f5!?⇄.

**29.♕b5 ♕xb5 30.axb5 ♖d8 31.♗h4
f6 32.e5 ♔f7 33.♖fe1 ♖d2 34.♖cd1
♖aa2 35.♖xd2 ♖xd2 36.exf6 gxf6
37.♖e4 ②d6 38.♖f4 f5 39.♗g3 ♔g6
40.h4 ♖d1+ 41.♔f2 ②f7 42.♗b8
♖a1 43.g4 fxg4 44.♖xg4+ ♔f6
45.♖f4+ ♔g6 46.♖e4 ♔f6 47.♖e8
♖a4 48.♖c8 ②e5 49.♖h8 ②xc4
50.♖xh7 a6 51.bxa6 ♖xa6 52.h4 ♔g6
53.♖b7 ②a5 54.♖c7** ½-½

Conclusion: With simple development
White can avoid complications, but he
cannot claim an opening advantage.

GAME 108
□ **Mieczyslaw Ciszek**
■ **Sjaak Pielaet**
Naleczow Open 1987

1.d4 ♘f6 2.c4 e5 3.dxe5 ♘e4 4.♘f3 b6

A new path. Shall we accept the invitation, gentlemen?

5.♕d5

We must always ask ourselves if there is a refutation or not, using Fritz 10 to avoid tactical mistakes. In a real game, practical players will tend to avoid complications. We should keep in mind that White can play the calmer 5.♘bd2!?.

analysis diagram

5...♗b7 6.e3 (6.g3 ♗c5!?) 6...♗b4 (6...♘c5!?) 7.♗e2 ♘c6 and now still engage his rival in complications with

8.a3!? (objectively better is 8.0-0! ♗xd2 9.♘xd2 ♘xd2 10.♗xd2 ♘xe5 11.f4↑) 8...♗xd2+ 9.♘xd2 ♘xd2

(**Tricks**: 9...♘xe5?? 10.♘xe4 ♗xe4 11.♕d4 1-0 Gagunashvili-B. van den Berg, Haarlem 2004)

10.♗xd2 ♘xe5 11.♗c3±.

5...♗b7

This is the most attractive option. The machine prefers 5...♗b4+!? 6.♗d2 (in reply to 6.♘bd2?! Fritz suggests 6...♗b7!? (or even 6...♘c5!?with the idea 7.♕xa8?? ♗b7∓) 7.♕xb7 ♘c6 8.♘d4 (8.a3 ♘c5) 8...0-0!∓) 6...♘xd2 7.♘bxd2 ♘c6⇄.

6.♕xb7

We are now in a dark cave.

6...♘c6

Tricks: 6...♗b4+? 7.♗d2+−.

7.♕a6??

A blunder. If 7.♗e3 ♗b4+!? 8.♘c3 (8.♘bd2 ♘xd2 9.0-0-0∞) 8...♘xc3 9.a3 ♗a5 10.b4 is very unclear.

The critical variation might be 7.♘d4!? ♗b4+ 8.♘c3 0-0!? (8...♘xc3 9.♘xc6) 9.a3! ♘xc3 10.e3!? and good luck with the rest...

And then we should always consider the intermediate move 7.e6!?.

7...♗b4+!

Now Black gains material.

**8.♗d2 ♘c5! 9.♕b5 ♗xd2+ 10.♘bxd2
a6 11.♕xc6 dxc6**   **0-1**

In all cases it is advisable to play 4.♘f3
b6 only when playing blitz or on the
Internet.

GAME 109
□ **Alexander Alekhine**
■ **Savielly Tartakower**
London 1932 (7)

1.d4 ♘f6 2.c4 e5 3.dxe5 ♘e4 4.♘d2

This was Alekhine's favourite move
against the FG.

4...♘c5!?

An interesting possibility, based on the
fact that the knight on d2 is slightly passive. Black invests a tempo but avoids
simplifications.

Do not exchange the Trojan Horse!
4...♗b4 5.g3 will be seen in Game 110;

for 5.♘f3 we refer you back to Game
106.

5.♘gf3

5.b4!? ♘e6 6.a3 d6?! (6...a5!? 7.b5
f6!?⇄; 6...f6!?) 7.exd6 ♗xd6 8.♘e4!
♗e5 9.♕xd8+ ♘xd8 10.♖a2 ♗f5
11.♘f3!± Herrmann-Fajarowicz,
Frankfurt II 1930.

5...♘c6

6.g3!?

6.a3 a5 (better is 6...♕e7! with the idea
7.b4? ♘xe5!→) 7.♘b3 h6?! 8.♗f4 ♘e6
9.♗g3± Bogoljubow-Richter, Swinemünde 1931; 6.♘b3 ♘xb3! 7.axb3

Savielly Tartakower (1887-1956) was the
first grandmaster who played the risky
Fajarowicz Gambit.

♗b4+ (7...f6!? 8.exf6 ♕xf6 to be followed by 9...♗b4+ seems reasonable) 8.♗d2 ♕e7 9.e3 0-0 10.♗e2 ♘xe5 11.♘xe5 ♗xd2+ 12.♕xd2 ♕xe5 13.0-0 (13.♖a5!?) 13...d6 14.♗f3 a6 15.b4 ♖b8 16.♖fc1 ♖d8 17.♖a3 ♗e6 18.♖d3 b6 19.♗d5 a5 20.bxa5 (20.b5!?±) 20...bxa5⇄ Moskalenko-G. Mohr, Belgorod 1990.

6...♕e7!?

Regaining the e5 pawn. An option to play more in FG style is the break 6...d6!?, with a typical game after 7.exd6 ♕xd6!? (7...♗xd6 8.♗g2 ♗f5 9.0-0 ♕e7 10.♘b3 0-0-0 11.♗e3 h5 12.♘fd4 ♗e4 13.♘xc6 ♗xc6 14.♗h3+? ♔b8 15.♘d4 ♗e4 16.b4 h4! 17.g4 ♘e6 18.♘f5 ♗xf5 19.gxf5 ♗xh2+ 20.♔xh2 ♖xd1 21.♖axd1 ♘g5–+ Cosma-Stefanova, Niksic 1994) 8.♗g2 ♗f5 9.0-0 0-0-0 10.b3 (10.a3 ♕f6!? 11.♘h4 ♗e6 12.♗xc6 bxc6 13.♕c2 g5 14.b4 gxh4 15.♗b2 ♕h6 16.♘f3 ♖g8∓ List-Richter, Swinemünde 1932; 10.b4!? ♘xb4 11.♗b2 ♕h6?! 12.♘d4 ♗h3 13.♘2f3 ♗xg2 14.♔xg2 ♗e7? 15.♕b1! ♕g6 16.♘f5 ♗f8? 17.♗xg7! 1-0 Graf-Lauer, Nuremberg 2006) 10...h5! 11.♗b2 h4→

analysis diagram

12.♕c1 hxg3 13.hxg3 ♕h6 (13...♕g6!?) 14.♖e1 ♘b4?! (14...♗e7!→) 15.♘h4 ♘bd3!?∞ 16.exd3 ♘xd3 17.♕c2□ ♗h7!? (17...♘c5!? 18.♘xf5 ♘xe1⇄) 18.♗h3+? ♔b8 19.♘e4 ♘xe1 (19...f5!↑) 20.♖xe1 ♗b4 21.♖e2 g5 (≥ 21...♗e7!?) 22.♗xh8 gxh4 23.♗e5 hxg3 24.♗g2 gxf2+ 25.♔f1 ♗e1 (25...♗f5!?) 26.♕b2 ♖g8 27.♗g3 ♖d8 28.♗xf2 ♗b4 29.♕f6 ♖d1+ 30.♗e1 ♕xf6+ 31.♘xf6 ♗d3 32.♔f2 ♗c5+ 33.♖e3 ♖xe1?? (33...♗xe3+ 34.♔xe3 ♗b1⇄) 34.♘d7+! ♔c8 35.♘xc5 ♖xe3 36.♔xe3 ♗b1 1-0 A.Shneider-Gutman, Bad Zwesten 2005.

7.♗g2 g6!?

Activating the f8-bishop and finishing his development, Black almost reaches equality; 7...♕e6!? is an alternative.

8.♘b1!?

With the idea of ♘c3-d5.

8...♘xe5 9.0-0 ♘xf3+ 10.exf3 ♗g7 11.♖e1 ♘e6 12.♘c3 0-0 13.♘d5

Incredibly, Alekhine won a lot of games with this manoeuvre in the BG, but it is not always so good. 13.♗e3!?.

13...♕d8 14.f4 c6!?

14...d6!? 15.f5 gxf5 16.♕h5 c6 17.♘f4 ♕a5∞.

15.♘c3

15...d6?!

Better was 15...♘d4!.

16.♗e3±

Now White keeps his pressure in the centre.

**16...♕c7 17.♖c1 ♗d7 18.♕d2 ♖ad8
19.♖ed1 ♗c8 20.♘e4 ♘c5?**

20...♖d7 was the only move.

21.♘xd6 ♘a4 22.c5?!

22.♕b4!.

22...♘xb2 23.♖e1

23...b5??

The decisive mistake. After 23...♗f5
24.♗f1 b6 Black would still be alive.

24.cxb6!

A piece of tactics.

**24...♕xd6 25.♕xd6 ♖xd6 26.bxa7
♗b7 27.♗c5 ♖dd8 28.♗xf8 ♔xf8
29.♗xc6 ♗xc6 30.♖xc6 ♖a8 31.♖b6
♖xa7 32.♖b8   1-0**

Mate.

Summary of 4.♘d2

This move is not as dangerous for Black or as flexible for White as 4.♘f3 or 4.a3. With 4...♗c5! (always the escape square for the Trojan Horse) Black can keep good chances in all lines.

GAME 110
□ Vladimir Epishin
■ Juan Manuel Bellon Lopez
Malaga 2000 (9)

With this instructive game we complete the study of typical positions in the Knight Poker game (4.♘f3/4.♘d2).

**1.d4 ♘f6 2.c4 e5 3.dxe5 ♘e4 4.♘d2
♗b4!?**

We must try everything.

5.g3!?

White is playing in the spirit of the old Catalan Opening. The move 5.♘f3 can be found in Games 106 and 107; and 5.a3!? is similar to Game 106.

5...b6

The FG expert Bellon Lopez presents us with an interesting battle along the Milky Way. In another game, after 5...♘c6!?, the legendary Danish grandmaster Bent Larsen confronted the FG with one of his famous concepts: 6.♗g2!

219

analysis diagram

6...♘xd2 7.♗xd2 ♕e7 (an easier road to equality is 7...♗xd2+ 8.♕xd2 ♘xe5=) 8.f4!? g5?! (8...0-0) 9.♗xb4 ♕xb4+ 10.♕d2 ♕xc4 11.♖c1 ♕xa2 12.♘f3 g4? (the superior 12...gxf4 is met by 13.♘g5, taking the initiative) 13.♘g5 ♕a5 14.♕xa5 ♘xa5 15.♗d5 (15.♖xc7!?) 15...f6 16.exf6+− c6 17.♗e4 d5 18.♗xh7 ♖xh7 19.♘xh7 ♔f7 20.e4 dxe4 21.♖c5 ♘b3 22.♖g5 ♗f5 23.♖xf5 ♔g6 24.♖g5+ ♔xh7 25.h3!

analysis diagram

with a thematic mate on the next move: 26.hxg4 1-0 Larsen-Romero Holmes, Las Palmas 1992.

The genuine FG move would be 5...d5!? 6.♗g2 ♘c6⇄.

6.♗g2 ♗b7

The Milky Way is on fire.

7.f3?!

Maybe for the above reason, Epishin begins to waver. The correct move was 7.♘f3!? after which White's army is very solidly placed.

7...♘xd2 8.♗xd2 ♕e7 9.e4?! ♘c6!
10.♘e2

10.f4 0-0-0.

10...♘xe5

The initiative is in Black's hands.

11.0-0 ♘xc4

Better was 11...♗c5+ 12.♔h1 ♘xc4∓.

12.♗xb4 ♕xb4 13.♕d4 c5! 14.♕xg7 ♕xb2 15.♕xb2 ♘xb2

Black has gained material and, later on, wins the game.

16.♘c3 ♗c6 17.f4 0-0-0 18.a4 ♘c4 19.♖fc1 ♔b7 20.♖ab1 d6 21.♘b5? ♘d2 22.♖b2 ♘xe4−+ 23.a5 f5 24.axb6 axb6 25.♖cb1 d5 26.♘a3 ♔c7 27.♖xb6 ♖b8 28.♖xb8 ♖xb8

29.♖xb8 ♚xb8 30.g4 ♘f6 31.g5 ♘h5 32.♗f3 ♘xf4 33.h4 ♚c7 34.♚f2 ♚d6 35.♚e3 ♘e6 36.♗h5 ♚e7 37.♗d1 ♚d6 38.♗h5 f4+ 39.♚f2 ♘d4 40.♗f7 ♘f5 41.♗g8 h6 42.♗h7 ♗d7 43.♘b5+ ♚e5 44.♗xf5 ♗xf5   0-1

Generally speaking, White has difficulties to obtain a serious advantage after 4.♘d2 and 5.g3, but we already know

that the same problem applies in the Catalan Opening.

Summary of 'Knight Poker'

White is very solid and it is hard to surprise him, but defending his extra pawn on e5 is not easy either.

Black has chances to equalize or to complicate in almost all lines.

Part III – The Milky Way

Introduction

The move a2-a3 looks slow, but it prevents quick development by the BG check 4...♗b4+, and so 5.♕c2 becomes an annoying threat. Black can react in several ways: with the immediate break 4...d6 (A), or first by developing with 4...♘c6 (B), attacking e5 as well, the aggressive queen sortie 4...♕h4 (C) or the modern 4...b6, opening the Milky Way (diagonal a8-h1).

Directions

A) 4...d6

After the typical FG break 4...d7-d6!?, taking on d6 is very dangerous for White.

It is clear that White must defend the e5 pawn with his knight (5.♘f3, A1, Game 111 Mayo-Herms) and attack the Trojan Horse with 5.♕c2 (A2, Game 112 Lukacs-Becker) or 5.♘d2. 5.♕c2 is the critical reply, after which Black must lose a tempo compared to Part I with ...d6-d5.

B) 4...♘c6 5.♘f3 d6

Natural development, but here things do not run so smoothly for Black, as White has some tricky queen moves (Game 113 Bisguier-Ljubojevic).

C) 4...♕h4

A very aggressive sortie, introducing tactics straightaway, seemingly in the spirit of the FG. But with natural moves, White can ward off the attack and develop (Game 114 Flear-Bellon Lopez). In this game I also analyse the alternative 4...a5 with which Black can safeguard the retreat of the Trojan Horse to c5.

D) 4...b6

This provocative move, opening the Milky Way, might be Black's best chance in this variation (Game 115 Kelecevic-Günsberg). This is quite a new idea with attractive points, which deserves closer examination.

The Milky Way – Games

GAME 111
□ **Marti Mayo Casademont**
■ **Jordi Herms Agullo**
Mataro 2004 (5)

1.d4 ♘f6 2.c4 e5 3.dxe5 ♘e4 4.a3 d6!?

A typical break in the FG. The idea is to attack the pawn on e5 and to create an exit for the c8-bishop: the idea is ...♗f5.

5.♘f3

🎩 **Tricks**: after 5.exd6?! ♗xd6 Black gets a dangerous initiative through the centre, for example: 6.g3?? ♘xf2! 7.♔xf2 ♗xg3+ winning the queen (0-1, Warren-Sellmann, Berlin 1930).
Another critical line is 5.♕c2!? as we will see in Game 112.

5...♗f5!?

First, Black activates his queenside pieces, preparing to castle there. The move 5...♘c6 will feature in Game 113.

6.e3?!

White wants to play ♗e2 and castle kingside, but this move locks in his c1 bishop, for which he will suffer in the middlegame.
The fianchetto may be more effective: 6.g3!?

analysis diagram

6...♘c6 (6...h5?! 7.♗g2 ♘c6 8.♘d4 ♘xd4 9.♕xd4 ♘c5 10.♕e3 dxe5 11.b4 ♘e6 12.♗b2 f6 13.♗xb7+− Levin-Gutman, German Championship, Altenkirchen 2001) 7.♘h4! (7.♗g2? dxe5∓; 7.exd6?! ♗xd6 8.♗e3 Danailov-Carpintero, Las Palmas 1992, and now 8...♕f6!) 7...♗e6 8.♗g2 ♘c5 (8...f5 9.exf6 ♘xf6 10.♘c3!? with the idea 10...♗xc4 11.♕a4 ♗e6 12.♘f3↑) 9.b4! (9.exd6?! ♕xd6) 9...♘d7 and now, after 10.exd6!? I prefer White.
An inferior continuation is 6.♘bd2?! dxe5 7.♘xe4 ♕xd1+ 8.♔xd1 ♗xe4 9.♘xe5 ♗d6 10.♘d3 ♘c6 11.♗d2 0-0-0 12.♗c3 ♗e5 (12...♘e5!?) 13.♔d2 ♖he8 with great compensation for Black, Gleizerov-Dausch, Cappelle la Grande 1995.

6...♘c6 7.exd6 ♗xd6

A desirable position for any FG player. Black will soon gain the upper hand thanks to his good development.

8.♗e2 ♕e7

An even more aggressive move is 8...♕f6!?, taking control of the f6-a1 diagonal, for example: 9.0-0 0-0-0 10.♕b3 g5! (this might be the stem game of the strong plan ...g5-g4, followed by ...♗xh2+; the alternative is 10...♕g6!?) 11.♘c3 g4 12.♘xe4 ♗xe4 13.♘d2 (13.♘e1 ♕h6!? 14.g3 f5–+)

analysis diagram

13...♗xh2+!! 14.♔xh2 ♕h4+ 15.♔g1 ♖xd2 (15...♗xg2! is the classical Lasker-Bauer continuation) 16.♗xd2 ♘e5 17.♕c3 f6 18.♕d4 ♗xg2? (the winning move was 18...♘f3+!) 19.♗xg4+! ♘xg4 20.♔xg2 ♖g8 (Fronczek-R. Hoffmann, Baden-Alsace junior match 1996) and now 21.♔f3 is unclear.

9.♘bd2 0-0-0 10.♘xe4 ♗xe4 11.♕a4 g5!

This powerful resource, similar to the thrust with the Black Jet in Chapter One, Part III, increases Black's initiative.

12.0-0 g4!

Attacking the only white piece that defends the kingside.

13.♘d2

13...♗xh2+!!

Some themes known since the Romantic Age keep returning. Minor pieces are sacrificed to break open the enemy fortress.

14.♔xh2 ♕h4+ 15.♔g1 ♗xg2! 16.f4N

Today, the idea of this fabulous attack is still alive on the Internet: 16.♔xg2 ♕h3+ 17.♔g1 g3 (17...♘e5!) 18.♘f3 ♖hg8 19.e4 gxf2+ 20.♔xf2 ♖g2+ 21.♔e3 ♕h6+ 0-1 Kreiman-Evertsson, blitz 2003.

16...gxf3

16...♖xd2!? 17.♗xd2 ♗e4–+.

17.♗xf3 ♗xf3 18.♖xf3

18...♕e1+!

Cutting off the king's road to safety is the key to victory.

19.♘f1 ♖hg8+ 20.♔h1 ♕h4+ 21.♘h2 ♕g5   **0-1**

White gets mated.

Summarizing the line 4...d6 5.♘f3 ♗f5, White has three natural plans:

A11) 6.e3?! allows a beautiful and powerful attack by Black;

A12) 6.♘d2?! simplifies and hands Black an advantage;

A13) 6.g3!? this plan is worthy of closer investigation from both sides, since it is the most critical in this line.

GAME 112
□ **Peter Lukacs**
■ **Walter Becker**
Germany Bundesliga B 1997/98 (9)

1.d4 ♘f6 2.c4 e5 3.dxe5 ♘e4 4.a3 d6 5.♕c2!?

Probably the critical reply to 4...d6.

5...d5

After this advance, White has gained a tempo compared to the line 4.♕c2 (Part I), even though he cannot take 6.exd6. Unfortunately, 5...♗f5?! does not work for tactical reasons, since after 6.♘c3!

analysis diagram

White is better in all variations: 6...♘g3 (or 6...d5 7.cxd5 ♘xc3 8.♕xf5 ♘xd5 9.e6! f6 10.e4+− Röder-Stefanova, Groningen 1996; 6...♘xf2 7.♕xf5±) 7.e4 ♘xh1 8.exf5 dxe5 9.♗e3 ♘c6 10.♖d1!± ♕f6 11.♘d5 ♕d6 12.c5

♕d8 13.♘f3 ♘d4 14.♘xd4 ♕xd5 15.♘f3 1-0 CapNemo-Der Rentner, playchess.com 2006.

Slightly better is 5...♘c5!?, but here White has the simple 6.exd6!? ♗xd6 7.♘f3 0-0 (7...♘c6!? 8.♘c3 ♕f6 9.♗g5 ♘d4 10.♘xd4 ♕xg5⇄) 8.♘c3± and Black has no full compensation for the pawn.

6.cxd5

Another important moment. An advantage may be more easily gained by playing 6.♘c3!? ♘xc3 7.♕xc3 d4 (Black just enters the Albin's Counter Gambit; 7...dxc4!? may be better here) 8.♕g3!? ♗e6 9.e4! ♘c6 10.♗d2 (10.f4!? f5) 10...d3 11.♗xd3 (11.0-0-0!?) 11...♘xe5 12.♗c2 ♘xc4 13.♗c3 ♗d6!? 14.♕xg7 ♗e5!⇄ S. Atalik-Fette, Groningen 1999.

Another option is the still untried but natural move 6.♘f3!?.

6...♕xd5 7.♘f3 ♘c6 8.♘c3

8.e3 ♗f5 (8...♘xe5!?) 9.♗c4 ♕a5+ (9...♕d7!?) 10.b4? ♗xb4+ 11.axb4 ♕xa1 12.0-0 (CapNemo-Yaacovn, playchess.com 2007) 12...♘g3!∓.

8...♘xc3 9.♕xc3

9...♗g4!?

9...♗e7 10.♗f4±.

10.b4?

More logical is the Rubinsteinian move 10.♗f4!? 0-0-0 11.e3 ♗e7!? and if 12.♗e2 g5! 13.♗g3 h5 14.h3 ♗e6, Black has a dangerous attack for the pawn. Another good question is raised by 12.♗c4!? ♕e4 13.♗e2.

10...0-0-0 11.♗b2 g6 12.b5 ♗xf3

13.bxc6??

A tactical blunder in a good position. The only move was 13.gxf3 ♗h6 14.e3 ♘xe5 15.♗h3+ ♔b8 16.♕xe5 ♕xf3 (16...♕d2+? 17.♔f1+−) 17.b6! axb6 18.♖c1 with an initiative.

13...♗h6!

An unexpected resource. The sudden threat of 14...♗d2+ is fatal.

14.cxb7+

If 14.e3? ♕d1+ 15.♖xd1 ♖xd1 mate.

14...♔b8 15.♕d4 ♗d2+ 16.♔xd2 ♕xe5 17.e3 c5   **0-1**

Summary of 5.♕c2: in the variations that arise after 5...d5 or 5...♘c5, Black obtains some compensation for the pawn, but White is quite solid and it is hard to surprise him.

GAME 113
□ **Arthur Bisguier**
■ **Ljubomir Ljubojevic**
Malaga 1971 (14)

1.d4 ♘f6 2.c4 e5 3.dxe5 ♘e4 4.a3 ♘c6

Simply developing a piece, but in the FG time is limited for this kind of moves.

5.♘f3

There are many hidden tricks in the variation 5.e3!? ♕h4!? (5...♘xe5?? 6.♕d4+−; 5...d6!?) 6.♕c2 (6.g3 ♕g5!?⇄) 6...♗b4+! 7.axb4 ♘xb4 8.♕e2 ♘xf2 9.♕xf2 ♘c2+ 10.♔e2∞.

5...d6

Also possible is 5...a5, although this spends another tempo: 6.♕d5!? (6.♕c2!?; less good is 6.e3 d6! 7.♕c2 ♘c5⇄) 6...♘c5 (6...f5!?) 7.♗g5 ♗e7 8.♗xe7 (more amusing would be 8.♕xc5!) 8...♕xe7 9.♘c3 0-0 10.♘b5 ♘a6 11.e3 ♖e8 12.♗e2 ♘xe5 13.♕xe5 ♕xe5 14.♘xe5 ♖xe5 15.♔d2 d6 16.b4!?± Bauer-Szabolcsi, Paris 2001.

6.♕c2!

The most dangerous move for Black.

🎩 **Tricks**: 6.exd6?! ♗xd6 7.e3?! (7.g3?? ♘xf2! 8.♔xf2 0-1 Marinelli-Osmanbegovic, Cannes 1995. Better is 7.♘bd2 ♗f5 8.♘xe4 ♗xe4 9.♗g5 f6 10.♗e3 ♕e7⩱ 11.♕a4∞ Degtiarev-Weitzer, Germany Oberliga 2005/06) 7...♗g4!? (for 7...♗f5! see Game 111, position after 7...♗xd6) 8.♗e2?! ♕f6 9.h3 0-0-0 (9...♗f5!) 10.hxg4 ♗g3! 11.fxg3?! ♖xd1+ 12.♗xd1 ♘e5 13.0-0 ♘xg3∓ Schlage-Richter, Berlin 1930.

If White plays Rubinstein's move 6.♗f4?! here, Black can reply 6...g5! with the same idea as in the Black Jet variation (Chapter One, Part III); 7.♗g3 h5 (7...♗g7!) 8.exd6 cxd6 (8...h4!?) 9.♕d5 f5 10.h4 ♕b6 with the initiative Montegre-X. Sanchez, Catalonia 1997.

6...d5

This looks forced, but now White has had an extra tempo for the useful move a2-a3 (see Part I – 3...♘e4 4.♕c2 d5), although he cannot take en passant now.

6...♗f5? does not work, since Black has the same problem he had in Game 112 after 7.♘c3! and now:

analysis diagram

7...♘xc3 8.♕xf5 ♘a4 9.♕c2 ♘c5 10.b4 ♘e6 11.exd6! ♗xd6 12.♗b2 0-0 13.e3+− Davies-Gatland, Trondheim 1997;

7...♘g3 is no better, for example: 8.e4 ♘xh1 9.exf5 dxe5 10.♗e3 ♗e7 11.♕e4 0-0 12.♗d3 f6 13.0-0-0 with a winning position for White, Montag-Heyer, corr 1994.

If 6...♘c5, then 7.b4!? ♘e6 8.exd6! ♗xd6 9.♗b2 0-0 10.e3 ♘g5 11.♘bd2±, Spraggett-Milla de Marco, Madrid 2000.

7.e3!

A critical position in this important line. Now Black must come up with a good idea.

After 7.cxd5 ♕xd5, the position from Game 112 would arise.

7...♗g4

This continuation has been proposed by GM Lev Gutman in his Survey in Yearbook 70 as offering Black some chances. But things are not so easy.

Just one game was played recently in the Germany Bundesliga with the line 7...♗e6 8.♗e2!? (also 8.♘bd2!?) 8...g5?! 9.cxd5 ♗xd5 10.0-0 g4 11.♘fd2 ♘g5 12.♖d1! ♘xe5 13.♘f1 ♘gf3+ 14.♔h1 c6 15.e4 ♗d6 16.exd5 ♕h4 17.♗f4 ♕xf2 18.♗e3 ♕h4

19.dxc6 ♞xh2 20.g3 ♛h3 21.♞xh2 1-0 Knaak-Pachow, Germany Bundesliga 2006/07.

Another try is the fianchetto, played several times on the Internet: 7...g6 8.cxd5!? ♛xd5 9.♗c4 ♛a5+ 10.b4! ♗xb4+ (10...♞xb4 11.♛xe4!?) 11.axb4 ♛xa1 12.0-0! ♗f5 13.♛b3 (13.♗b2+−) 13...♞c5 (13...a5 14.♗xf7+ ♚e7 (CapNemo-Yaacovn, playchess.com 2007) 15.♗b2+−) 14.bxc5 ♛xb1 15.♗b2 ♛c2 16.♗xf7+ ♚e7 17.♛xb7 ♚xf7 18.♞g5+ ♚g7 19.e6+ ♚h6 20.♞f7+ ♚h5 21.♗xh8 ♖xh8 22.♞xh8 ♛xc5 23.♛xc7 ♛e5 24.♛xh7+ 1-0 CapNemo-Yaacovn, playchess.com 2007. If 7...♗f5?! 8.♗d3 and White is better.

8.cxd5
8.b4!?.

8...♛xd5 9.♗c4 ♛a5+

White has two ways to meet this check.
10.b4!
This is the main response, attacking the queen and the Trojan Horse at the same time. Another good and more solid option is 10.♞bd2!?. After the forced 10...♗xf3 11.gxf3 ♞xd2 12.♗xd2 ♛xe5 I believe that White is much better after13.♗c3!?.
10...♗xb4+
10...♞xb4 11.♛xe4! ♞c2+ 12.♚e2+−.

11.axb4 ♛xa1 12.♛xe4
The Trojan Horse is eliminated!
12...♗h5

13.e6!
This old move is perfectly possible. Also good is 13.0-0!? ♗g6 14.♛f4 ♛xb1 15.b5 ♞d8 16.♗a3 ♛f5 17.♛h4 f6 18.e6 (18.♗d5!+−) 18...c5 19.bxc6 ♞xc6 20.♞d4 ♛a5 21.♞b5+− G.Flear-Leygue, St Affrique 2002.

13...♗g6
If 13...0-0-0, 14.♛c2!? seems good for White.
14.exf7+ ♚f8 15.♛f4 ♛xb1 16.0-0 ♛e4 17.b5 ♛xf4 18.exf4 ♗xf7 19.♗xf7 ♚xf7 20.bxc6+− bxc6
20...b5 (Matsukevich) 21.♞g5+ ♚g6 22.♞e6.
21.♞g5+ ♚g6 22.g4 h5 23.h3 a5 24.♗a3 a4 25.♖c1 ♖a6 26.♖e1 c5 27.♖e7 ♖b8 28.♖xc7 ♖b3 29.♗xc5 ♖c3 30.f5+ ♚h6 31.♞f7+ ♚h7 32.♖c8 ♖c1+ 33.♚g2 g6 34.♞g5+ ♚h6 35.♞e6 1-0

Analysis after 12...♗h5
In the above diagram position I have discovered a new winning line for White.
13.b5!

This strong intermediate move has been missed in all analysis so far.

13...♘a5

If 13...♗g6 14.♗xf7+! ♔xf7 (14...♗xf7 15.♕c4+ ♔f8 16.bxc6 ♕xb1 17.0-0+−) 15.bxc6 ♗g6 16.♕d5+−.

14.e6!

14.0-0!? ♘xc4 15.♕xc4 ♕xb1 16.♗a3 ♕f5 17.♕c5+−.

14...0-0-0 15.e7 ♖de8 16.♗d3!

Keeping an extra piece. For example:

16...♗g6

16...♔b8 17.♕b4+−.

17.♕d5 ♖xe7 18.♗f5+ ♔b8 19.0-0+−

White has a winning position.

Summary of Game 113: it seems that the move order 4.a3 ♘c6 5.♘f3 d6 is even worse for Black than 4.a3 d6.

Black can complicate, but he cannot equalize.

Summary of 4/5.a3 d6 or ...♘c6/d6: White is always threatening ♕c2, so Black will have to lose a tempo to defend his knight with ...d7-d6-d5. If we compare the positions in Part I, the extra move a2-a3 will always be very useful for White.

That is why Black has been looking for new plans in this line.

GAME 114
□ Glenn Flear
■ Juan Manuel Bellon Lopez
Bern 1991 (7)

1.d4 ♘f6 2.c4 e5 3.dxe5 ♘e4 4.a3 ♕h4

Why not go for mate immediately, tell me, please! From now on, both sides have plenty of resources and as soon as one of them misses a chance... such a miss can be immediately decisive in the FG.

Black has also tried 4...a5 (preparing the retreat of the Trojan Horse to c5) 5.♕c2!? ♘c5 (5...d5 is very similar to Games 112 and 113) 6.♘f3 ♘c6 7.♘c3 ♘e6 8.♘d5 (8.e3!?) 8...d6 9.exd6 ♗xd6 10.e3 0-0 11.♗d3 h6

229

12.♗d2 ♘c5 13.♗c3 ♘xd3+ 14.♕xd3 ♗g4 15.0-0-0! ♗h5 16.c5 ♗xc5 17.♗xg7! ♚xg7 18.♕c3+ f6 19.♕xc5+− Neverov-Pletanek, Pardubice 1992.

5.g3!?

Pawns can defend as well as attack. The other option is 5.♗e3!? ♗c5!? (5...♘c6 6.♘f3±) 6.♗xc5

(**Tricks**: 6.♘f3?? ♕xf2+! 7.♗xf2 ♗xf2 mate)

6...♘xc5 7.e3!? (7.♘d2 ♘c6 8.♘gf3 ♕e7 9.b4 ♘e6± Siegel-Bellon Lopez, Havana 1998; 7.♘c3!) 7...♘c6 8.♘f3 ♕h5 9.b4 (9.♘c3!? ♘xe5 10.♘d4±) 9...♘e6 10.♕d5?! a5 11.b5 ♘e7 Ward-G. Flear, Oakham 1994.

5...♕h5

6.♗g2

6.♕d5 ♘c5 (threatening ...♘b3) 7.♘d2 (7.♘c3!? ♘b3 8.♖b1±) 7...♘c6 8.b4!? ♘a4 (the lesser evil is 8...♘e6 9.♘gf3±) 9.♘gf3 ♕g6 10.♗g2 d6 11.exd6 ♕f6 12.♘b3 (12.♕e4+!) 12...♕c3+ 13.♘fd2 cxd6 14.0-0 ♗e7 15.♕b5+− Naumkin-G. Mohr, Voskresensk 1990; 6.♘f3!? ♗c5 7.e3±.

6...♕xe5

Recovering the pawn. If 6...♘c5?! 7.♘c3! ♘c6 8.f4 d6 9.♘b5 ♘e6

10.♗f3 ♕g6 11.e4 f5 12.♗h5 1-0 Gyimesi-Kahn, Budapest 1995.

7.♘f3

The result of the black actions is a lag in development.

7...♕h5

7...♕c5 8.♘d4 ♘f6 9.♘c3↑.

8.0-0 d6?! 9.♘d4 ♘f6 10.♘c3 ♗e7 11.e4

Summarizing the opening (4...♕h4): after the material balance is restored, on move 11 we end up in a position similar to a Philidor Defence, but not in the spirit of our gambit. White has played natural moves whereas Black has only moved his queen (...♕h4-h5-e5-h5) and king's knight (...♘f6-e4-f6). This is in White's favour.

11...♕xd1 12.♖xd1

Obviously, White dominates throughout the remainder of the game.

12...0-0 13.♗f4 a5 14.♘db5 ♘a6 15.c5!

In our days, this resource is almost forgotten.

15...dxc5 16.♘xc7 ♘xc7 17.♗xc7 ♗e6 18.e5 ♘e8 19.♗b6 a4 20.♘d5 ♗xd5 21.♖xd5 ♖a6 22.♗xc5 ♗xc5 23.♖xc5 ♖b6 24.♖d1! g6 25.♖d2 ♘g7 26.♖c7 ♘e6 27.♖xb7 ♖xb7 28.♗xb7 ♘c5 29.♗d5 ♖b8 30.f4 ♔f8 31.♔f2 ♔e7 32.♔e3 f6 33.♖c2 ♖b5 34.exf6+ ♔xf6 35.♔d4 ♘b3+ 36.♗xb3 ♖xb3 37.g4 h5 38.♖c6+ ♔f7 39.gxh5 gxh5 40.♖c2 ♔g6 41.♔e4 h4 42.f5+ ♔g5 43.♖f2 ♔f6 44.♔f4 h3 45.♔g4 ♔f7 46.♖f3 ♖xb2 47.♖xh3 ♖b3 48.♖g3 ♔f6 49.♔f4 ♖b2 50.♖g6+ ♔f7 51.♖a6 ♖xh2 52.♔g3 ♖h1 53.♖xa4 ♔f6 54.♖a5 ♔g5 55.a4 ♖f1 56.♖c5 ♖a1 57.a5 ♖a3+ 58.♔f2 ♔f4 59.f6 ♖f3+ 60.♔e2 ♖e3+ 61.♔d2 ♖e8 62.a6 **1-0**

A last chance for Black might be the opening of the Milky Way.

We will conclude the study of 4.a3 with a quite modern and hitherto little-used idea.

GAME 115
□ **Nedeljko Kelecevic**
■ **Alexander Günsberg**
Lenk 1995

1.d4 ♘f6 2.c4 e5 3.dxe5 ♘e4 4.a3 b6!?

The Milky Way, diagonal a8-h1, is opened. This move is now more to the point than in the event of 4.♘f3.

5.♘f3!?

The most natural response. We will examine:

A) **Tricks**: 5.♕d5?!

analysis diagram

5...♘c5! (knight fiction; 5...♗b7?! does not work in view of 6.♕xb7 ♘c6 7.♘c3! ♘c5 8.♗g5!) 6.♕xa8? ♗b7 7.♕xa7 ♘c6∓ wins the queen. The only escape square, a3, is occupied by a pawn of her own army;

Gerard Welling (b. 1959) is a Dutch master who likes to experiment in the opening – sometimes also with the Budapest Gambit.

B) 5.♕c2 ♗b7 6.♘c3 ♘xc3 7.♕xc3

analysis diagram

🎩 **Tricks**: 7...a5!? (an interesting alternative is 7...♘a6 8.b4 c5 9.b5 ♘c7) 8.♘f3?? (8.♕g3 ♕e7 9.♘f3 ♘a6⇄) 8...♗b4! 0-1 Schmied-Schlindwein, Untergrombach 2003;

C) 5.♘d2 ♗b7 (5...♘c5!?) 6.♕c2 ♘xd2 7.♗xd2 a5 8.f3?! ♗c5 (8...♘c6!?) 9.e4 ♘c6 10.♗c3 ♕e7 11.♘e2 ♘xe5 12.♘d4 f6 (12...♕h4+!? 13.g3 ♕f6↑) 13.♘f5 ♕f7 with mutual chances, Gen. Timoschenko-Welling, Ostend 1991;

D) 5.♘h3?! a5 (5...♗b7⇄) 6.♘d2 (6.♕d5?! ♗b7!) 6...♘c5 7.♘f3 ♗b7 8.♘f4 a4 9.♘d5 ♘c6 10.♗g5 ♗e7 11.♗xe7 ♘xe7= Narciso Dublan-Bücker, Martinenc 2001.

5...♗b7 6.e3?!

This move, which has the drawback of locking in the c1 bishop, harks back to the ideas investigated in Game 111.

Most probably the critical line, as in the line with 4.♘f3 b6, is 6.♘bd2!? and now:

analysis diagram

A) A complicating option is 6...♘c5!? (dancing with the Trojan Horse) 7.b4 ♘e6 8.♗b2 d6!? 9.♘b3 ♘d7 10.exd6 ♗xd6♚ Hartmann-W. Stein, Griesheim 2003;

B) 6...d6?! 7.♘xe4 ♗xe4 8.♗g5±;

C) 6...♕e7?! 7.♕c2 ♘xd2? 8.♗xd2 ♘c6 9.♗c3± Hillarp Persson-Romero Holmes, Benidorm 2003;

D) 6...a5!? 7.♘xe4 ♗xe4 8.♕d4 ♗b7 (8...♗g6!?) 9.♕g4 ♕e7 10.♗g5 ♕e6 11.♕xe6+ dxe6♚ Eliet-Herbrechtsmeier, France 2001.

A note of advice: Not many games have been played with this important line. It merits further investigation from both sides.

6...d6!

This extremely important resource in the FG may turn the 4.a3 variation around in Black's favour.

Less good is 6...♘c6? 7.♘bd2 (7.b3 d6!⇄) 7...♘c5 8.b4! ♘e6 9.♗b2± a5 (9...g5?! 10.♘e4 ♗e7 11.♘f6+ ♗xf6 12.exf6 d6 13.♗d3 ♕d7 14.♗f5 0-0-0 15.♘xg5+− CapNemo-TheButcher, playchess.com 2007) 10.b5 ♘e7 11.♗d3 g5? 12.♘e4 ♗xe4 13.♗xe4 ♖b8 14.h4 1-0 Postny-Herges, Andorra 2005.

7.♗e2

7.♘bd2 dxe5⇄.

7...♘d7! 8.exd6 ♗xd6

The position is quite similar to the one in the main game in Game 111.

9.0-0 ♕f6!?

This is not the only possible plan; 9...f5!? 10.♕c2 ♘df6?! (10...♕f6!⇄) 11.♕a4+? (11.c5!?) 11...♘d7

12.♘bd2 0-0 13.♕c2 ♕f6⇆ Alfredsson-Oskarsson, Linköping 1996. Why not try 9...0-0!? 10.♘bd2 ♘dc5 (or 10...f5!?) 11.♘xe4 ♘xe4 and White is hemmed in.

10.♘bd2 0-0-0!

10...♕h6!?; 10...♕g6!?.

11.♘xe4 ♗xe4 12.♕d4 ♕g6 13.♘h4 ♕e6 14.♘f3

14...g5?

Black was ready for a strong attack, but not like this. Better was 14...♘c5!? with a clear initiative.

15.♘xg5 ♗xh2+ 16.♔xh2 ♕h6+ 17.♘h3 ♗xg2 18.♔xg2 ♖hg8+ 19.♔h2 ♘c5 20.♕f4 ♕f8 21.e4 ♘e6 22.♗g4 ♕c5 23.♗e3 ♕e7 24.♖ad1 ♖df8 25.♖g1 **1-0**

Summary of 4...b6: I consider this a very fresh and interesting option. Although the opening lasts for just a few moves, Black has many ideas and plans to develop. If White wants to play for the win, the position gets quite complicated and the result is hard to predict.

Summary of 'The Milky Way'

- Undoubtedly, the move 4.a3!? is very useful for White. Without the BG check ...♗b4+, the Trojan Horse on e4 gets no support from the rest of the black pieces.

- Pawn support by ...d7-d6-d5 or ...f7-f5 does not seem to be sufficient.
- The attack with 4...♛h4?! is probably a waste of time.
- However, opening the Milky Way with 4...b6 is an interesting option which is little-explored and leaves room for quite a bit of creativity.

Kurt Richter (1900-1969), the second pioneer of the Fajarowicz-Richter System.

Statistics of 3...♞e4

The total number of games in the Megabase is 1870, and Black has a slightly worse result compared to the BG with 3...♞g4:

White wins: 46% (861 games) =59%
Average Elo   2172
performance   2171
Draw: 27% (498 games)
Black wins: 27% (511 games) = 41%
Average Elo   2115
performance   2073

General Conclusion of Fajarowicz-Richter System 3...♞e4

We can hardly speak of a classical game here. Hostilities arise as early as move 4 and tend to end quite quickly; there are very few long games with this line.

This interesting system is not well-developed yet, neither theoretically nor practically, compared to 3...♞g4.

White players are usually not well-prepared theoretically and must play according to concepts, so the FG can be used as a surprise weapon.

I still think that the critical line is 4.a3, since in all other lines Black gets his chances.

Sometimes the complications are not enough for Black to equalize, but in practice Black wins many games if he plays in true FG spirit!

⚠ Keep in Mind!

- While in the BG with 3...♞g4 Black can play solidly since there are enough resources, in the FG he does not get so much time and must proceed at extreme risk. Anyway, in the FG a lot also depends on the white player's choices.
- My final recommendation is that if you like the idea of the Budapest Gambit (1.d4 ♞f6 2.c4 e5!?), but you also want to learn a bit more about chess, you should study first 3...♞g4 and then try out the sharp ideas connected with 3...♞e4.

I wish you good luck with it!

Epilogue

What is the essence of the Budapest Gambit? The main objective is to quickly eliminate White's queen's pawn, even though Black loses some tempi by doing so. On the other hand, practice has demonstrated that the move 4.e4 isn't so dangerous for Black.

Therefore, the Budapest Gambit is a success from an opening-theoretical point of view, as it breaks down White's centre with a few moves. The tempi which are lost are compensated for by superior piece activity, especially from Black's kingside knight.

Which are the Budapest weaknesses? The queenside, the d-file and the d5-square. White's key pieces are the c-pawn, which can advance to c5; the b1 knight which can leap to d5 and the a1 rook which can exert pressure on the c- and d- files. Along with the queen, these are White's most active pieces. If Black is able to neutralize them, I think he can obtain a great game.

Bibliography

For this book, the author has made use of the following sources for reference:

- programs ChessBase 9 and Fritz 10
- ChessBase: Mega Data Base 2007, Opening Encyclopaedia 2007 and CBM magazines 114-119
- CD Budapest Gambit, Oleinikov Dmitrij, ChessBase 2005
- TWIC issues January-August 2007
- 'The Budapest Gambit' by Otto Borik, Batsford, 1986
- 'Budapest - Fajarowicz' by Lev Gutman, Batsford, 2004

New In Chess Code System

White stands slightly better	⩲
Black stands slightly better	⩱
White stands better	±
Black stands better	∓
White has a decisive advantage	+−
Black has a decisive advantage	−+
balanced position	=
unclear position	∞
compensation for the material	⩹
strong (sufficient)	>
weak (insufficient)	<
better is	≥
weaker is	≤
good move	!
excellent move	!!
bad move	?
blunder	??
interesting move	!?
dubious move	?!
only move	□
with the idea	△
attack	→
initiative	↑
lead in development	↑↑
counterplay	⇄
correspondence	cr

A brief biography of the Author

Viktor Moskalenko
born April 12, 1960 in Odessa, Ukraine

Champion of Ukraine in 1987
Champion Catalonia (Spain) in 2001, 2005, 2007
Chess Grandmaster since 1992
Residing in Barcelona, Spain, since 2000
Winner of numerous international tournaments
Chess coach
Specialist in theoretical articles
Elo rating on July 1, 2007: 2560
E-mail: vmoska@terra.es

Index of Players

The numbers refer to pages